Essential Off-road RC Racer's Guide

Dave B Stevens

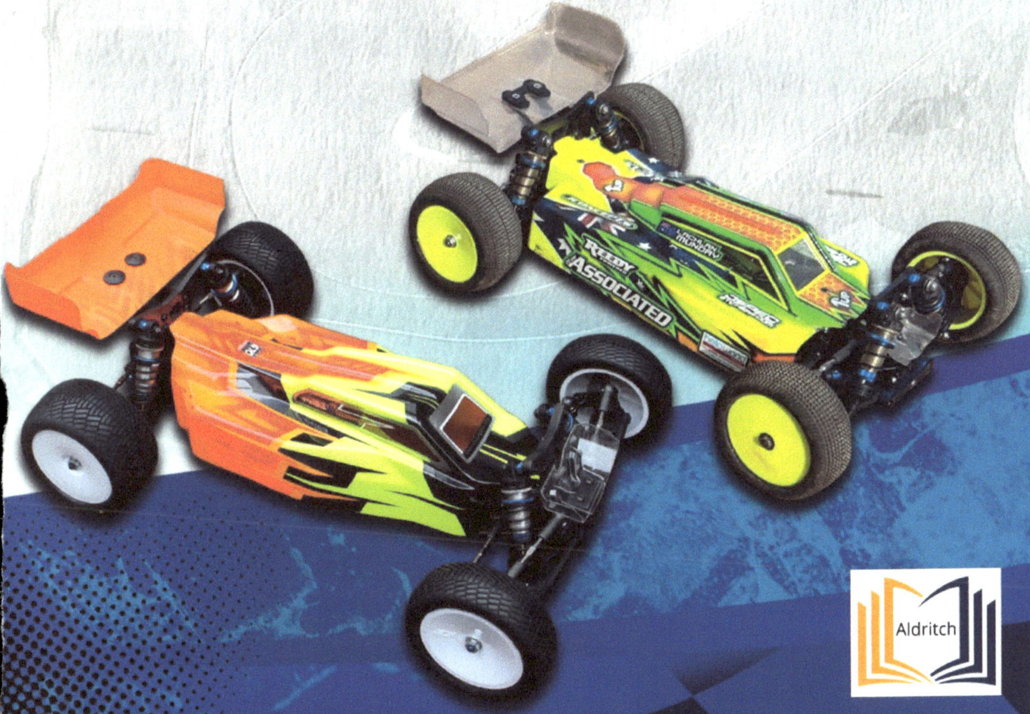

Copyright © 2021 David Bryan Stevens. www.DaveBStevens.com

Tech Talks © Ray Munday. @AskRayMunday
Speed Secrets © Ryan Maker. www.RCMaker.com.au

All rights reserved. No part of this publication may be reproduced, stored in a retrieval system, or transmitted in any form or by any means, electronic, mechanical, photocopying, recording or otherwise, without the prior permission of the copyright holder.

ISBN 978-0-6485811-4-7. Published by Dave B Stevens, Aldritch Publishing, Australia.

Technical Contribution: Bruno Coelho (br1rc.com), Billy Easton (www.serpent.com), Ray Munday (@AskRayMunday), Ryan Maker (www.RCMaker.com.au).
Additional Case Studies: Martin Bayer, Brett Butter, Adam Drake, Dakotah Phend, Charlie Maiorana, Matthew Gonzales, Max Götzl, Aydin Horne, Sam Isaacs, Lee Martin, Colin Morse III, Michal Orlowski, Jesper Rasmussen, Brennan Schimmel, Kevin Siller, Tater Sontag, Dreighton Stoub, Yusuke Sugiura, Matt Williard.
Beta Readers: Ryan Harris (@RyanStilesHarris), Tony Parreiro, Paul Sims.
Proof Reading: Rhiannon Raphael.
Graphic Design: Evie Diakogeorgaki.
Illustrations: Ruwan Prasanga.
Jumping Graphs: Chris Stevens.
Additional Contribution: Andy Cooke, Paul Sims (bezerk.com.au), Aaron Stevens.

Photo Credits: Thank you to the following for their kind permission to reproduce their photos and images in this book. The page numbers for each of their photos are listed after the contributor's name (t=top; m=middle; b=bottom; l=left; r=right):

Martin Bayer: 271; Bruno Coelho: cover self image, 12, 20, 21; Aleandro De Lorso: cover 1/8 buggy, 22; Adam Drake: 288; Billy Easton: cover self image, 13, 18, 19, 65; EOS (www.eurorcseries.com): 71, 216b, 248, 258, 261, 263, 265, 267, 270, 272, 273, 274, 276, 277, 279, 280, 282b, 284, 303, 327, 324; Euro RC (www.EuroRC.com): 81, 88, 89, 90; Nathan Facciol (www.nathobuilds.com): 115, 131, 132, 147, 151; Max Götzl: 281t; Aydin Horne: 93tr, Infield Media (@RCRacingPhotography): cover Truck, 10t, 23, 44, 48t, 104, 208, 224, 299; JConcepts (www.jconcepts.net): 80, 93tl, 94, 98, 227t, 237, 245, 249, 250, 251, 285; LCRC Raceway (lcrcraceway.com): 286, 290; Lee Martin: 270t, 270m; Ray Munday (@AskRayMunday): cover 4WD, title page 4WD, 57, 59, 61, 98, 101, 113, 138, 140, 193, 312; Michal Orlowski: 252, 268; Ashley Peeler: cover SCT, 10b; Dakotah Phend: 226, 227m, 228, 238; Joe Pillars (1upracing.com): 200, 215t, 232, 234, 242, 243; 231, 246, 254; Red RC (eos.redrc.net): 262; Redcat Racing (www.redcatracing.com): 217; Toni Rheinard (www.tonisport.de): 164, 194, 309; Serpent (www.serpent.com): 105, 155, 209, 212, 218, 220, 221, 222, 223; Kevin Siller: 294; Paul Sims (bezerk.com.au): 207; Tater Sontag: 247; Dreighton Stoub: 241; Aaron Stevens: cover top, 14, 15, 32, 34, 35, 36, 38, 39, 48b, 50, 53, 54, 58, 66, 68, 70, 82, 85, 87, 93b, 95, 103, 108, 110, 114, 115, 120, 123, 125, 137, 143, 144, 145, 166, 168, 178, 182, 189, 195, 201, 210, 211, 214, 215, 216t, 216m, 298, 324; Matt Subotsch: rear cover top, title page background, 73; Yusuke Sugiura: 255; Matt Williard: 291.

All other photography is by the author.

Special thanks to Michael Sherman (www.speedyrc.com.au) and Team Zombie for providing batteries/motors and for photos 76b and 91.

Table of Contents

chapter 1

Introduction ... 11

Foreword – Bruno Coelho ... 12
Foreword – Billy Easton ... 13
Foreword – Ray Munday ... 14
Author's Preface ... 15
Introduction ... 16
How To Use This Book ... 17
The Vehicles ... 18

chapter 2

The Process of Driving Faster ... 23

Introduction ... 24
Setup Theory ... 24
Setup Sheets ... 26
Weight Transfer – the Holy Grail ... 27
The Racing Line ... 28
  Braking Point ... 28
  Turn-in Point ... 29
  Apex ... 30
    Wide Corners ... 30
    Geometric Apex ... 31
    Late Apex ... 32
    Early Apex ... 32
    Overtaking on a Corner ... 33
    The Karting Apex ... 33
    Driving Tips ... 34
    Chicanes ... 34
    Sweepers ... 35
    Hairpins ... 36
Slipstream Overtaking ... 36
The Position of the Next Corner ... 37
Increasing Corner Speed ... 37

Table of Contents

Perfect Practice Makes Perfect … 39
Fast Lap Times … 40
   How to get a fast lap time? … 40
   What is acceleration? … 40
Driver Etiquette and Traffic … 45
   Lapping … 45
   Staggered Start Passing … 45
   How to Pass … 46
   Resolving Disputes … 46
   After a Crash … 46
   Hitting Someone From Behind … 46
   Marshals … 47

chapter 3

Jumping … 48

Jumping Basics … 49
   Introduction … 49
   Jump Types … 50
   Control in the Air … 52
Jump Distance … 54
Science of Jumping … 56
   Run-up and Take-off … 56
   Flight Path … 57
   Throttle Control … 59
   Steering Control … 61
   Combination Throttle/Steering Techniques – the "Whip" … 62

chapter 4

The Track … 65

Mapping the Track … 66
Track Walk … 67
Conquering a New Track … 71
Putting It All Together … 73

Table of Contents

chapter 5

Tyres 76
Tyres Introduction 77
Tyre Gluing 77
Beadlock Wheels (Short Course Trucks) 80
Tyre Direction 80
Inserts 81
Additive 82
Tyre Warmers 84
Wheel Balancing 84
Tyre Cleaning 85
Tyre Storage 85
Tyre Selection 86
Track Terminology Definitions 86
Wheel Sizes 88
   1/10 Vehicles 88
   1/8 Vehicles 90
   Wheel Offset 90
Tyre Selection Criteria 91
   1. Compound Selection 92
   2. Tyre Profile 92
   3. Rear Tread Selection 93
   4. Front Tread Selection 95
   5. Setup Changes 95
1/10 JConcepts Outdoor Tyre Guide 96
Tyre Tech 99
How Does a Tyre Create Grip? 99
Tyre Slip – How to get the maximum grip out of the tyre 100
Tyre Energy – Looking after Tyre Temperature 101
The Friction Circle – Getting the most out of the tyre at all times 102

chapter 6

Car Setup Reference 104
Introduction 105
Parts of the Cars 105
Ackermann 107

Table of Contents

Anti-dive (front) ... 111
Anti-squat/Pro-squat (Rear) ... 111
Arm Sweep ... 112
Axle Height ... 113
Battery Position ... 114
Bodies ... 114
Bump Steer ... 117
Camber ... 118
Camber Gain ... 121
Chassis Stiffness (Flex) ... 122
Caster ... 124
Centre of Gravity ... 125
Damping ... 126
   Oil ... 126
   Piston Holes ... 127
   Position ... 128
   Preload ... 129
   Rebound ... 130
   Springs ... 132
   Damper Theory ... 134
Differential ... 141
   Gear Diff ... 142
   Ball Diff ... 145
   Diff Height ... 146
   Diff Tech ... 146
Droop (Down Travel) ... 152
ESC Settings ... 158
Flex ... 160
Gearing and Rollout ... 160
   Final Drive Ratios ... 161
   Gear Mesh ... 162
   End Bell Timing ... 163
   Tuning Gearing for the Lowest Lap Times ... 163
   Motor Temperature ... 164
Kick-up/Anti-dive (Front) ... 165
Pro-squat ... 166
Radio Settings ... 167
   Too Much Steering ... 167
   Too Much Power for the Conditions ... 167
   Exponential (Expo) ... 168

Table of Contents

Ride Height 169
Roll Bars 173
Roll Centre 177
Rollout 180
Shock Absorber 180
Slipper Clutch 180
Solid Axle (Spool) 182
Steering Arm Ball Cup Location 182
Steering Linkage Angle 182
Steering Throw/Lock 183
Toe 185
Transmission (2WD) 188
Track Width 188
Tyres and Additives 191
Up Travel 191
Weight 192
Wheelbase 196
Wings 197

chapter 7

Tweak 201
What is Tweak? 202
Tweak Causes 202
Chassis Tweak 203
Suspension Tweak 205
Equipment 207

chapter 8

Trucks 208
Short Course Trucks 209
What's Different About SCT? 209
Driving SCTs Quickly 209
Jumping 211
SCT Setup 212

Table of Contents

Stadium Trucks _____ 215
Monster Trucks _____ 217

chapter 9

1/8 Scale _____ 218
1/8 Buggy _____ 219
1/8 Truggy _____ 222

chapter 10

Case Studies _____ 224
Clay Case Study _____ 226
Packed Dirt Case Study _____ 249
Carpet Case Study _____ 257
Astroturf Case Study _____ 273
1/8 Case Study _____ 285

appendix A

eBook _____ 295

appendix B

Glossary _____ 296

appendix C

Beginner's Guide _____ 301
Buying Considerations _____ 301
Learning to Drive on a Track _____ 302

Table of Contents

Beginner Advice _____ 302
Common Build Errors _____ 304
Tyres Unglued _____ 308
Setup Diary _____ 308
Tools _____ 308
Lipo Battery Safety _____ 309

appendix D

Checklists _____ 310

Maintenance _____ 311
  After Run Checks _____ 311
  Maintenance Checklist _____ 312
  Rebuilding a Car _____ 313
Correcting Key Balance Issues _____ 314
  Traction – How to Increase _____ 314
  Steering _____ 315
    Too Much Steering (Oversteer) _____ 315
    Not Enough Steering (Understeer) _____ 317
  Easier to Drive – How-to _____ 319
Troubleshooting _____ 320
  Acceleration/Forward Traction _____ 320
  Bump Handling _____ 320
  Change of Direction (Chicane) _____ 321
  Changing Tracks – Low-Grip to High-Grip (or vice versa) _____ 321
  Fast Sweeper Cornering _____ 322
  Flipping _____ 323
  "Hops" or "Chatters" Across the Track _____ 323
  Inconsistent Handling _____ 323
  Jumping Issues _____ 324
    More Distance _____ 324
    Hard Landings _____ 324
    Jumps Nose Up _____ 324
  Traction Rolling _____ 325
  Unexplained – Handling Changes for No Apparent Reason _____ 326
    Lacking Acceleration or Started Oversteering _____ 326
    Steering Response Changes for No Apparent Reason _____ 326
    Traction – Unexplained Loss of Traction _____ 327
  Wanders on the Straight _____ 327
Quick Reference _____ 330

Chapter 1
Introduction

Foreword – Bruno Coelho

I've raced many classes with my dad, off-road and on-road. I wouldn't be where I am today without him. For more than ten years, all my support came from my family. They believed in me and helped me to get where I am today.

In 2014 I TQ'd and came 2nd at the Euros in Spain. Xray invited me to go to the Touring Car World Championship in Florida, all expenses paid. However, I had no holidays at my job and couldn't go. My dad encouraged me to quit my job and, following a good performance at the worlds, I became a full-time pro driver for Xray. I've worked with them ever since. Being part of a team is fantastic for sharing experiences and setups. I encourage new drivers to make friends with other drivers who use the same chassis and share their ideas and experiences. This will help to make you a better driver.

There is no substitute for practice and hard work. Before I travelled to my first world championship, I practised from 7 a.m. to 11 p.m. for two weeks.

Everyone needs support of one kind or another. I hope that this book provides you with support by providing ideas and knowledge to take your racing to the next level.

Bruno Coelho

- ✓ 2 x 4WD IFMAR World Champion
- ✓ Touring Car IFMAR World Champion
- ✓ 4WD European Champion.
- ✓ 1/8 European Champion
- ✓ European Nitro Touring Champion

Author's note:

One of the best all-round drivers in the world, Bruno is one of the very few to have achieved world titles in both off-road and on-road. He is the current world champion for both 4WD off-road (2019) and touring car (2018) [not held in 2020 due to COVID-19]. Bruno sells the RC products he uses at br1rc.com. He was not paid to support this book.

Foreword – Billy Easton

I won the IFMAR 2WD World Championship in 2003 in Clearwater, Florida. It's ironic I now live in Florida and regularly race not far from Clearwater. It's possible that subconsciously I just love Florida dirt!

Since then, I've spent more than ten years designing Serpent's off-road vehicles, including 1/10 and 1/8 scale, electric and nitro. I still love to race, but now I race to make my designs better and to help our customers with new products.

Winning a race is awesome, but knowing I did a great job on a product and helped others to win is an even greater reward. Helping racers is one of the reasons I wanted to support this book.

When we start a completely new design, we purchase all the current cars on the market to see what works and what can be improved. There are only so many ways to approach RC car design, but we always come up with new and innovative features. We model a lot of alternatives using Pro-E CAD software, Solid Works for bodies, Gear Trax for the drivetrain, MathCAD and other software for any additional calculations.

Whether it's to make the car easier to work on or to enhance performance, we're always looking to improve and provide cars that are at the top of their class.

Billy Easton

- ✓ 2WD IFMAR World Champion
- ✓ 2WD Palmetto Classic winner
- ✓ 1/8 IFMAR World Championship A-finalist
- ✓ 1/8 Silver State Champion
- ✓ 1/8 Force Spring Series winner
- ✓ 3 x ROAR 1/10 Gas Truck National Champion (back-to-back)

Author's note:

Billy Easton competes at the top level across many off-road classes. He works full-time for Serpent RC (www.serpent.com) as their lead designer of off-road vehicles and therefore brings a unique perspective. He was not paid to support this book.

Foreword – Ray Munday

When Dave first approached me to contribute to this book, I felt honoured to be involved in a project like this.

There are a lot of textbooks out there, but in my experience, they are either too theoretical and hard work to read or too generic with incorrect explanations.

Over the years, I have created a series of "Tech Talks" designed to go through the basics of vehicle dynamics, demystify the way to go about driving, and how and why to change setup with less guesswork. Many of these Tech Talks are included in this book, and I hope they assist you in bridging the gap between theory and practice in RC cars.

I hope you enjoy this book and it helps you with your racing.

Have fun at the track!

Ray Munday

- ✓ 4WD Australian Champion
- ✓ 2WD Australian Champion
- ✓ 29 x State Champion
- ✓ Top 30 at the Worlds
- ✓ Reedy Race of Champions A-main Finalist
- ✓ 4 x Keilor Invitational Winner

Author's note:

With titles spanning three decades, Ray is one of the most successful off-road drivers in Australia. He is also a mechanical engineer, having worked on full-scale race cars for many years. He has a talent for explaining complex topics in simple terms. You can ask Ray questions via his Facebook page @AskRayMunday. He was not paid to support this book.

Author's Preface

In 2007, my 11-year-old son, Aaron, bought an RC car on eBay. As soon as I saw it I had to have one for myself, and Aaron and I spent most weekends at the track from then on.

There is a lot of information on the web about setting up RC cars. However, it is often hard to find, incomplete, brand-specific, out of date or on a forum where the discussion lacks the context to make it truly useful.

I wrote this book to create a comprehensive manual that racers can follow to improve their lap times, regardless of their skill level or the car they drive. I spent 30 years as a business consultant, and part of my skill set is to extract technical experience from experts in the field, pull in relevant information from multiple sources, and present it in an easy to apply "how-to" format.

About the Author

This is the third book in Dave's Essential RC series which has sold in 29 countries. Following the success of his first RC book **Essential 1/12th and F1 RC Racer's Guide** released in 2019, Dave released **Essential Touring Car RC Racer's Guide** in 2020.

In 2013 he set a Guinness World Record for "the longest distance covered by a battery-operated remote-controlled car"; a record he held for three years.

In 2012 Dave launched www.RCformula1.com. In the early years, it was the only dedicated RC F1 website and it is still the most read, with nearly 8 million page views as of late 2021.

Dave is a former president of the Templestowe Flat Track Racers RC club and a former board member of the Victorian On Road Tracks Executive Committee.

He also writes fiction and lives in Melbourne, Australia with his wife and sons.

Connect with Dave via:
Facebook   facebook.com/DaveBStevens.Author
Web   www.DaveBStevens.com

Introduction

Every weekend, you will find off-road racing at club tracks throughout the world. Some drivers are racing with their friends to have fun, while others are trying to win at club level or a local competition. Most countries have regional racing, nationally organised competitions and, of course, there are world championships.

The 2WD and 4WD Modified Electric Off-road buggy classes have been International Federation of Model Auto Racing (IFMAR) World Championship classes since 1987.

A fantastic range of off-road classes are raced at local clubs including 2WD and 4WD Buggies, Vintage, Stadium Truck, Short Course Truck, 1/8 Buggies and Truggies, and others. A range of motors are also available in 1/10 scale, from the sedate 21.5 turn to the super quick Modified/open motors like the 6.5 turn. No matter your level of skill, and how fast you want to go, off-road has a class to suit!

Whether you are a complete beginner or an experienced racer looking for an edge over your competition, this book was designed to provide the answers you're looking for. It provides a complete, step-by-step reference to these fantastic vehicles.

In-depth information is included on off-road electric vehicles, focusing on:

- 1/10 scale two-wheel drive (2WD) buggies
- 1/10 scale four-wheel drive (4WD) buggies
- 1/8 scale four-wheel drive (4WD) buggies

Short Course Trucks (2WD and 4WD), Stadium Trucks (2WD) and 1/8 scale Truggies are referred to as needed and also have their own sections.

Buggies and trucks are both referred to as cars throughout this book.

4WD cars are fantastic for beginners as they are relatively easy to drive. 2WD cars are less expensive and easier to build.

Whether 2WD or 4WD, it is very achievable to have a car that has sufficient rear end grip and still has enough steering to turn tight corners under almost all track conditions. This guide provides you with the information to set up your car to be easy and fun to drive fast.

How To Use This Book

Appendix B – Glossary, starting on page *296,* defines core technical terms referred to in this book.

The Process of Driving Faster, beginning on page *23,* covers setup theory, a driving tutorial and how to apply this theory to any track.

If you are a beginner, your next step is to check out *Appendix C – Beginner's Guide*, on page *301*. If you're not sure what all the parts of the car are called, there are diagrams on page *105*.

Jumping techniques and the fastest way to jump, starts on page *48*.

The Track, beginning on page *65*, covers mapping the track, walking the track and putting together all the cornering and jumping techniques covered previously, using an example track.

Tyres are a complex area and we cover everything you need to know, beginning on page *76*.

Car Setup Reference, starting on page *104*, covers the A–Z of setup settings from Ackermann to Wings and everything in between. I've also labelled each setting option as Basic, Intermediate or Advanced.

Tweak, starting on page *201*, covers how to ensure all your tyres touch the ground with equal pressure and what happens if they don't. It also describes how to identify the cause.

Trucks (Short Course Trucks, Stadium Trucks and Monster Trucks) have their own section, beginning on page *208*.

The *1/8 Scale* Buggies and Truggies chapter starts on page *218*.

Case Studies, starting on page *224*, describes actual race meetings, how pro drivers approached their setup, what changes they made, why and the results.

Appendix D – Checklists, on page *310*, covers all the common problems and situations you might encounter. Car is spinning out? Wanders on the straight? Doesn't have enough steering? We've got you covered.

This book is available as an eBook for ease of reference at the track. The eBook is available at a discount for those who have purchased the physical book (page *295*).

Introduction

The Vehicles

This book covers all 1/10 and 1/8 scale off-road electric vehicles with a particular focus on buggies.

2WD Buggy (Billy Easton's Serpent SRX2 Gen3 Dirt)

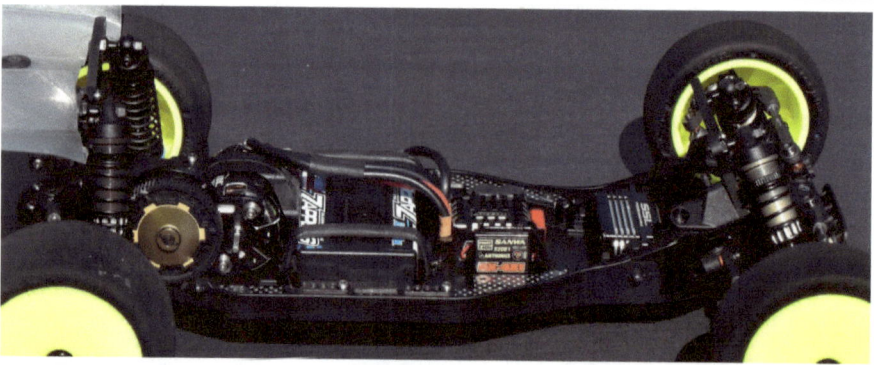

4WD Buggy (Bruno Coelho's World Champion Xray XB4 '20)

1/8 Scale 4WD Buggy

In this book, whenever a 1/8 buggy setup option is different from the main text it is also specified. 1/8 Scale has its own chapter beginning on page *218*.

Trucks (2WD/4WD)

In this book, whenever a truck setup option is different to the main text it is also specified. This primarily relates to tyres and bodies. Trucks have their own sections as follows:

- Short Course Trucks (SCT) on page *209*.
- Stadium Trucks on page *215*.
- Monster Trucks on page *215*.

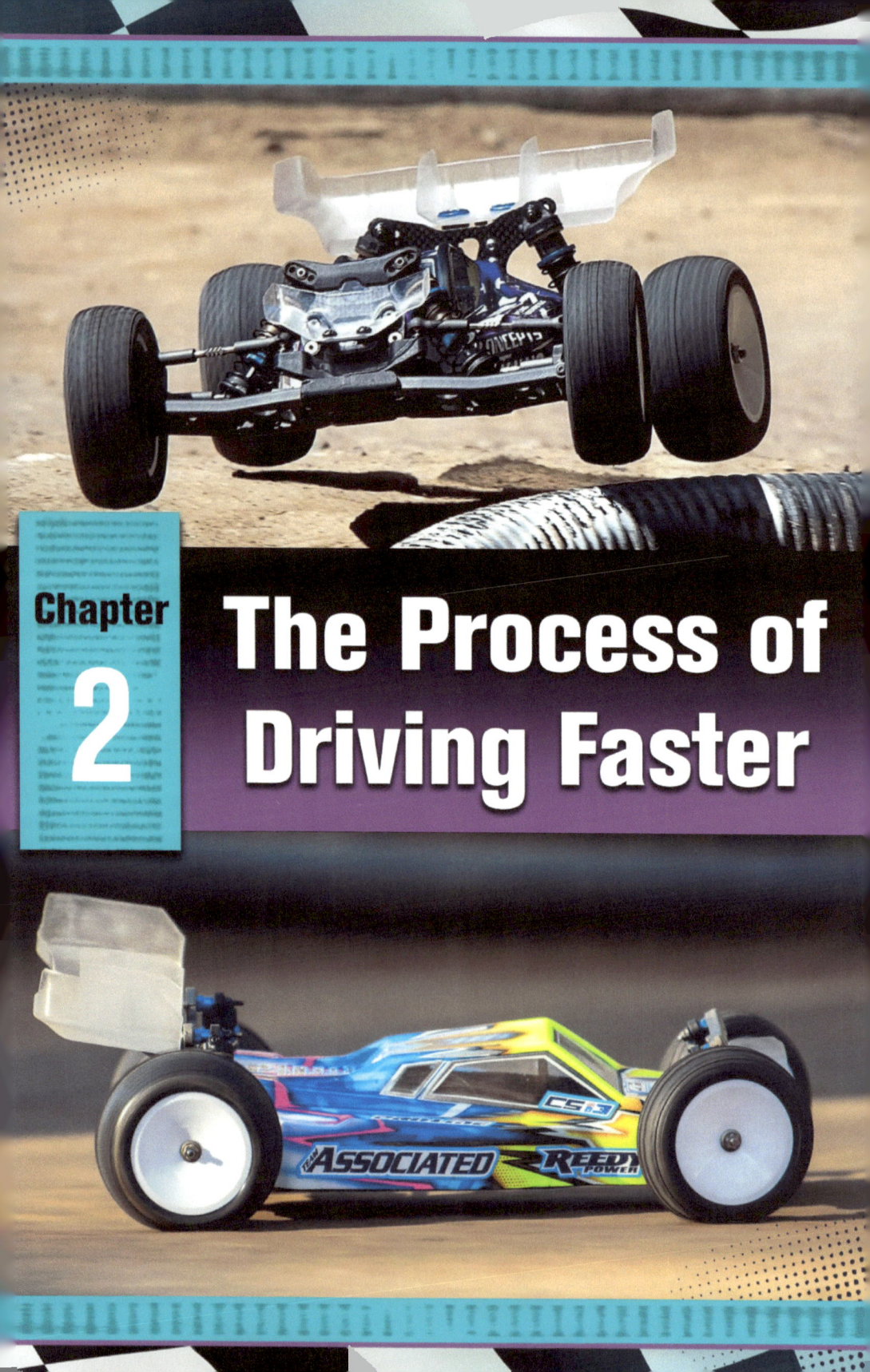

Chapter 2
The Process of Driving Faster

Introduction

Being able to drive faster on a given track is a process that involves the following steps:

1. Determine a base setup for the track.
2. Map the Racing Line for the track.
3. Practice the Racing Line for the track.
4. Tune your car's setup so you can drive it as quickly as you are able and as close to the Racing Line as possible.
5. Practice the Racing Line for the track until qualifying starts.

Setup Theory

A car's handling is determined by the contact patch of the tyre on the racing surface. In a full-size production car, that area is about the same as a size 10 shoe. In an RC car, it might be the size of your fingernail or smaller.

How the tyres interact with the track determines how the car corners, accelerates and brakes, so tyre choice is the most important factor in car handling. However, at many large race meetings a control tyre is used, meaning everyone has the same brand and compound of tyre. Therefore the advantage will go to the driver who sets up their car so that these tyres provide the right amount of grip at the right time.

Ignoring other factors for the moment, the easier the car is to drive, the faster you will be able to drive it. Changing the car's setup will make the car easier to drive near its performance limit. This should allow you to drive it faster.

In this book we explain what each setting is, why it changes the behaviour of the car, how to make each change and the result you should expect.

Make small changes one at a time and measure the result based on what you were trying to achieve (refer to Mapping the Track on page 66). Note whether the car felt better or worse and any impact on lap times. If the car does not feel better, then undo the change.

We say small changes because adding a 0.5mm shim or changing a setting by 0.5° may make a noticeable difference, and if you skip to a 2mm shim or 1.5° change, then you may miss the sweet spot. You can also go too far, which may cause the opposite of what you're trying to achieve. Small incremental changes are best.

We recommend that you keep track of your setup changes and record which setups work best at different tracks under various conditions.

A car that "feels" faster is not necessarily turning faster lap times. Use a stopwatch or timing system to check if it really is quicker and not just easier to drive.

For the car to respond correctly to setup changes, it must be in good working order. In other words: the car is not tweaked (page 201), the suspension is free, dampers (page 126) and differential (page 141) are correctly built, there are no broken binding or loose parts, and the car has proper weight balance left-to-right (page 192).

Many setup adjustments interact with other settings. For example, changing the ride height will also change the droop. These interactions are explained under the relevant headings.

Finetuning the setup will make the car easier to drive near its performance limit. This should allow you to drive it faster.

Start with a base setup, make changes so that the car drives the lines you want (see The Racing Line on page 28), then stiffen the car up as much as practical while making sure it is still as easy for you to drive as possible. As you gain experience, you will be able to shortcut this process.

Use our After Race Checklist on page 310 to identify problems before the next run.

Setup Sheets

Team Driver Setup Sheets can be a useful reference, and it is helpful to see what changes professional drivers have made. However, copying another driver's setup sheet without understanding why each change was made can cause a car to be undriveable. The track conditions are probably different, they may not have recorded their setup completely accurately, their driving preferences and skill level are almost certainly different to yours. Note: setup sheets are normally based on finals, once the best setup has been determined.

Different cars have unique handling characteristics. Even with the same chassis, driver style varies. That is why it is not recommended that you copy a world champion's car setup without understanding the settings. Instead, identify the differences between their setup and your car's setup and make one change at a time. Determine whether your car handling is better or worse, based on your skill level and driving style, and finetune from there.

It is better to make small incremental changes. Often a chassis will have one basic setup for carpet/astroturf and another for dirt, and this is usually a better place to start than how a pro driver sets up their car. These setup sheets may be found in your car's manual or be available on the manufacturer's website. If your manufacturer only has a dirt setup, then refer to Carpet Case Studies on page 257 for guidance on the difference between dirt and carpet setups and how others have approached this issue.

Don't hesitate to ask for setup tips from the local fast drivers. Treat their advice like a pro driver's setup sheet by making one change they suggest at a time and noting the result. By doing this, you are refining your own setup knowledge.

Weight Transfer – the Holy Grail

Weight transfer refers to the redistribution of weight supported by each tyre during acceleration, braking and cornering. Understanding weight transfer is the key to understanding car setup and handling.

When a car is at rest, it has a certain amount of weight on each tyre. By transferring weight from one tyre to another (front-to-rear or side-to-side), the loaded tyre will be pushed harder onto the racing surface and, therefore, will have more grip. Equally, the inside tyre on a corner will have less grip.

This book explains all the setup settings available to you, how changing these will allow the transfer of more or less weight, during racing and how this affects the handling of your car.

Car setup is a matter of compromise. For example, transferring more weight to the front tyres will provide more initial steering, but reduce rear traction. The aim is to set up your car so it is easy for you to drive quickly and consistently from lap to lap while providing sufficient rear traction and sufficient steering. Of course, your definition of driving quickly will depend on your experience and skill as a driver. Regardless of how well you drive, it is possible for you to set up your car so you can drive it as quickly and consistently as your current ability allows.

Good setup is all about controlling weight transfer.

The Racing Line

The racing line is the fastest path through any corner, and identifying it is an essential skill for any driver wanting to lower their lap times.

Driving the fastest laps possible is a combination of two competing goals:

1. driving the shortest possible distance around the track, and
2. keeping the car's cornering speed as high as possible by minimising the angle of the corners.

By using all the space available on the track, your car can travel in a straighter line and therefore drive through the corner at a faster speed (keeping in mind *Wide Corners* on page *30*).

You should experiment with different lines, watch the fast guys and talk to other drivers at the track. On some tracks, the most common racing line will show up as a darker, or even black, area on the track (called the groove).

Ignoring traffic for the moment, the racing line is determined by the following factors:

- Braking point.
- Turn-in point.
- Apex.
- The position and direction of the next corner.
- The acceleration a car has available (a Modified car's racing line may differ from a Stock car's racing line).

We will now break down each of these factors.

Braking Point

The aim when braking before a corner is to slow down just enough to clip the apex (defined on the next page). If you enter the corner too fast, you will miss the apex (understeer). If you enter the corner too slowly, you may need to accelerate mid-turn. Both scenarios mean you won't be going as quickly as you could be.

It makes sense to brake earlier when learning the track and getting familiar with your car, then gradually reduce the braking distance as your confidence and experience grows. Ideally, you should be off the brakes before turning into the corner. For pro drivers, a slight brake pressure on entry can help to reduce understeer and provide a better turn-in (this is known as trail braking).

Other factors include:

- Modified motors have greater braking power than Stock class motors.
- Braking too early may result in a slow lap.
- Braking too late may result in overshooting the corner and a slow lap (or in the worst-case scenario, a broken car).

For each corner, choose a braking marker. This is a specific point on the track (or to one side of it) that doesn't move, which you can use as a consistent reference for precisely where to brake.

Turn-in Point

To get the racing line right, it is vital to turn-in at the correct point. Leave it too late and you'll understeer, missing the apex. Turn-in too soon and you'll clip the apex/curb, upset the car and have to adjust your line mid-corner, losing speed.

Pick a spot on the track as your turn-in point and note it on your track map (refer to *Mapping the Track* on page 66). Adjust this turn-in point during practice until you're happy with your line through the corner.

Apex

The apex is the point at which you are closest to the inside of the corner (also known as the clipping point). Once you have hit the apex, you should be able to reduce your steering input and increase the throttle as the car exits the corner.

In general terms, there are three different types of apex. These are summarised in the table below. You would normally select the best apex for a corner depending on traffic and the position of the next corner.

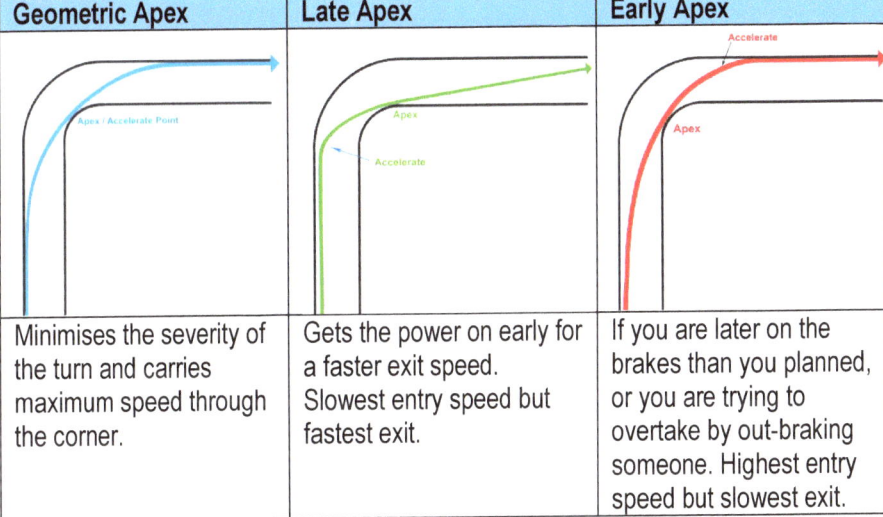

Geometric Apex	Late Apex	Early Apex
Minimises the severity of the turn and carries maximum speed through the corner.	Gets the power on early for a faster exit speed. Slowest entry speed but fastest exit.	If you are later on the brakes than you planned, or you are trying to overtake by out-braking someone. Highest entry speed but slowest exit.

As previously stated, by using all the space available on the track, your car can travel in a straighter line and therefore drive through the corner at a faster speed.

Each of the above is discussed in more detail on the following pages.

Wide Corners

In real racing, using the full width of the racetrack is normally faster, but in RC this is not necessarily the case. Refer to the optimal line around the example track on page 73.

If the entry or exit of a corner is very wide (the track width is wider than required for the racing line) then touching the outside of the track on the way in and the outside of the track on the way out increases the distance travelled and slows the overall lap time. In this situation, some trial and error may be required to determine the optimum time to turn in.

Any part of the track that is not on the racing line is often dirty, with reduced grip, and should be avoided.

Geometric Apex

The geometric apex of a constant radius corner is the central point on the inside of the corner.

Hitting the geometric apex is good for carrying speed and minimising turn severity.

The fastest way through a 90-degree corner is to touch the outside of the track on the approach, hit the geometric apex of the corner, and then swing out in an even curve to meet the outside edge of the track. By following a symmetrical, curved line you will take the corner as fast as possible by minimising the tightness of the corner. This minimises cornering force, freeing up grip for maintaining speed.

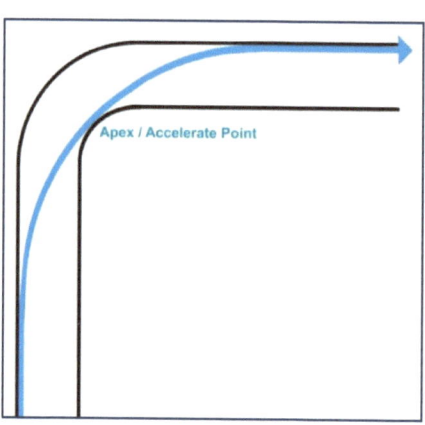

The geometric apex is exactly halfway around this corner.

Advantages:

- Smooths out the corner efficiently.
- Maintains momentum (particularly useful for Stock/lower powered cars).
- Reduces the chances of understeer or oversteer (especially helpful in low-grip conditions).
- Preserves tyre life.

Disadvantages:

While it is the fastest way to drive the current corner, it is not necessarily the fastest way to drive the next part of the track and therefore may not produce the fastest lap times in all situations.

Late Apex

If a straight follows the corner, then the ideal racing line for maximum speed over the corner, plus the straight, is a late apex. Although the car is slower into the corner when compared to a geometric apex, it positions the car to accelerate much earlier. Overall, the time over that part of the track (from the corner entry to the end of the straight) is quicker.

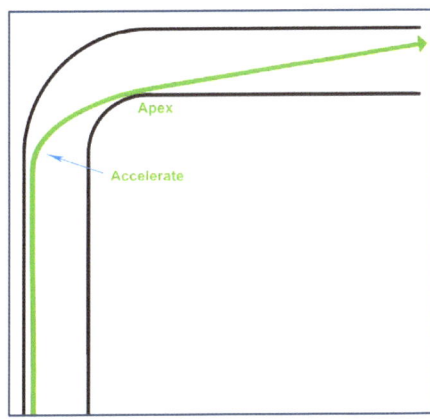

Accelerating early as the car passes the clipping point means it will be faster down the following straight. The driver who accelerates sooner and/or harder has a large advantage, and a late apex may help maximise that advantage.

Advantages:

- Increases the chances of a fast lap in a powerful car (Modified).
- Allows the power to be applied earlier.
- Maximises the use of any straights following the corner.

Disadvantages:

- Requires earlier braking.
- May not be the fastest path in a lower powered car.

Early Apex

An Early Apex can be faster for an understeering car.

We can also use it for overtaking, as described below.

Overtaking on a Corner

We've seen that the fastest way around a track is to follow the racing line. If you are closely following a car that is following this racing line, then they may approach the corner from the outside of the track. This provides an opportunity to brake late and take an early apex, darting up the inside of your opponent (the red racing line on the diagram below right). Although you will probably run wide to maintain your corner speed, you should have nosed in front of the other car. You may also have disrupted their concentration and/or forced them off the line that they wanted to take. Pass accomplished.

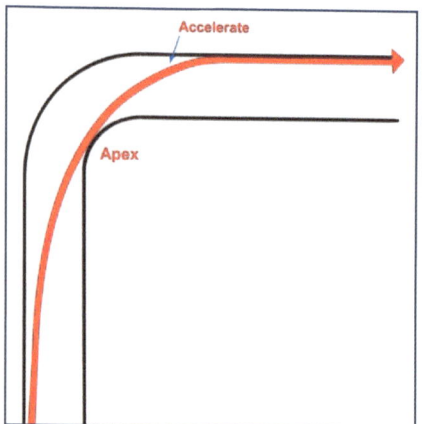
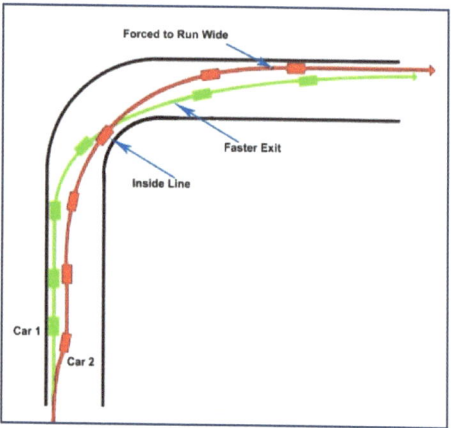

To defend against the above, you need to take a late apex while slowing sufficiently not to hit the car passing you, and then accelerate early and shoot back past them while they are running wide.

Of course, once you have another car close on your tail, you leave yourself open to the above passing scenario if you stick to the racing line. Therefore, you may wish to drive closer to the inside of the track to prevent the above overtaking move. Your choice to not drive the racing line will slow your lap times, but by not leaving a gap, you should retain the position.

The Karting Apex

The best racing line for a low-powered car (such as a 21.5 motor) can be the Karting Line (in some circumstances). This is a wider line that doesn't hit the apex. Karts don't have good brakes or quick

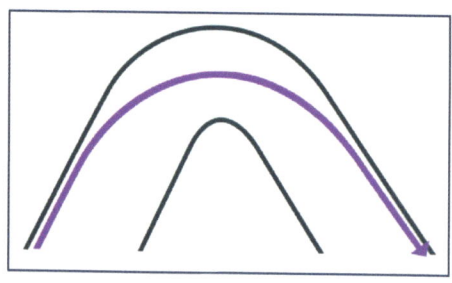

acceleration and therefore focus on maintaining momentum around the track.

Faster cars can also use the Karting Line when traction is low, as it maintains as much momentum as possible without relying heavily on acceleration.

Driving Tips

- Only brake in a straight line and don't jam the brakes on. Reduce the radio's brake End Point Adjustment (page 167), if necessary, until you get used to smooth braking.

- Accelerate smoothly out of corners so you don't lose the back end.

- Experiment to find the best line around each corner for your driving style.

- If you can't turn as tightly as you would like, slow down. Otherwise, overshooting a corner will more than lose any gain from entering the corner faster. Then adjust your setup for the next run so you have sufficient steering to take the corner the way you want to.

- A common mistake in off-road is to apply full steering lock (on the radio) at every corner. Use more steering lock in tight corners, less in fast corners.

Chicanes

A chicane is a shallow corner in one direction, followed by a shallow corner in the other direction. Depending on the corners preceding and following the chicane, it can often be driven at high-speed. This requires a car which will change direction quickly (refer to page 321) and examination of the chicane for the straightest possible line through it (refer to the example on page 73). Chicanes can be a difficult part of the track to drive quickly due to the fast steering inputs required without upsetting the car.

Sweepers

A sweeper is a long corner. Because the corner is not very sharp, the steering input is less, and therefore the corner may be taken much faster than a sharper corner.

With some sweepers it is faster to follow the corner as closely as possible, while with others running wide may lead to a faster exit. Unfortunately, it is not practical to provide diagrams for every scenario.

Sweepers are often at the start or end of the straight.

If the sweeper is entered relatively slowly because of the prior corner, then you are often accelerating during most of the sweeper and may hug the inside throughout and still be at full speed as early as possible on the straight – example on the left below.

If the sweeper is entered at high-speed, then it may be easier to think of the sweeper as two separate corners – example on the right below.

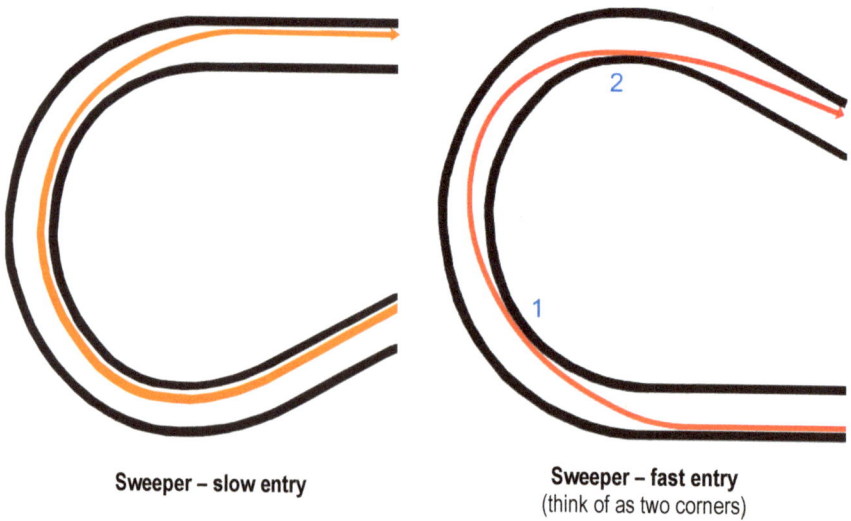

Sweeper – slow entry

Sweeper – fast entry
(think of as two corners)

Diagrams are examples only and will not apply to every sweeper.

Hairpins

A hairpin is a corner which changes the direction of the car by 180-degrees. Assuming the track is smooth and clean, the fastest line around a hairpin is a very late apex (about three-quarters of the way around the bend). A guide point is that halfway through the turn, you should be roughly in the middle of the track.

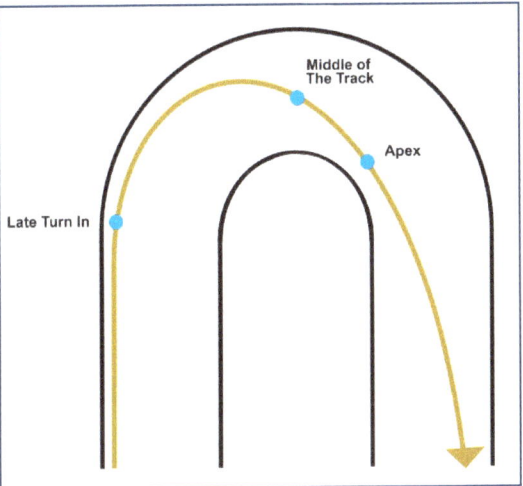

However, in off-road the surface of the track that close to the edge may be slippery, so a tighter line is more common. Try to have the car pointing towards the next straight as early as possible.

Slipstream Overtaking

In RC racing, using the slipstream of the car in front is not commonly practised at club level. It is very difficult to get right, and the straights are not usually long enough for it to make a significant difference. There are exceptions, but in general tucking your car closely in behind the car in front is difficult and risky to both cars in RC.

The Position of the Next Corner

The fastest way through a 90° corner is discussed above under the heading Geometric Apex. However, we aren't just trying to take one corner as fast as possible, we're trying to drive a complete lap as fast as possible, and the position and direction of the next corner affect the racing line of the current corner. For example, if the next corner is a left-hander you'll need to move over to the right-hand side of the track (orange line below), and therefore will need to apex later and take a tighter, slower line. However, if the next corner is another right-hander, a wider faster line can be used (red line below):

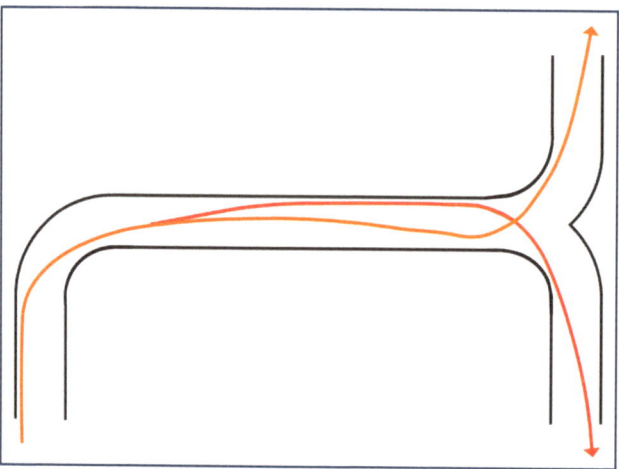

When there are a series of corners, it is better to view them as one large corner and focus on maximising your exit speed from the last one. Both red and orange cars take the last corner with a late apex for maximum acceleration onto the straight. The red car could possibly go faster by using an early apex for the first corner.

Increasing Corner Speed

Now that we know how to find the best line through a corner, the next step is to drive it as quickly as possible.

"Slow in, fast out" is the strategy of slowing more on the approach to the corner to ensure that you hit your apex and get back on the throttle as soon as possible. It is a useful mantra to keep in mind when first learning about cornering. However, we don't want to enter the corner slowly. We only want to slow the car the minimum amount so we can hit the chosen apex. Priorities are:

1. Slowing down early enough to be on the correct line mid-corner.
2. Practicing how hard you can exit the corner.
3. Practicing how hard you can enter the corner.

The Process of Driving Faster

The fastest lap means always driving your car on the absolute limit of the available grip. When you brake, leave the braking as late as possible so you can use all the grip available to brake the car down to the speed you wish to take the corner (which is ideally the fastest speed that your car can take the corner). When you stop braking, this makes grip available for turning (which is why hard braking and turning at the same time can make you lose control, as well as scrubbing off speed). As you pass the apex, reduce the steering input to make grip available for acceleration.

Pro drivers sometimes reduce the Steering Throw (page *182*) to maximise corner speed.

Sections of a Corner

Ideally, braking should be smooth and fluid. Steering should also be smooth and fluid. Sudden or jerky braking/steering can upset the balance of the car, causing it to oversteer or understeer.

Tapping the brakes transfers weight forward for cornering, which gives the car more grip available for steering.

The perfect corner involves tightening the steering until the apex and then gradually reducing the steering as you accelerate. If you find yourself increasing or correcting the steering during the corner, after the initial turn-in, you've probably taken the wrong line.

The greatest demand on the tyres' grip occurs between the turn-in point and the apex. It is important not to accelerate or brake during this part of the turn; you want to maintain a constant speed.

When accelerating, you will not be able to use all the power of a Modified car until you're completely in a straight line. However, if you're in a less powerful car, you can apply the throttle much closer to the apex.

Smooth braking and steering are factors that separate the professional driver from the club racer.

Perfect Practice Makes Perfect

We can break practice into two types:

- **Driving Practice** – learning the track and practising braking, cornering, and acceleration.

- **Testing** – identifying areas of the track where your car's handling could be improved, changing the setup and retesting to see if the change is better or worse.

Experienced drivers will often combine these two types of practice, but when learning it can be easier to focus on one.

Practice is only useful if done as close to race conditions as possible. If you use tyre additive and tyre warmers at a race meeting, then make sure you do this when practising. If you are practising for an event, then use the same brand and model of tyres for practice that you will use during the event. Otherwise, you may waste your time as your car's grip is likely to be completely different.

Fast cornering takes practice. Identify the racing line you want to take and practice it. Change the setup of your car to make your ideal racing line as easy and fast to drive as possible. It is often easier to focus your practice on getting one or two corners right each lap rather than trying to get every corner perfect. Once you are happy with the corners you've been practising, focus on the next couple of corners. The goal, of course, is to lower your lap times.

Practising the way you will race and focusing on getting one corner right at a time until you can string them all together is "Perfect Practice", hence the title of this section.

Fast Lap Times

Ray Munday – Tech Talk

The objective of any form of racing is the same – get around a circuit in the least possible time with your equipment (and hopefully in less time than your competitors!). Sounds pretty simple right? Here we will talk about what it actually means to get a fast lap time, and how you can adjust your driving to the track's features and your car's strengths to minimise your lap time.

How to get a fast lap time?

Quick physics refresher: Time = Distance / Speed

In other words, go twice as far, and you will take twice as long to get around the track; go twice as fast, and you will get around in half the time. In summary, we want to go as fast as possible and take the shortest possible route.

In reality, our race tracks are made of a series of corners and straights all connected together. Our lap time is the total of how much time we spend in each section. Going as fast as possible isn't as simple as just having the most top-end speed – we have to slow down for corners or we will spin out, and top-end is no good if it takes our car a long time to get up to speed. Therefore, what we want is a car that gets up to speed/slows down on the straights in the shortest time and goes around corners as quickly as possible (which not only means we spend less time in the corner but also means we are travelling faster when we get onto the straight).

What does that mean? We want to maintain the highest acceleration at all points on the track to minimise lap time.

What is acceleration?

A lot of people confuse speed and acceleration. Speed is how fast you go in a straight line (for the physics nerds out there, it is more correctly referred to as velocity, which is how fast you are going and in which direction). Acceleration is how quickly you change speed (or velocity) and there are two types of acceleration we need to consider: forward acceleration and cornering acceleration.

Forward Acceleration = (Change in Speed) / Time

In other words, it is a measure of how quickly your car will build up speed in a straight line (under power) and also how fast it will wash it off (under braking). It is a function of motor torque that is being applied at the wheels and how much traction your car has.

Not everyone realises it, but cornering is also a type of acceleration (referred to as centripetal acceleration). When you are cornering, you are actually slowing down in one direction and increasing speed in another. If you think about what happens when you go around a 90-degree corner at a constant speed, you have actually completely washed off your speed in the direction of the first straight and increased your speed in the new direction you are travelling. This happens progressively as you go through the corner, and the direction of this acceleration force is pointing towards the centre of the corner at all times. The formula for this is:

Cornering Acceleration = (Speed)^2 / Radius

There are two very important points to note from this:

1. If we want to go twice as fast around a corner, the acceleration is 4 times higher
2. A small radius (tight corner) will require a slower speed for the same acceleration.

Cornering acceleration is generated by the side grip of the tyres (page 99).

As a quick summary:

- Fast lap time = maintaining maximum acceleration around the track.
- Higher cornering acceleration = less time in the corners.
- Higher forward acceleration = less time on the straights.

What makes cornering more challenging than straight-line driving is that generally, there are multiple ways of going around a corner. Let's take two examples:

1. **Driving the classic "racing line"** – sweeping from the outside to the inside and back to the outside through a corner (refer to the Geometric Apex on page 31). By taking the classic sweeping racing line, we are maximising the radius (making the turn as big as possible) which allows us to carry more speed through the corner. However, it also requires us to drive a further distance and because you are on the limit of cornering traction, you can't accelerate until you have finished the corner (refer to the friction circle of the tyre discussed on page 102).

2. **Taking the "tight line"** – aiming straight for the inside of the corner, hugging the corner as tightly as possible all the way around, then reaccelerating out of the corner. By hugging the inside of the corner, you are making the turn as tight as possible, which means you can't carry as much speed through the turn. However, you don't spend as long in the turn and are able to accelerate sooner out of the corner.

When should you use these methods? It's not always black and white, but we need to look at the performance envelope of your car and drive to its strengths.

Performance Envelope

Each tyre has a "friction circle" (described on page 102). In summary, a tyre will have a certain amount of traction in each direction – if we draw this from above, it looks like a circle. We can expand this to create the "performance envelope" of the car. This is a function of the tyre grip and the motor power available.

For cornering, it will look like a friction circle as all four tyres create the grip. Under acceleration, a 4WD car will have close to twice as much grip as a 2WD car, so there is a lot more acceleration traction available. Under brakes, a 4WD car (with a locked centre diff) will also have a lot more braking power available than a 2WD car. If we look at the power available between a 21.5 car and a Modified car there is a significant difference – under acceleration, a mod car can generate enough power to reach the limit of the tyres, whereas a 21.5 car will be limited by the motor rather than the tyres (especially at higher speeds).

In summary, a 4WD car will have more forward braking/acceleration than a 2WD, and a motor with low power will have less forward acceleration available.

How do we apply this to our driving line? Going back to our earlier statement – we want to maximise acceleration at all times.

If you have a car with good forward acceleration, then you want to get through the corner quickly so you can use that forward acceleration for as long as possible. In this case, you should take a tight line, so that you finish the corner as quickly as possible and use the forward acceleration as soon as you can to slingshot you down the straight.

If you have a car with less forward acceleration (such as a Stock or 21.5 car) then you should take a more flowing line to keep up the corner speed and minimise how much forward acceleration you have to do on the corner exit.

A classic example (that I have seen many times) is the change you need to make to your driving style when changing from Stock to Modified. In Stock, you are maximising corner speed, but when you go to mod, your car will not corner any faster. You are also entering corners faster as the speed down the straight is higher. Generally, when moving to mod people tend to end up going way too fast into the corner, which means that they run a wider line and spend more time than they have to in the corner, and are late getting back on the power (or they put too much power on too early, spinning the wheels and losing grip).

A mod car doesn't go through corners any faster and as we have just described, you are actually better off using a slightly slower mid-corner speed to allow yourself to use the power more effectively out of the corner. It's funny in some ways, the car with the least power (e.g. 21.5) should actually be travelling the fastest through the corners!

You also need to consider the track layout when you plan your racing line. If you have a series of tight hairpins leading into each other, you are better to keep a tight line in each so you can punch it between each one and have the shortest distance possible. If you have a corner leading onto a long straight, you should take a more flowing line to keep the speed up through the corner and carry that onto the straight.

You should also consider the track layout when you set up the car. In a 2WD especially, weight distribution has a big influence on forward traction and cornering power. If the track has many flowing corners, you will be spending more time in the corner and should focus on maximum corner speed (i.e. move the weight forwards). If the track is a "point and shoot" layout with lots of tight corners and hairpins, you will be spending more time under forward acceleration so you should focus your setup on maximum forward acceleration (i.e. move weight backwards).

If you compare mid-motor 2WD buggies and rear-motor buggies, you can see a similar trend. Mid-motor buggies tend to require a more flowing line to maximise their corner speed compared to a rear-motored car.

Doing a track walk (refer to page 67) is critical to planning your racing lines and your setup. Think about the nature of the track – is it mostly flowing or tight? Which corners have straights after them, and which ones are followed by tight corners? Where is the surface grippy or loose? Where can you maximise your acceleration as much as possible around the track?

If you plan your racing line, driving style and setup to maximise your acceleration, I'm sure you will see your lap times drop and enjoy your racing more!

– Ray Munday

Driver Etiquette and Traffic

If your car is involved in an incident, you are losing time. This section covers proper driving etiquette and how you can use it to prevent incidents.

The following provides guidance on how to handle common situations when racing:

Lapping

Drivers that are being lapped must give way to the lapping car. The race software may call cars that are about to be lapped when they cross the start/finish line, but of course, the leaders can catch people at other parts of the track. It can sometimes be confusing whether you are being lapped or not. If you are lapping someone and they are not moving aside, then call out "red car lapping blue car", for example, so that the blue car knows the situation. The blue car must allow the red car to pass without blocking them. Of course, if you are racing for position and not being lapped, then block away.

Staggered Start Passing

Staggered starts for qualifying (also called IFMAR Called starts) can create an interesting situation when passing or lapping. This is how they work.

If you wait until your name or car number is called before starting, then it is a staggered start. Staggered starts are a time trial where you race against the clock. A "heat" or "qualifier" contains a number of drivers because it would be time consuming for every driver to take their turn individually. Once your name or number is called, you start your time trial. Your personal timer starts when you cross the start/finish line for the first time and ends when the race software calls the end of the race plus the lap you are on (always keep going until your name or car number is called as finished) If it's your first time to this track, check out one of the qualifiers before yours to get a feel for how it starts and observe where the cars are lining up (for example, does it call your name or car number and is there a short or long pause between each car starting its run?).

As you are racing the clock, if the driver behind catches you, they have already passed you on the clock, so racing to try and keep them behind only hurts your own time. Let them by and take this as an opportunity to follow the faster driver and learn some racing lines that you may have missed in your study of the track. Most of all, be patient whether you are the slower or faster driver, call out for the red car to pass the green car on the next corner and allow them through. Getting tangled up with each other isn't going to help either of your times! You must not block people in staggered start qualifying. If someone catches you, then let them pass.

How to Pass

How to let other cars pass deserves some discussion. When you are learning to drive, it's difficult to move out of someone's way without crashing. The best way to let someone pass is to go slightly wide at a corner allowing the other car to pass on the inside. Sudden changes in speed or direction can cause a crash. For example, slowing down suddenly might cause the passing car to crash into the back of you.

If you let the person know when you will go slightly wide, then they can take advantage of it to pass. If the lapping car is blue, then say "pass me on the inside blue car at the next corner" or simply "inside blue car". If you know the person's name, then use it to be even clearer e.g. "inside Jim". The passing racer will appreciate it, and it will have the least impact on your own qualifying time.

Resolving Disputes

You may have heard the term "hacked" or "taken out", for example, "he hacked me". This slang means the person feels someone crashed into them. If there is a racing incident that affects you, why not speak to the person involved immediately after the race? Racers who are new to the hobby sometimes need guidance on what is acceptable behaviour. As long as this guidance is provided in a positive and friendly manner, then most of the time the person will change their behaviour. Sometimes people get angry in the heat of the moment. Walking away and trying to talk to them later, when they've cooled down, often works. If the behaviour continues, then notify the Race Director.

After a Crash

If you cause an accident, then the correct behaviour is to wait for that person to continue before you continue. An apology after the race never hurts either. We should all be aware that the speeds and distances involved mean that mistakes happen, and that's racing. It's how we handle it that matters.

Hitting Someone From Behind

If you hit someone from behind, then it's always your fault. You control where your car is at any given time on the track. If the car in front brakes unexpectedly, then that may well cause an incident, but that you ran into the back of them is your fault. If you are coming up behind someone you've never raced with before, then it pays to be more cautious.

Marshals

If your car has left the track or is on its roof, then hopefully a marshal will assist you as soon as possible.

If a marshal doesn't see your car is in trouble, then a single call of "Marshal" is acceptable to draw their attention to it. Remember that if you hadn't crashed, a marshal wouldn't be necessary, so treat marshals with the respect they deserve.

The marshal's priorities are their safety and not to cause issues for the drivers who haven't crashed. So marshals will not rush in front of other cars on the track to get to your car. Nor should you expect them to fix any issues with your car.

Do not hit the throttle until your car is back on the track (you could injure the marshal), and do not pull out in front of another car. Wait until there is a gap.

Chapter 3

Jumping

Jumping Basics

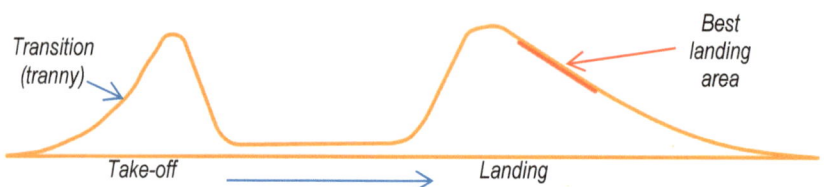

Introduction

Infinite variation can be found in the shapes and sizes of jumps, but the same basic principles apply to them all:

1. Flying over a jump is normally faster than driving over it.
2. While you are in the air, you are slowing down due to air drag. Less time in the air is faster.
3. While in the air, you are unable to accelerate as your wheels aren't touching the ground. The lower the height that you jump, the sooner you will be back on the ground, and therefore the faster your lap time. The higher you jump, the slower your lap time.
4. Landing:
   - The objective is to land fully in control and to smoothly continue your lap.
   - Landing with all four wheels on the ground allows the suspension to best absorb the landing. Otherwise, the car may be unsettled and could crash.
   - Landing on the downslope of the jump is recommended as it requires less suspension compression than landing on a flat piece of track.
   - Landing with wheels turning at the correct speed for the forward motion of the car allows acceleration or braking after the jump in the most efficient manner.
   - Apply the throttle just before you land to try to match the wheel speed with the ground speed. This is very important: Landing with some power on also helps the suspension to "bind up", which reduces bottoming out.
5. Take-off:
   - Approach the jump straight on, i.e. if you are in the middle of the track as you take-off, then you should land in the middle of the track (assuming the track is straight and the jump is perpendicular to the track).

Jumping 3

- More crashes occur at jumps than at any other part of the track. If your car is not completely under control as you approach the jump, then consider driving over it rather than jumping it. You will lose less time that way than if you crash and need to be marshalled.

Jump Types

The following covers the most common types of jump. You can see real life examples on page 73.

How you take each jump is dependent on what comes before and after it (a straight, a corner, or another jump). Below is general guidance for the fastest lap time, assuming the jump is not immediately followed by another jump or a corner.

Low Single

Accelerate over the jump. The trajectory through the air should be fairly close to the ground and therefore little time is lost in the air (as in the photo below).

High Single

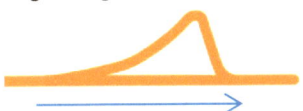

A slower approach can minimise time in the air, allowing you to accelerate away as early as possible.

50

A faster technique is called **Scrubbing** – brake just before the lip of jump to mimimise time in the air while approaching as fast as possible. This can also be used for longer jumps to minimise time in the air. This is a pro driver technique and takes a lot of practice.

Drop Off

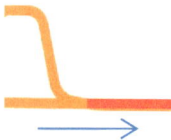

Land flat in the red zone, as close to the bottom of the drop off as practical which allows you to accelerate away as early as possible.

Double

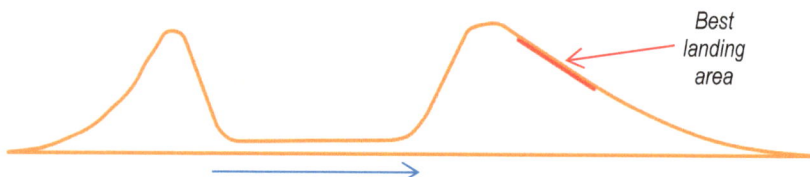

Note that the best landing area minimises time in the air.

Table Top

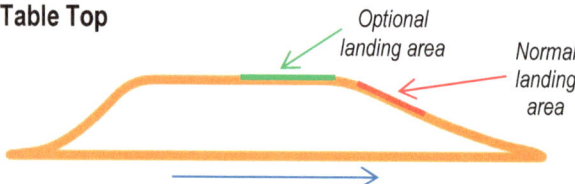

Normally the fastest way over a table top is to treat it like a double and land in the red zone. However, if there is a corner immediately afterwards you may need to "flat land" in the green zone to let the car settle before taking the corner.

Triple

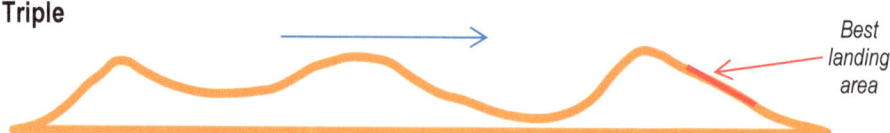

Land on the downslope of the third mound. Lower powered cars may not be able to make the triple in one jump. In that scenario, split the jump into two (a double and a single).

Quad

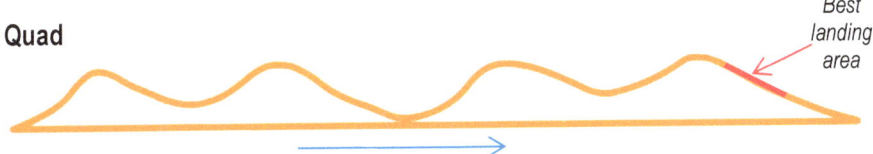

Best landing area

Land on the downslope of the fourth mound. Lower powered cars may not be able to make it in one jump. In that scenario, and depending on the power available, split the jump into two doubles, or a triple and a single.

Rhythm section

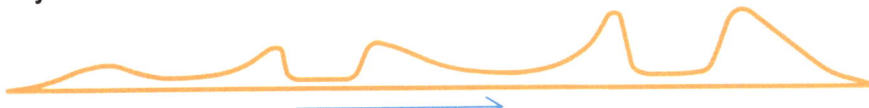

A rhythm section is multiple jumps back to back. Refer to *Putting it All Together* on page *66* for an example.

On some tracks a rhythm section may be introduced by adding corner dots all over the track, forcing the suspension to work hard.

Control in the Air

Pitch

In the air, your car can rotate horizontally around the Centre of Gravity (page *125*). Pitch-up is when the front of your car is pointing slightly towards the sky, while pitch-down is when the front is pointing slightly towards the ground.

Your car will normally leave the face of the jump pitch-up and should naturally pitch-down for the landing (if it doesn't, then refer to Jumping Troubleshooting on page *324*).

You can change the pitch of the car in flight by:

- Increasing throttle – pitching nose up.
- Reducing throttle – pitching nose down slightly.
- Braking – pitching nose down.

This can be useful to adjust the pitch for landing so that all four wheels hit the ground at the same time. This allows the suspension to best absorb the landing.

Changing pitch does not change the direction the car is travelling.

Because 4WD cars drive both the front and rear wheels, changing the throttle or brake will change the pitch to a greater degree than for a 2WD car.

Roll

Roll in the air has the same meaning as roll on the ground. The car rolls to the left or right around the Centre of Gravity (page *125*). However, the suspension doesn't compress because the car is in the air.

If the front wheels are spinning, then you can change the roll of the car in flight by:

- Steering left – car rolls right.
- Steering right – car rolls left.

This can be useful if your car didn't leave the jump squarely and has rolled in flight.

> **Whipping** – When there is a corner just after you land the jump, you can turn the car towards it by changing the roll and pitch of the car in combination so that the car faces the corner as it lands. This takes a great deal of practice and is an advanced technique used by pro drivers. Refer to *Combination Throttle/Steering Techniques* on page *62*.

Jump Distance

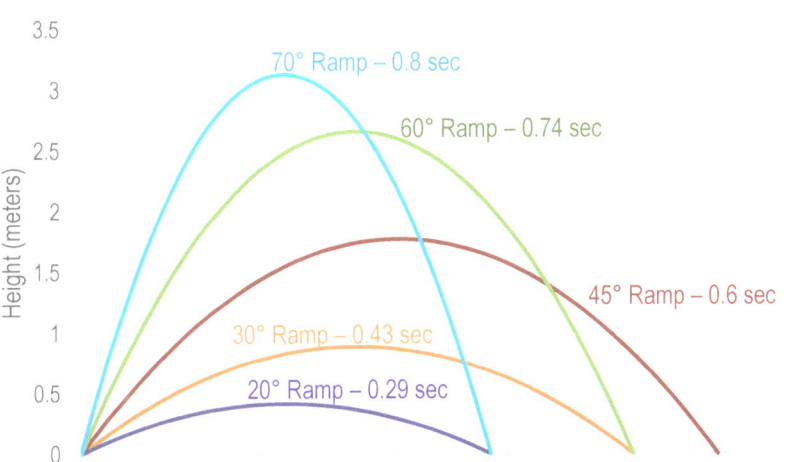

The graph above shows a car travelling 30km/h (about 19mph), taking five different jumps with various ramp angles between 20° and 70°. The jump type is a High Single and for ease of calculation, drag/air resistance has been ignored.

For example, a car leaving a 45° jump at 30km/h will travel just over 7m (about 23 feet) in 0.6 seconds.

Of course, as drivers, we can only vary the speed and not the ramp angle itself, but it does demonstrate that if you have the option, it is faster to minimise your time in the air and that a 45° path of travel will provide the greatest distance.

Below is the same graph at 20 km/h (roughly 12 mph) for comparison:

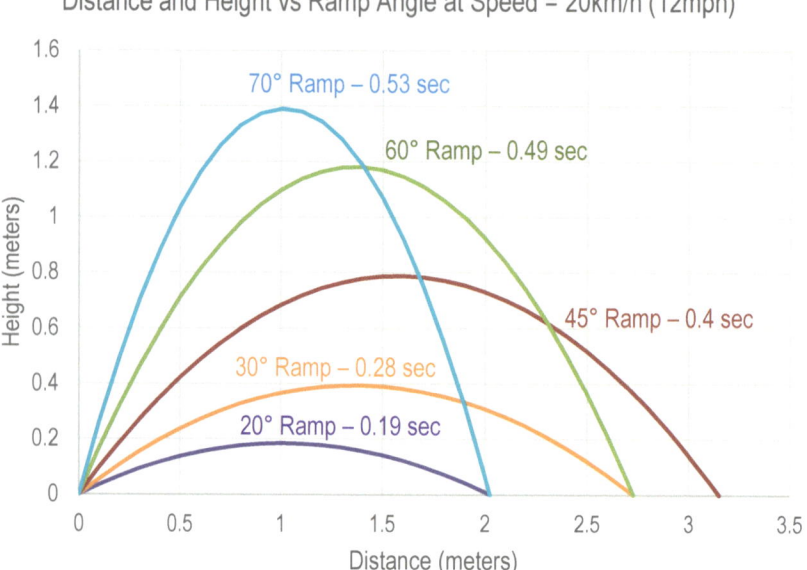

Here are some interesting facts:

- Leaving the jump 50% faster more than doubles the distance jumped and the car spends approximately 50% more time in the air.

- Remember that we have ignored drag/air resistance. In the real world the car will slow down due to air resistance and will not quite reach the distances shown. The longer the car is in the air, the greater the speed reduction due to air resistance. Air resistance will affect the car more if its trajectory is not flat (i.e. if the car flies parallel to the ground then air resistance will be less than if it flies nose up or nose down).

- A car launched at 70° travels the same distance as a car launched at 20°. In fact, any angle greater than 45° has a corresponding angle less than 45° which will result in the same distance. This angle can be found by taking 90° minus the larger angle to find the smaller angle, e.g. 90°−70°=20°.

    The smaller angle will always be faster, e.g. on our 20km/h graph the car travels 2m in 0.19 seconds at 20°. However, the same distance takes 0.53 seconds at 70°. If you've ever seen the leading car jump high and the chasing car jump low to take the lead, this is why.

Science of Jumping

Ray Munday – Tech Talk

Many people refer to jumping an RC car as "an art". When you watch a top driver throw their car through the air, you can appreciate that there is an art to it, and some are much better than others. I would like to explain the science behind how to control your car in the air, so you can help make your jumping more subconscious.

The basic components of jumping I will run through are:

1. Run-up and Take-off.
2. The Flight Path (Trajectory) and Landing.
3. Throttle Control.
4. Steering Control.
5. Combination Throttle/Steering.

Run-up and Take-off

The approach to the jump and the take-off are critical as they define the next phase of the jump (the actual flight path). It's always good practice to do a track walk (refer to page 66) to determine the ideal line through a jump, taking into consideration any uneven jump faces, which direction the corner after the jump is, and how much run-up you have.

When you hit the face of the jump, your car is forced hard towards the track. At this point, as long as your chassis isn't bottomed out, you actually have the greatest traction available around the entire track. Your tyres are being pushed hard into the ground, which gives them the most grip. This means you can actually build up a lot of speed on the face of the jump itself if you time your throttle application correctly – punch it as the car is forced into the ground. If you set your slipper clutch too loose (page 180), you will lose a lot of punch on take-off as the slipper is limiting how much torque can reach the wheels – if you are having trouble clearing a jump, slipper clutch tightness is the first place to start.

Generally, you want to be perpendicular to the jump. If you hit the jump at an angle, your car will tend to corkscrew. You also want to hit the track with the car going in a straight line. If it's sliding when it hits the jump, it will suddenly change direction (due to the high-traction from the tyres being forced into the ground) and often jump off the side of the track.

Flight Path

The flight path (or trajectory) is basically defined by the speed and direction of the take-off. The jump face transfers your car's speed from going forwards (i.e. parallel to the ground) to being partly forward, partly upwards. The steeper the jump, the more vertical speed your car has, but the less horizontal speed.

Once your car leaves the face of the jump, there are only two forces that act on it:
1. Gravity (pulling the car back towards the ground).
2. Air drag/lift (drag slowing the car down, lift trying to push the car up or down).

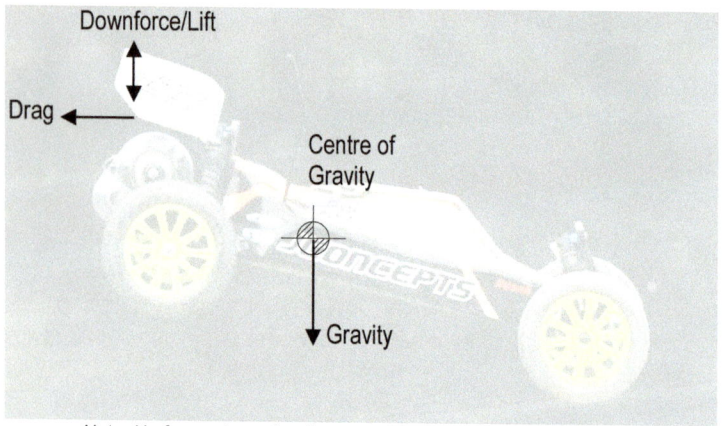

Note: No forward acceleration as tyres are not on the ground!

No matter what you do with the throttle or the steering, you won't change the direction of the car in the air, and you will only change the flight path if pitching the vehicle's nose up or down changes the aerodynamics of the vehicle (as it does with Short Course Trucks). Think of it like throwing a ball – once the ball has left your hands, the ball goes up, then comes down – the harder you throw it, the further it goes, the steeper your throw, the longer it stays in the air.

The trajectory defines how long you will be in the air, how far you will jump and how hard you hit the ground. If the jump is steep, you will jump higher and be in the air for a longer time, but not necessarily jump very far. If the take-off is flat, you will jump a long way, but not necessarily very high.

What is the optimum trajectory? That is something you need to determine case-by-case. You want to jump far enough to clear the jump itself, but usually no further. When you are in the air, your tyres are not touching the ground, so you can't accelerate. Therefore during your time in the air you aren't increasing speed (you are actually getting slower due to air drag).

Jumping 3

Ideally, if the jump has an appropriate downslope, you want your trajectory to be coming down so that you land on the downslope, which makes for the most gentle landing and allows you to build up speed quickly (you have a lot of traction as you come off the downslope of a jump).

There are some extreme cases where you want to take a less conventional line.

Example #1 is coming out of a tight corner with a high single jump immediately afterwards. If you punch it hard up the jump, you may get a lot of air, but you will not be accelerating and therefore you may lose a lot of time (with electric motors, the acceleration is strongest at low-speed). In this instance, it can be better to hit the brakes just before you jump and actually get no air – then you can accelerate hard down the back of the jump. Braking just before the lip of a jump is called **Scrubbing,** and it minimises time in the air while approaching as fast as possible. It is particularly useful for singles or for longer jumps to minimise time in the air. This technique takes a lot of practice to perfect.

Example #2 is a low single jump on a fast straight. If the jump has a shallow take-off angle, it can be better to hit it fast and jump a long distance as you will still be going fast, and if you are already close to top speed, you won't be losing acceleration being off the ground. A downside of this is you might be "flat landing" which can cause heavy bottoming, so you may need to adjust your setup to compensate. Again, a quick track walk will highlight this before you start racing.

Throttle Control

Once your car is in the air, we can use physics to change the angle of the car in pitch using the throttle. As described in the previous section, this won't change the trajectory, but has two important advantages:

1. You can control the angle so that it matches the downslope of the jump, giving you maximum control.
2. You can get the car to point nose down to give some extra downforce which will reduce the time spent in the air (especially critical for Short Course Trucks).

How does it work? We are relying on a physical phenomenon called "Conservation of Angular Momentum". Angular momentum is the rotational inertia of a part multiplied by the speed it is spinning.

Throttle on: When our car is in the air, if we hit the power and make the wheels speed up, they gain angular momentum. This creates an equal and opposite reaction which tries to keep the total angular momentum constant – in this case, it will make the chassis (which has a much higher rotational inertia than the wheels) rotate backwards in sympathy.

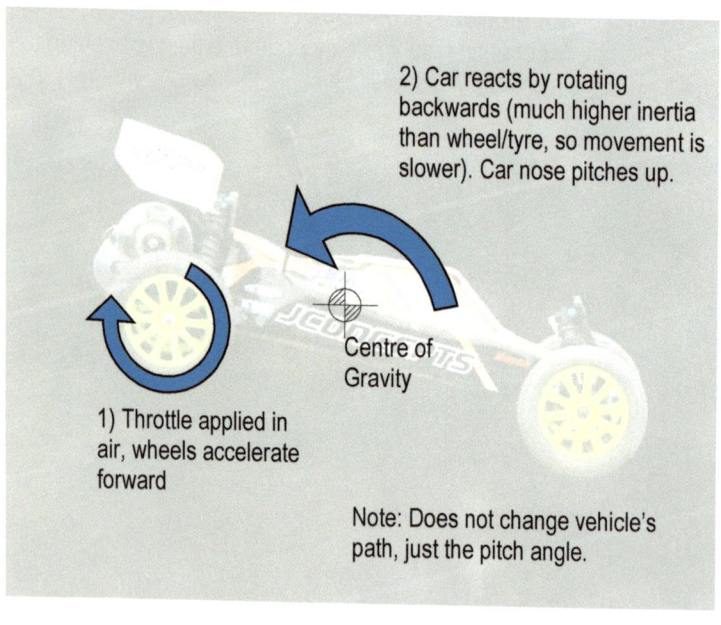

Brake on: If the wheels are spinning fast and we hit the brakes in the air, the wheels have lost angular momentum. To compensate, the body will start to rotate forwards (the opposite of the Throttle On diagram above). Remember to apply the throttle just before you land to try to match the wheel speed with the ground speed.

Note that it is not just the wheels that contribute to the angular momentum; any part that rotates within the drivetrain (motor, gears, diffs, driveshafts, etc.) all contribute to this effect. Transmission gears are a case in point. With a regular 3 gear transmission on a 2WD, the motor spins in the opposite direction to the wheels. While the motor has much less rotational inertia than the wheels (as it is much smaller) it also spins about ten times faster. Thus when you apply the throttle/brakes, it counteracts the rotational inertia of the wheels somewhat. Whereas, with a 4 gear transmission, the motor spins in the same direction as the wheels and therefore adds to the effect.

It is also worth noting that this effect does not just happen in the air. When the car is on the ground, there is also a reaction torque which tries to make the vehicle pitch backwards as the wheels accelerate. This creates additional weight transfer to the rear under acceleration and is another key reason for 4 gear transmissions on mid-motor cars.

What are the factors affecting how sensitive a car is to throttle on/off in the air?

1. **4WD vs 2WD** – A 4WD car accelerates/decelerates all four wheels, making the effect twice as sensitive as with a 2WD. Many years ago it was common to run one-way bearings in the front driveshafts of a 4WD so that there was full power to the front but no braking (reducing understeer) – but the jump control with this setup was very poor and is one of the reasons 4WD cars usually don't use these.

2. **Less pitch inertia** – A vehicle with its mass spread out along the chassis (e.g. an older rear-motor 2WD buggy) has very high pitch inertia. It takes a lot of effort to get this type of chassis moving in pitch as the heavy motor is a long way from the centre of the car. Cars with the mass concentrated closer to the centre (i.e. a typical 4WD or mid-motor 2WD) will be much more sensitive to throttle application in the air. In the same vein, wheels/tyres with higher rotational inertia (i.e. heavier or larger) will have more of an effect on the pitch control.

3. **Motor power** – A vehicle with high motor power will be able to accelerate the wheels much faster and therefore give you more opportunity to bring the nose up.

4. **Take-off speed** – The faster you are travelling when you leave the jump, the faster the wheels are spinning in the air and therefore, if you hit the brakes, the

more they slow down and cause more of a nose down effect. You have less possibility to bring the nose down on slower jumps.

5. **Timing of the throttle/brake application** – The earlier in the flight path you apply the throttle or brakes, the more effect it will have on the vehicle's pitch when you land. As soon as your car leaves the jump, you need to be able to judge if it is starting to nose up or nose down and react with the throttle immediately. Keep in mind, if all four wheels stop spinning, the car has no gyroscopic energy in the air and can start to float around, especially on outdoor tracks when it's windy. It is always best to keep the wheels spinning, even if not at full speed.

Steering Control

While you can't make the car steer in the air (the trajectory will be in a straight line unless there is a strong crosswind), you can control the roll angle of the car in the air using the steering. This is handy to recover the car in the air if, for some reason, it has started to roll (for example, not hitting the jump square, hitting an uneven take-off surface, or because the landing surface is not level).

How does it work? We are relying on a physical phenomenon known as "precession" which involves a lot of complicated mathematics, which I won't try to describe here!

In summary: if a wheel is spinning and is turned to the left, it will react by trying to roll to the right. Therefore, steer to the right, and the car rolls to the left. Steer to the left, and it will roll to the right.

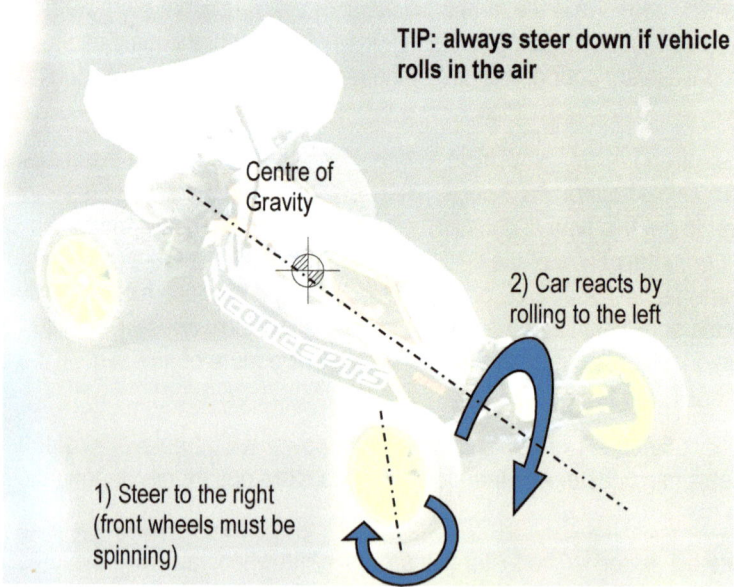

Note: Does not change the path of the vehicle, just the roll angle.

So if the car rolls in the air and you wish to level it out, then steer down (towards the ground). Another way to remember it is to steer into the roll.

What are the factors affecting how much steering control you have in the air?

1. How fast the front wheels are spinning: The faster they are spinning, the more effect they have. If you have already hit the brakes on a 4WD and the front wheels have stopped, there will be no effect.
2. The rotational inertia of the front wheels: The more inertia they have (larger diameter or heavier), the more the car will react to steering inputs in the air.
3. The roll inertia of the car: If the car has a low roll inertia (i.e. all the mass is down the centreline of the car), it will react quicker to steering inputs. This is why 2WD cars tend to react well to steering inputs (plus, their front tyres are spinning fast, regardless of the rear tyre speed).
4. Steering lock: The further you turn the steering, the more roll you will generate.

The use of steering in the air is a more advanced technique, and I would suggest only trying it out after you have mastered the pitch control techniques.

Combination Throttle/Steering Techniques – the "Whip"

After you have mastered Throttle and Steering control by themselves, you can try some more fancy combination techniques. It's best to have a car in your hand to visualise these examples. When it comes to manoeuvres in 3D, A plus B does not equal B plus A!

When you have a corner immediately after a jump, it often helps to have the car pointing towards the apex when you land. This is called a "whip" or "whipping", and this is how it works.

We will refer to our example track (from page 73). Below is a photo of the Triple (#18) followed by a 180° Hairpin (#19):

Normally, we would jump the triple and then turn in to the hairpin. However, it is faster to "yaw" the car in the air, so it is facing the apex of the hairpin when it lands. A yaw is when the car rotates left or right around a vertical axis (imagine a spike hammered through the centre of the roof around which the car yaws).

Whipping is an advanced technique and requires a lot of practice. But, once mastered, it reduces lap times.

"Whipping" Example

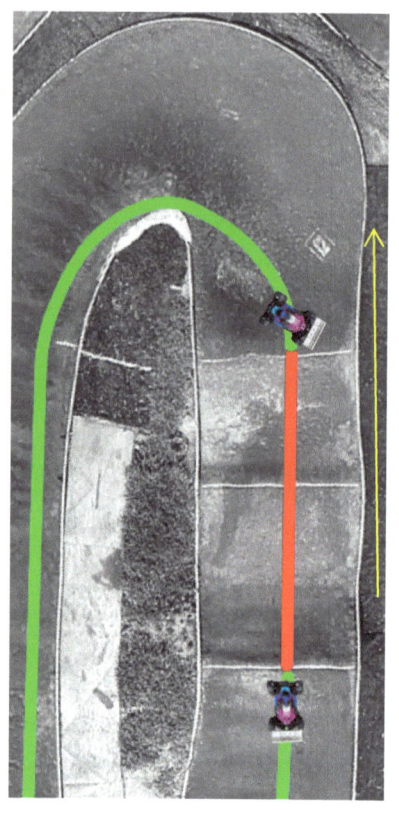

1. Car leaves the jump.
2. If it's a 2WD, apply full brake to stop the rear wheels (this will make the car roll faster and car will nose down). Skip this step for 4WD.
3. Steer to the right (car rolls left). It will also yaw to the left (due to the caster of the front wheels).
4. Straighten the wheels just before the car lands. Car will roll back to level. You may need to finetune the steering angle/roll in order to land all four wheels on the downslope at once.
5. Accelerate so that the wheels will be turning at the correct speed when the car lands.

The car is still travelling forward (trajectory is straight), but we have been able to yaw the car in the air to point it towards the apex of the next corner.

Make sure you land on the downslope of the jump or the car is likely to flip.

When done correctly "whipping" looks very cool, but it can be risky. If you make a mistake it can cause a crash. So practice until you can do it automatically (without thinking about each step) before you try it in a race.

If you are on Facebook you can watch a video of Lachlan Munday demonstrating whipping, here:
https://www.facebook.com/LachlanMundayRC/videos/1185962588582426

2WD "Whip" example: Brake then steer – In 2WD if you hit the brakes in the air, the front tyres are still spinning, and the rears are stopped, so any steering in the air will have the greatest effect. Hit the brakes just after take-off and then apply the steering. You will find the car rolls in the air much faster than if you steered first then hit the brakes.

4WD "Whip" example – In 4WD it's important to keep the wheels spinning if you want to whip the car, so I try not to brake in the air with a 4WD unless I really need to bring the nose down. You won't need to use as much steering as you would with a 2WD.

– Ray Munday

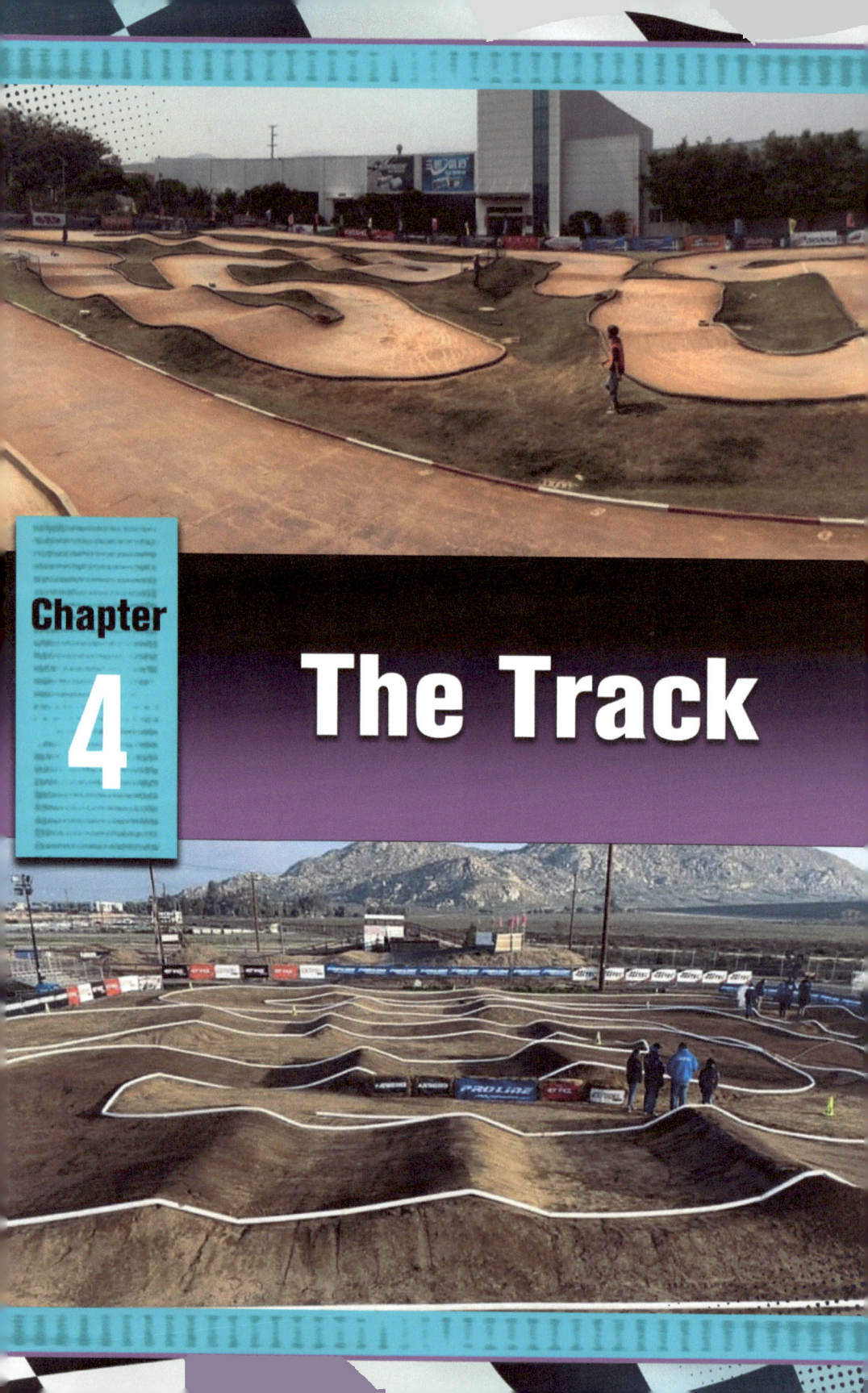

Chapter 4

The Track

Mapping the Track

Now that you know how to determine the racing line for any corner (refer to page 28) you should sketch out the racing line for the entire track. Draw the track on it, including all the features you have seen, and draw your planned racing line on the track. This is especially useful the first time you go to a track and you want to have a plan for how to attack the track from the start.

This is your map of the track. Now practice driving it.

If it's your first run at a track, take the first couple of laps very slowly (say 30% or so). Try to rub every kerb or pipe at every corner on the track so that you know you have judged the edge of the track correctly. Try to drive to the lines you have worked on during your track walk, but be flexible – sometimes, you need to adapt a little. After your run, make more notes on your track map. You will find this valuable the next time you go to the track.

Once you are comfortable that you are driving the racing line as close as possible, it may become obvious that the car is not following the racing line in certain sections as closely as you wish. By changing the setup of the car, you can make it easier to drive the racing line. For example, the car may not follow the sweeper the way you'd like, or it may take hairpins too wide. These issues may be corrected by changing the car setup to allow you to drive the racing line you have selected more closely and therefore reduce your lap times.

Refer to *Appendix D – Checklists* on page 310 for how to correct various issues with car handling.

On most tracks, your car will spend more time in the low-speed corners than in high-speed corners or on the straight. Therefore, that is where your biggest time gains might be made. For that reason, you may wish to adjust your gearing (refer to page 160) to increase acceleration out of corners at the expense of top speed on the straight.

Track Walk
Ray Munday – Tech Talk

Racing involves you (the driver) racing a car around a track against the clock. We spend a lot of time on our cars and maybe some time on our driving, but how many of us focus on the track itself?

No matter what scale of racing you are involved in, a track walk is one of the most effective ways to learn a new track and improve your lap times for zero cost and only a little effort. Fortunately for RC racers, our tracks are relatively small and easy to walk around. Yet, I am continually amazed by how few people I see actually doing them. Below I describe how I go about a track walk, what I am looking for and how to use this information.

Why do a track walk?

Without sounding too obvious, it gives you a better view of the track! If you do it properly, you can get a lot of information that can help with line selection, driving technique, even setup and tyre choice. This is especially important when you visit a track for the first time and practice time is limited, but I also recommend it anytime you visit a track (or even during a race meet as track conditions can change regularly). It's also valuable if you are struggling with a particular part of the track. Instead of changing your car for this section and potentially making it worse on other parts of this track, have a look at the track and see if you aren't missing something at ground level.

I recommend doing a track walk before anything else. Get your gear out of the car, batteries on charge and register, but don't touch your equipment until you have done a track inspection. You might find something that necessitates a change in setup from the start, and it gives you more time to be mentally ready for your first practice session.

Step 1 – Confirm the track direction.

Step 2 – View the track from the driver's stand. Look for any sections that might be obscured or lines that may be difficult to see. Can you see the jump faces? Are there tall kerbs that are potentially blocking the view through a corner?

Step 3 – Inspect the track from the base of the driver's stand. Is there any elevation change that wasn't obvious from the stand? Is the track flat or on a slope?

Step 4 – Walk the track itself. Note: if the track has been watered, or if the ground is muddy, it's best not to walk on the actual surface but keep to the edging. Also, if there is a race on or others are practising on the track, be respectful and don't get in their way. Pick a point to start from and move around the entire lap in the direction of travel.

Things to check for at each section:

Surface

1. Is it smooth or bumpy? If it's bumpy, are the bumps uniform across the whole track or are they just on one line? Is there a different line you can take to avoid the bumps? If the track has many bumps around the whole track, consider adding more camber (page *118*), more droop (page *152*) and running bigger hole pistons in the shocks (page *127*).

2. How does it feel? Rub your finger on the surface to see if it dusts up, crumbles, is slippery or abrasive. Can you push your fingernail into the surface or is it very hard?

3. Is the surface the same all around the track? Many tracks have variable surfaces, which may affect tyre traction and handling. The surface in the corners or corner exit is more important than the surface halfway down the straight when you are already at speed.

4. Is the surface consistent across the width, or is there a specific racing line?

5. Is the track flat, or are there off-cambers, dips and rises? Get down on your knees, and you will see this more easily (as well as any bumps).

Jumps

1. Is the face of the jump consistent across the width of the track? Many jumps have faces with holes that should be avoided or one part of the jump that will give more air or a steeper take-off.

2. What is the landing of the jump like? Can you downslope it, or will you need to flat land? This can have a big effect on the shock setup you start with.

3. Does the jump have any options? Some jumps should be hit flat out, where others may reward a slower approach then punching out of the first jump. This is especially important in longer rhythm sections.

4. What is the run-up to the jump like? Will you need to take a different line through the previous corner, or can you take the correct racing line?

5. Is the jump square to the track? I have driven several tracks where the jump isn't perpendicular to the direction of travel, and it makes the car jump very strangely.

6. Can you see the face of the jump from the driver's stand? If not, pay more attention to that section.

Layout

This is probably the most important part of the track walk. There are many things you can look for, but the key ones are:

1. How can you enter the straight carrying the most speed? Top speed isn't important, but carrying speed into the faster sections helps a lot with lap time.

2. What line should you take through each corner to flow most cleanly into the next section? I try to look for the line that isn't necessarily the quickest for that corner, but for the overall speed through the two or three corners afterwards.

3. Which corners should you take tight to keep the tightest line? Which ones may require a more flowing line?

4. Is the general layout flowing or point and shoot? This will have a big influence on the weight distribution you may choose.

5. Look for the straightest path through the chicane(s).

Kerbs

Kerbs come in many shapes and sizes. The main things to look for are:

1. Can you ride the kerb? In faster sections, this can help you take a straighter line.
2. Will the kerb flip the car? If so, make sure you stay a little wider.
3. Will the kerb grab the car? If so, it's best to leave a little bit more room.
4. Can you see the car behind the kerb from the stand? Some kerbs/pipes which are tall can block your view from the stand even though the car is on the racing line. This is something you would never find out without a proper track walk.

Step 5 – Go back to the driver's stand after your track walk and take another look. Do you notice any additional features you didn't see before? It's a good idea to walk to each end of the stand at this stage. Sometimes you get a much better view from one spot on the stand, but you can't always get that spot every race.

Step 6 – If there are any spots on the track that are hard to see from the stand, ask someone to take your car and place it on the racing line at those places. You might find that on the racing line, all you can see is the wing!

During large events (or weather changes), the track can change a lot. It's good practice to do a track walk each day or even between qualifying and finals. Look for changes to the track – new bumps, loose surfaces, broken up jump faces – and make a plan how you will change your driving or setup to compensate. Also, keep an eye on the surface itself by rubbing your finger on the track as the day or event progresses. Look for it feeling dustier or tackier and change tyres to compensate.

As with many of the most effective techniques, a track walk costs nothing other than a little time. Practice using it each time you go to the track (especially a new track), and you will find it becomes second nature.

– Ray Munday

Conquering a New Track

Ryan Maker (4 x On-road Modified Australian National Champion) describes how to approach a new track. This is very relevant for off-road racing.

Arriving at a new track that you haven't driven a lap on can be quite intimidating, especially when the locals are already flying around. Don't let it get to you. Just start slow and do your own thing.

First, take a Track Walk (refer to page 67). Look closely at each of the curbs. Sometimes a track will use various curb sizes in different parts of the track. It is important to know which curbs you can drive over and which are too high. If the track has a white painted line, note where it is in relation to the curb (useful for judging distances when you are on the driver's stand).

Pick your driver's stand position. Everyone is different, but I like to position myself relative to the centre of the track, which is not necessarily the centre of the driver's stand. If there's a particular part of the track I'm struggling to see or drive, then I may move 1–2m towards that section for a better view. It's amazing how different a track can look depending on where you stand!

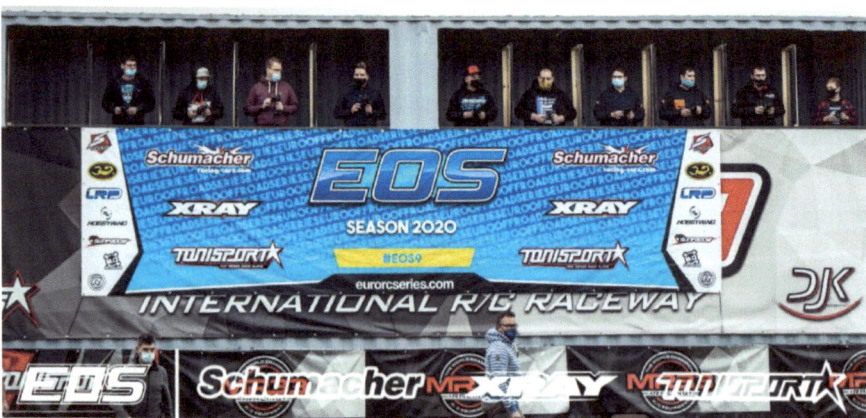

Initially, you should focus solely on your driving; ignore car setup until you've learnt the track. I make sure I can drive for five minutes without mistakes before changing my car setup. Start slowly and don't drive too fast, as you need to learn the confines of the track. A track can sometimes drive very differently from how it looks, and sections that look easy can sometimes be hard to navigate.

Once you're up to speed (usually 3–4 battery packs), you can start to look at your car setup. Don't get too carried away. Make sure you stay close to the normal setup that you run at home (assuming it's a similar track).

Make changes. If they don't work, then change them back. Something I see many people doing is making a change, and if they don't know if it's better or not, they just leave it. Bad move! If something isn't an obvious step in the right direction, then you should change it back to what you know. Otherwise, you will end up on some crazy setup that you have no idea how to finetune once racing starts.

Use your practice sessions wisely and, if possible, go out on the track when it isn't too busy. Use old tyres at the start when you are learning the track, and when the track is at its most "race-like" condition. Later, use new tyres in order to get a feel for the car's full potential at race speed.

If using a tyre additive (refer to page 191), you will also need to find one that works; you should do this once the track is in good condition. It's often trial and error to find one that comes on nicely at the start of the run and doesn't fade too much by the end. How you apply it is also critical. If you are struggling to find something that works, ask a local fast racer. They've probably tried everything and should be able to point you in the right direction. On some tracks, certain additives only work because all the locals are using it, and it's what is on the track.

Top tips:

- Try to get as many runs as possible during the practice day. Familiarise yourself with the facility and track to ensure that you are comfortable to start racing.
- Use the tyre preparation for racing that you developed during practice.
- Use what you learnt during practice and replicate it for racing.
- During racing, don't make any significant changes that you "think" might work.
- Often once the track surface is in good condition, you only need to make very small changes to tune your setup, as the car will be more sensitive.
- Keep in mind that track conditions can change during the day. This may mean that your ideal racing line could change:
    - The track surface may break up or rut in places due to traffic.
    - Cars may throw dust onto the racing line.

Putting It All Together

Our example track is KEORCA in Keilor, Melbourne, Australia. The racing line is in green, and time spent in the air (over jumps) is red.

Track Condition: Outside, clay, oiled, high-grip, very little surface dust.

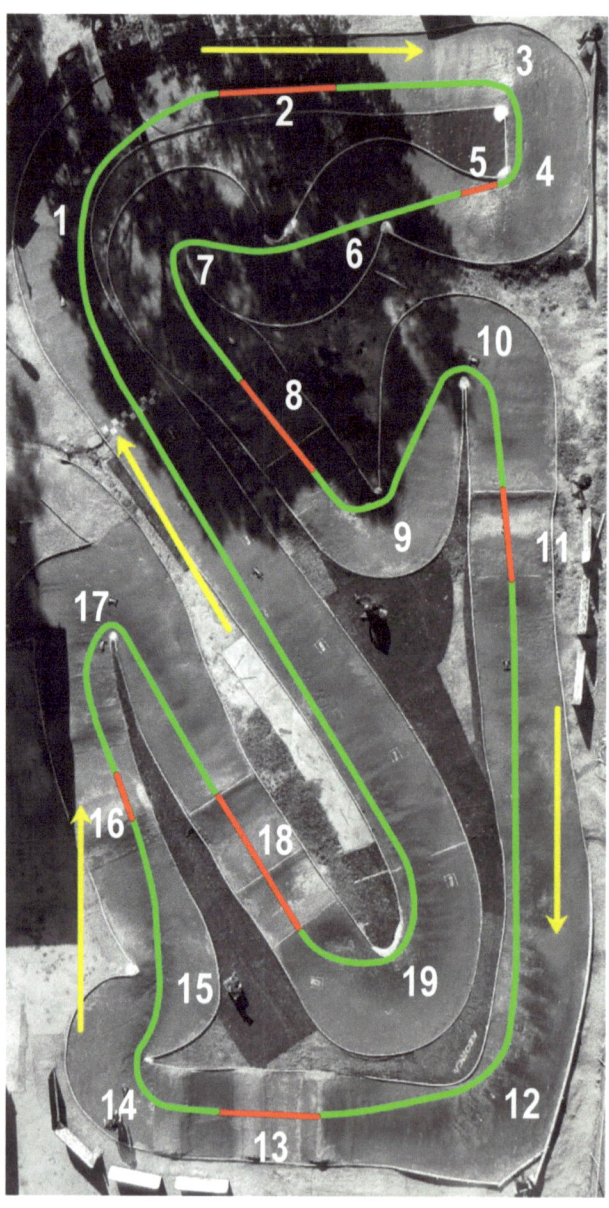

We took drone footage from directly above the track to map the racing line. Thanks to drone pilot Matt Subotsch for arranging permission as KEORCA is close to the flight path for Melbourne International Airport. Thanks also to the KEORCA club.

The example track is quite wide in places, and it would be much slower to use the full track width when cornering (as discussed under *Wide Corners* on page *30*).

Tips below from Ray Munday are a good starting point and can be adjusted to suit your skill level and driving style.

1	Fast Sweeper (page *35*).
2	Table Top (page *50*).

3	Uphill 90° corner. Take it a little wide to take the ideal line through the following corner (4). Late apex.
4	Exit the corner pointing towards the apex of corner 6. Geometric apex.
5	Drop Off (page *50*).
6	Chicane (page *34*). This can be taken in a relatively straight line provided you nail the exit from corner 4 and drop off (5). The right-hand kerb in the middle of the chicane is low, and the next corner (7) is tight, so best to cut across this kerb.
7	A tricky corner because of the entry angle. It's about 135°. We take an earlier apex on this corner as it lines you up better for the next jump into corner. We try to exit mid-track aiming towards apex 8.
8	This Single jump is followed by a Table Top. The downslope of the Table Top is very close to corner 9, and therefore it is fastest to jump the Single and land in the middle of the Table Top. If you land on the downslope of the Table Top, you will overshoot the apex of corner 9.
9	Another 135° corner. Late apex.
10	Hairpin (page *34*).
11	Double (page *50*). Make sure your car is completely straight before hitting this jump or it will kick sideways. Aim for the middle of the track as the following straight has a kink in it.
12	Geometric apex. As the track drops away on the exit, you need to be patient before getting back on the power as the suspension is unloaded and the tyres can't grip as much until you have reached the bottom of the hill.

13	Triple (page *50*). However, the downslope of the third mound is very close to corner 14, so it is faster to jump it as a Double, roll over the third mound and take the ideal line into corner 14.
14	Corners 14 and 15 act as a Chicane (page *34*). Geometric or Late Apex for corner 14.
15	This corner is substantially off-camber (the apex is much higher than the middle of the track). For this reason it is faster to stay closer to the middle of the track which is at the same level as corner 14 and allows you to set up for jump 16.
16	Single (page *50*). As there is a corner immediately after the jump, steer to the left in the air to point the car to the right.
17	Hairpin (page *34*). In the Stock class, it's important to not make the corner too sharp. Keep up your momentum to allow you to clear the following triple.
18	Triple (page *50*). Approach mid-track (as the left side of the jump is a little low). As there is a left-hand corner immediately after, whip the car to the left by steering to the right (example page *62*). Remember to straighten the steering just before landing.
19	Hairpin (page *34*). Be patient and let the car rotate around the apex before applying the throttle. You want to stay on the left-hand side of the straight to prepare for the right-hand turn 1. If you get on the throttle too early, the car pushes wide, which will hurt your entry to turn 1.

Chapter 5

Tyres

Tyres Introduction

The correct tyre choice is critical to your setup. Some major races will specify control tyres so that all racers are on an even playing field. However, this is often not the case. If you have the choice of tyres, then ask the local fast drivers what they are using.

This section is both a tyre selection guide and provides information on getting the most from the tyres you use.

As a general rule, the softer the tyres are, the more grip they will provide. However, the softer the tyre, the higher the wear and the greater the likelihood of overheating on a hot track.

Tyres may come unglued from the wheels and should be checked after each run and reglued if necessary.

Ride height settings should stay consistent since they do not reduce in diameter significantly from run to run. However, as a general rule, grip tends to reduce with wear.

Tyres on outdoor tracks are more susceptible to track temperature changes than on indoor tracks.

For examples of tyre usage refer to the Case Studies chapter beginning on page *224*.

Tyre Gluing

Some tyre combinations are available as premounts, with the tyre already glued to the wheel. However, most tyre combinations must be glued.

Use a good quality CA glue. I prefer thin glue so that it will run between the tyre and rim, but some prefer a medium glue. With the thin glue, I use an applicator nozzle which allows greater control over the location and flow.

This is how I glue my tyres:

1. It is important that the rubber tyre makes a solid connection with the wheel rim:
    a. Check the wheel rim for any burrs and remove with a knife or file.

b. Check the lip of the rubber tyre for any burrs and remove with a knife.

2. If using a glossy or chromed wheel, then rough up the part that glues to the tyre with sandpaper. This will improve the bond. Clean thoroughly afterwards.

3. Ventilation holes – These allow air in the tyre to vent when running on bumpy surfaces or landing jumps. Without vent holes the tyre is more likely to come unglued or even tear the sidewall. Some events may have rules on ventilation holes, so check this first:

   a. **1/10** – If the rim does not have ventilation holes, then create them by reaming two small holes on opposite sides of the wheel. If you are using closed cell inserts, then punch 2 x 3mm holes on the inner tyre sidewall as well as having the holes in the rim. This helps the tyre to ventilate better and gives more traction on bumpy tracks.

   b. **1/8** – instead of venting the wheel, vent the tyre itself by punching two small holes in the tread (on opposite sides of the tyre) with a leather punch.

4. Wipe down the inside of the rubber and the rim with Simple Green, glass cleaner or isopropyl alcohol (motor spray) on a clean rag to remove any mould release agent (left behind from the casting process).

5. Fit the insert inside the tyre (ensuring it is evenly seated all the way around). Closed cell inserts do not require trimming. Open cell inserts may benefit from trimming the square edge from the insert to better fit the selected Tyre Profile (page 92).

6. Fit the tyres to the rim, making sure the insert is not bunched up anywhere, and the tyre fits snugly on the wheel. If the tyres have a directional tread, then make sure the left and right are both facing the same direction (see Tyre Direction below).

7. Glue one side (I start with the inside of the wheel). I run glue all the way around the bottom of this channel. I then run another bead of glue all the way around the vertical channel to glue the side, as follows:

   a. Stand the tyre up on the pit table.

   b. Note your starting point on the circumference of the rim. There's often a manufacturer's logo or another mark you can use for reference. Or you can make a dot on the rim with a sharpie/marker pen.

c. Use your thumb to pull the tyre bead back from the rim slightly until you can get the glue nozzle between the tyre and the bottom of the channel.

d. Place a drop of CA glue onto the rim in the bottom of the channel. The thin glue will run around the rim to the bottom of the tyre so don't use too much and ideally it should only run in one direction (which is the direction you'll turn the tyre to continue gluing).

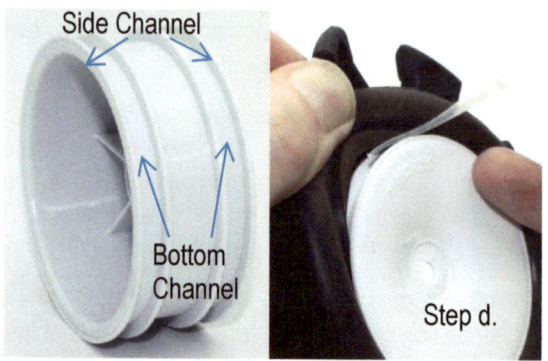

e. Fully reseat the tyre.

f. Turn the wheel/tyre slightly and repeat (c–e above). Keep going all the way around.

g. You have now glued the tyre to the bottom of the wheel channel. I now also glue it to the side of the wheel channel by repeating steps c–e while running another bead of glue all the way around the outside of the internal tyre bead to fix it to the inside of the vertical wheel channel.

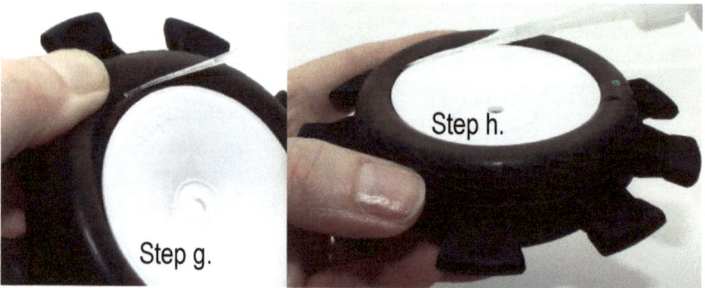

h. Run a thin layer of glue around the outer edge of the bead.

NB: Wipe any excess glue away with a clean rag. Pay careful attention not to get any glue on the surface of the tyre (the part which meets the track).

8. I use rubber bands to apply light pressure to assist the bonding process. Rubber bands that are too tight may distort the tyre and cause the glue to set with the tyre out of position. Many tyre manufacturers sell rubber bands of the correct diameter for the type of tyres you are gluing (pictured).

9. I let it dry overnight. However, CA glue normally dries within minutes (refer to the directions on the bottle). I don't recommend a CA accelerant to make it dry faster as this can weaken the bond (although it can be useful if your race is coming up shortly).

10. Turn the tyre over and repeat steps 6–8 on the other side.

11. Use a sharpie or marker pen to write inside the rim any information you wish to remember, such as the tyre compound, tread pattern and insert used.

Tyres glued like this should last many runs before showing signs of coming unglued. But it's a good habit to check your tyres after each race just in case and reglue as needed.

Beadlock Wheels (Short Course Trucks)

A tyre is not glued to a beadlock wheel. Instead, it is secured by screwing a circular flange to the wheel, which captures the bead of the tyre. They look cool and allow the re-use of wheels but are too heavy for racing and will slow your truck down. Check your local rules to see whether they are legal to use.

Tyre Direction

Many tyres have a directional tread pattern or side lugs which face in a particular direction. Make sure when gluing your tyres that the tread pattern for both the left and the right face in the same direction. If your left and right tyres have the tread pattern facing in opposite directions, then your car may handle inconsistently.

Refer to the manufacturer's instructions to determine which way to run the tyres based on the track conditions.

You can use a sharpie or marker pen to draw an arrow inside the rim showing the normal direction. That way you won't have to think about it and risk putting them on backwards in the rush to prepare for a race.

Inserts

Unlike full-scale tyres, RC tyres are not filled with air. Instead, they have foam inserts that provide support to the tyre. Most tyres come with an appropriate insert from the manufacturer.

Changing the density of the foam changes how the tyre reacts on the track. Changing inserts to a foam of higher or lower density is an advanced setup option. Inserts will not normally affect handling as significantly as changing compound or tread selection.

Softer Inserts	Harder Inserts
• In off-road racing, a softer insert will give you better side bite. • Better for bumpy tracks or when traction is lower. • If an insert is too soft the tyre will become inconsistent as it transitions between turns.	• Increases forward grip by maintaining tyre shape under acceleration. • Less likely to fold over in a corner.

The softer the tyre compound, the denser the foam insert tends to be to provide more support to the tyre.

Open Cell	Closed Cell
• Cheaper to produce than closed cell. • Expands and contracts easily during use. • Porous, so will absorb water. • Easy to cut and shape. • Good for bumpy tracks.	• The most common insert for racing. • Can be moulded into unique shapes for specific handling characteristics. • Good for wet tracks as they don't absorb water. • Tend to hold their shape better than open cell.

Changing the insert can be an expensive tuning option because once the insert is glued into the tyre, you can't change it. Most drivers will be satisfied with the insert which comes with the tyre. However, pro drivers (especially those sponsored by tyre companies) often try different inserts looking for the best one for their setup.

Closed Cell Advanced Technique – An advanced tuning option is to cut the foam insert into a pattern, such as cutting a V into the inner ribs of the insert, which makes the insert a little softer vertically to ride bumps better. Always cut the same pattern in the left and right tyres and make sure the V faces the same direction on both sides.

Cutting the square edge off of the outside of a foam insert can produce a slightly softer tyre sidewall and slightly more rounded profile when using square tyres. This can make the tyres more consistent through corners, and less likely to grab and flip on a rutted track (refer to Tyre Profile on page 92).

Always use the same type of insert in the left and right tyres. Front and rear tyres may use different inserts.

Additive

Tyre additive (also called tyre sauce or traction compound) softens the tyre and increases grip but shouldn't be used on dusty or loose dirt tracks as the dust/dirt will stick to the additive, reducing traction.

Additive	No Additive
• Carpet – depends on the type of carpet but can make a significant difference. • Smooth track with low abrasion and little dust.	• Dusty track. • Loose dirt abrasive track.

Additive can be used with or without tyre warmers.

Normally a track's grip will increase during the race meeting as rubber and additive are laid down on the track (and for outdoor tracks, as the temperature increases during the day). This may mean reducing the application of additive as the meeting progresses to maintain the level of grip for which you have set up your car. Additive is normally applied sometime before the race and allowed to soak into the tyres, softening the rubber. How long before depends on the tyre compound, the additive, the track surface and temperature, air temperature, and whether tyre warmers are used. However, leaving the additive on for at least 15 minutes is a good starting point. Manufacturers produce different additive products for different types of track.

It is normal to apply additive across the entire surface of the rear tyres and to some or all of the front tyres, depending on how much steering is needed. If applying additive only to a portion of the front tyre, then always start at the inside of the tyre (the part closest to the chassis) as this part of the tyre should be touching the track before the car starts to turn in (refer to Camber on page *118*) and should continue to touch the track throughout the turn. In comparison, the outside of the tyre might only touch the track close to the corner apex.

Don't drown the tyres in additive. Use enough to cover the tyre, but only as a thin film and not too thick and wet. This way, it should mostly evaporate by the time you race.

You want to make sure the tyres are tacky when they come off the tyre warmers; if they aren't, then you probably don't have the right additive for the particular tyre you are using.

There's no rule on which additive you should use in the cold, but often a thinner, less oily additive is the best option.

In hot conditions, you should use a thicker, oily additive, so you may need to wipe the tyres before your run.

You want the tyre relatively dry and tacky when you hit the track.

For examples of additive usage, refer to the Case Studies chapter beginning on page 224.

If you don't have access to tyre additive, WD40 may also work.

Tyre Warmers

Tyre warmers aren't commonly used in off-road. When they are used they have the following purposes:

1. Warm tyres to their operating temperature so they provide good grip as soon as the car is placed on the track. Useful on a cold track.

2. To improve the absorption of additive. By heating the tyre while the additive is absorbed, the additive should soften the tyre to a greater degree than without tyre warmers. If you notice grip diminishes towards the end of the run, and you're using additive without warmers, then using warmers should increase how long the additive lasts.

For examples of tyre warmer usage refer to the Case Studies chapter beginning on page 224.

Cold weather:

In cold weather, try to keep the tyres warm right up until your race starts. Warm on 60°C (140°F) for 10–15 minutes before your race, and take the warmers off as late as possible before your race. This ensures the heat stays in the tyre, and you don't have to do more than one warm-up lap to warm your tyres. Excessive warm-up laps compromise your increased pace at the start of a race by wearing off the additive.

If traction is high, you may not want to warm for quite so long, as this could cause the tyre to over-grip.

Wheel Balancing

When installing a new set of tyres, pro drivers often check the wheel balance. If a wheel is significantly out of balance, they might add lead tape to ensure the wheel runs true. Unbalanced wheels can affect the perfect handling of your car. However, if the wheel is not too unbalanced, then it is common not to balance it. Check whether wheel balancing is allowed under the race meeting rules.

Tyre Cleaning

Keeping your tyres clean is a free way to be faster and is essential for both racing and bashing. Dirty treads reduce the contact patch and therefore traction. If you use tyre additive, it will not soften the tyre uniformly if it is blocked by dirt.

Use a cleaning fluid such as Simple Green, which is non-toxic, cleans well and will not dry out your tyres.

Do:	Do Not:
• Clean your tyres as soon as practical after your run. The longer the dirt stays on, the harder it will be to clean off. • It is easier to clean tyres by first removing them from the vehicle. • Brush off loose dirt with a nylon brush. • Spray cleaning fluid onto the tyre surface and wipe off thoroughly with a towel. • Be careful not to get any fluid inside the tyre.	• Submerge the tyre in water or cleaning fluid. The fluid will enter the vent hole (or any cracks in the gluing) and will be trapped between the tyre and wheel. This adds mass and the tyre will probably become unbalanced. If this occurs, cut a small hole in the surface of the tyre and run your car to let centrifugal force expel the fluid. • Leave dirt on your tyres over time. This can dry out your tyres. • Scrub the tyres too hard, damaging the tread.

Note: On some grooved tracks, cleaning may not be necessary and may even reduce performance as additive from earlier runs is removed. Test what works best for your track.

Tyre Storage

If you are storing your tyres for any length of time then add tyre additive (or WD40) to the surface and seal the tyres in a zip lock bag. This way the tyres will not dry out. Keep them out of high heat or sunlight.

You may wish to use a sharpie or marker pen to write on the bag the type of tyres, date or number of runs they've been used for.

Tyre Selection

There are a significant number of good tyre brands on the market to choose from. This section discusses the selection process, regardless of the brand you use.

Track Terminology Definitions

Surface	Description
Astroturf	Artificial grass track surface. Sometimes abbreviated to Turf.
Carpet	Either specialist RC carpet or ordinary carpet.
Clay	Clay tracks tend to be smoother, with higher traction than Dirt (untreated) tracks. They tend to be more consistent and not break up as easily.
Dirt (treated)	Track surface is sprayed with a chemical to improve traction. This can give it similar properties to a Clay track. When the surface has been freshly oiled, you can use a very soft compound even if it is very hot as the oil takes away the abrasion of the surface. But once the oil has dried, you will need to run a slightly firmer compound again.
Dirt (untreated)	Worst traction. Tends to break up as the day goes on. Wetting the track (damp not drenched) can assist with traction. Loose dirt may allow drifting around corners.

Traction or grip:

Traction	Description
Forward Traction or Forward Bite	The amount of traction available when accelerating in a forward direction.
Side Traction or Side Bite	The amount of traction available when a tyre experiences side loading, such as through a turn.
Overheating	A tyre that gets too hot loses grip. If this occurs, try a harder compound.

Other Terms	Description
Abrasion	The more abrasive the surface, the greater the tyre wear and therefore the fewer runs you will get from your tyres.
Moisture	Wet or dry.

Dirt or Clay tracks may have the following conditions:

Condition	Description
Bumpy	Not smooth, making the suspension work hard. A track might have Bumpy sections.
Dusty	Either a thick or thin layer of surface dust over much of the track.
Grooving	A dark groove is beginning to show.
Grooved – Blue	Rubber has been laid down on the surface creating a dark groove. May have some dust on it.
Grooved – Black	Rubber has been heavily laid down on the surface creating a very dark groove. Very little dust normally.
Loamy	Wet, loose dirt covers most of the surface.
Packed or Hardpacked	Hard surface which is less likely to break up or Rut.
Ruts	Potholes or wavy lines in track surface.
Sandy	Loose sand covers part of the surface.
Smooth	A smooth track with few bumps or Ruts.
Wet	Surface has moisture on the track or in it.

Tyres 5

Wheel Sizes

Tyres are glued to the wheels (also called rims). Refer to your vehicle's manual for the size of wheels you should use. The dimensions given are for the outside diameter of the plastic wheels/rims. The tyre's inner diameter (the hole) must match the diameter of the wheels. For historical reasons, off-road manufacturer's usually refer to wheel diameters in inches (abbreviated as ").

1/10 Vehicles

1/10 Vehicle	Wheel Size
Buggies (2WD and 4WD)	Most buggies use 2.2" wheels/rims front and rear. The rear wheels of a buggy are wider than the fronts. Fronts also come in normal width and narrow width. Narrow width tyres/rims are typically used when racing on carpet. Left-to-right below: 2WD front, 4WD front, 2WD and 4WD rear:
Truck 2WD (Stadium Truck)	Wheels are typically the same 2.2" size as buggies. The width is the same on the front and rear. Fronts are usually grooved. Rears typically have a larger outer diameter and are wider than both buggy tyres and Short Course Truck tyres. Left-to-right below: Rear and Front.

88

Essential Off-road RC Racer's Guide

1/10 Vehicle	Wheel Size
Short Course Truck (SCT)	These vehicles have unique wheels. Short Course tyres can only fit onto short course rims. Below is a photo of both sides of the same tyre. The inside and outside diameter of the tyre is different. Left-to-right: Inside diameter 3.0" (tyre towards chassis) and Outside diameter 2.2". An example wheel is shown below (far right).

As a size comparison – left-to-right below: 1/10 buggy front, buggy rear, stadium truck and short course truck.

Hex Sizes

1/10 vehicles typically have a 12mm or 14mm hex at the end of each axle for mounting the wheel. Some cars may use different hex sizes (or even a pin or bearing mount instead), so when you're about to buy new rims, check your vehicle's manual. Below: inside of wheel with 12mm hex on the left and 14mm hex on the right:

1/8 Vehicles

1/8 Vehicle	Tyre Size
Buggy 4WD	These wheels tend to be a uniform size between manufacturers. Front and rear wheels are the same size.
Truggy 4WD	Truggies have much larger and wider tyres than buggies. Front and rear wheels are the same size. The outer diameter of truggy rims vary and it is therefore best to use the same manufacturer for the rim and tyre. Check the measurements against your vehicle's manual when purchasing.

Left-to-right below: 1/8 buggy and truggy wheels.

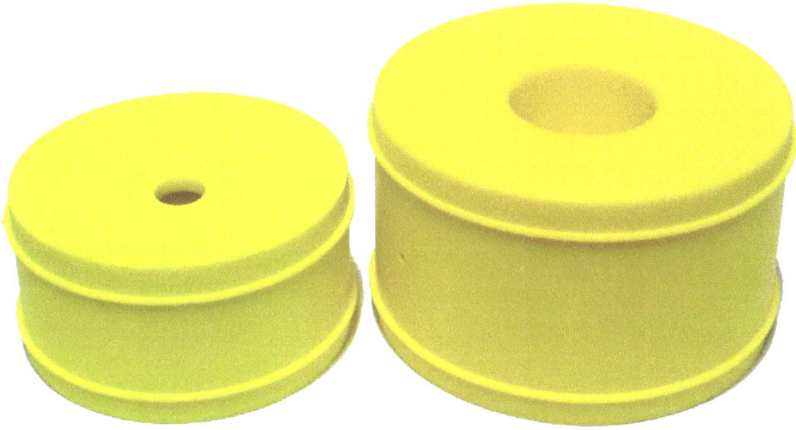

Hex Sizes

1/8 vehicles typically have a 17mm hex at the end of each axle for mounting the wheel. Refer to your vehicle's manual.

Wheel Offset

A wheel with 0mm offset does not change the width of the car. A wheel with positive offset, for example, 0.5mm, will increase the width of the car by 0.5mm on each side (1mm total). However, Track Width is more commonly changed in other ways (refer to page 188).

Tyre Selection Criteria

If your tyres provide too much grip then you will be inconsistent.

If your tyres have too little grip then you will be slow.

Selecting the right tyre for the conditions will provide the correct amount of grip and allow you to drive fast.

How tyres generate grip is discussed in detail on page 99. In summary, the compound grips the track surface and the tread digs into the surface. Both need to work together to provide the optimal grip.

Factors to consider include:

- Track temperature – the colder the track, the softer the compound needed. The hotter the track, the harder the compound.

- Track abrasion – the more abrasive the surface the harder the compound needed (running a soft compound on an abrasive track will wear out your tyres more quickly).

- Whether the track is wet, damp or dry – the more slippery, the softer the compound required.

- Track surface, including the amount of dust on the racing line – the tread needs to dig into the surface.

- For 1/8 scale, the length of the race is also a factor as the tyres must last the distance and not overheat.

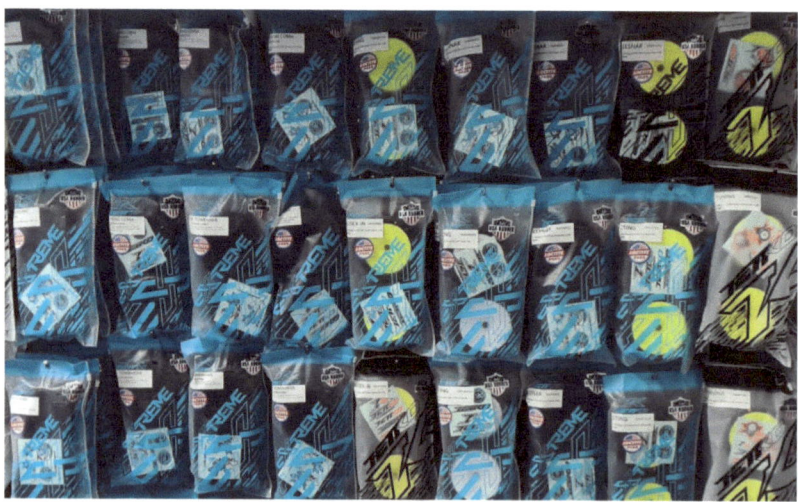

Tyre selection process:

1. Compound Selection

Compound is the softness of the tyre. A softer tyre is not necessarily better. Compound is generally more important than tread pattern, especially on harder surfaces. Run the hardest compound which still provides good grip. The ideal compound varies depending on temperature, track moisture and abrasiveness, but here is a guide:

Compound	Track Condition
Soft	• Good for well packed track surfaces with some loose material on the surface. • Good for dusty conditions. • A number of manufacturers offer both Soft and Supersoft compounds. If in doubt try a softer tyre first.
Medium	Good when the track condition is poor. For example, • A lot of loose material on the surface. • Track starts to break up. • Moderately wet conditions.
Hard	Hard tyres are rarely used. Use when: • Track temperature is very hot. • Surface is very abrasive.

2. Tyre Profile

The tyre profile is the shape of the tyre surface. Profile can be split into two broad categories: square or rounded.

A **square** tyre is flat across the entire surface and will normally stand up by itself on your pit table. It has a large contact patch. A **rounded** tyre has a curved surface and is not as easy to stand up on your pit table by itself.

Profile	Description
Square	• Excellent forward traction. • In smooth track conditions provides good traction throughout the corner. • Not as good when a track starts to break up. Can catch an edge in ruts/holes, causing the car to get out of shape or flip. • Not as good when car is constantly sliding sideways as may slide unpredictably.
Rounded	• Predictable through corners. • Excellent in rough, rutted conditions. • Not as good at generating forward traction in smooth conditions.

3. Rear Tread Selection

To maximise traction, we want as much of the tyre to touch the track as possible. The tread pattern is chosen based on how hard or soft the surface is. In general, the less dust there is, the more surface area of the tyre you want on the track. In these conditions a bar tyre or densely packed pin could work well and the closer together the pins can be on the tread. When it is dusty the pins should be wider apart so that they can dig through the dust to the hard track underneath. The density of the pins depends on the hardness of the surface underneath. When the track is loamy (there is a layer of loose dirt on the surface) try a bigger pin which is spaced out in order to dig through the loam.

Surface: Carpet/Astroturf	Surface: Pure Clay, Racing Carpet or Asphalt
Well spaced, rounded, small pins. E.g. JConcepts Pin Downs. 	On a smooth non-dusty track, a slick tyre may work well. Some racers grind the pins/tread to make slick tyres (pictured).  Some manufacturers sell slick tyres.

Tyres

Surface: Soft	**Surface: Wet**
Needs a sharp pin to dig in. E.g. JConcepts FlipOut.	Needs open-spaced pins to minimise clogging of the tread. E.g. JConcepts DoubleDee.
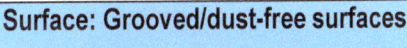	
Surface: Hard based surfaces with loose or dusty tops	**Surface: Grooved/dust-free surfaces**
Needs dense pins. E.g. JConcepts Sprinters.	Likes lots of surface area and bars. E.g. JConcepts Ellipse.

4. Front Tread Selection

- Front tread pattern is chosen to give a good balance to the rear so that the car has sufficient steering without oversteering or understeering.

- 4WD cars normally run the same pattern on the front as on the rear.

- 2WD buggy/truck often run a different front tread pattern depending on the amount of steering desired. Ribbed tyres are a common choice on dirt (and also work well when bashing in sand or snow).

- Narrower front tyres tend to be the most stable, while a wider tyre may provide more steering.

- Low profile or tall front tyres are available. However, you should always run the same diameter tyres front and rear. Check your local rules for tyre diameter restrictions.

5. Setup Changes

Each tyre/surface behaves differently, and you may need to adjust your setup and driving to compensate. When changing tyres, you may wish to review your weight bias (page *194*), rear toe (page *187*) and/or rear roll centre (page *177*). Read on for examples.

1/10 JConcepts Outdoor Tyre Guide

Ray Munday

Author's note: Ray is sponsored by JConcepts and has many years of experience with their tyres.

One of the appeals/challenges of outdoor off-road racing is the variation in track conditions that occur (even on the same day). Tyre choice is critical to get the best lap time and enjoyment out of your buggy, but with so many tyres available, it can be overwhelming to stay in front of the track conditions.

This guide details how we choose our JConcepts tyres for outdoor off-road here in Australia (where pretty much every track is outdoors dirt of some kind) based on countless hours of testing. Many of our race days start wet, then start to dry out, then groove up, then cool off again in the evening, so you need to be prepared for these situations.

Through our testing, we have narrowed down the tyres we carry to four tread patterns. There are other patterns in the range which sometimes work in specific conditions, but the four patterns in the guide below should cover almost every condition you will experience in this type of racing.

Four Step Process

I have broken the selection into four steps in the order I follow when choosing tyres:

1. Compound selection.
2. Rear tread selection.
3. Front tread selection.
4. Setup changes.

Compound

- Compound is generally more important than tread pattern, especially on harder surfaces. The ideal compound varies depending on temperature, track moisture and abrasiveness.
- Generally if it's wet, green is the go-to compound. Blue is used if it's dry. Black if it's very cold, R2 if it's very hot or abrasive. We use green and blue 90% of the time here in Melbourne, Australia.

- There has been a trend towards oiled dirt surfaces (using a vegetable oil such as canola). When the surface has been freshly oiled, you can use a very soft compound even if it is very hot as the oil takes away the abrasion of the surface. But once the oil has dried, you will need to run a slightly firmer compound again.

Tread Pattern

- Tread pattern is chosen based on how hard or soft the surface is:
    - Soft surfaces need a sharp pin to dig in = FlipOut.
    - Wet surfaces need open-spaced pins to minimise clogging of the tread = DoubleDee.
    - Hard based surfaces with loose or dusty tops need dense pins = Sprinters.
    - Grooved/dust-free surfaces like lots of surface area and bars = Ellipse.
- The Sprinter is a great all-round tyre which I usually start with unless it's very wet. If you can only have one tyre in your bag, it's this one!
- As soon as the track looks to be grooving, switch to Ellipse. We use Sprinters and Ellipses most of the time, but I keep some Flip Outs and DoubleDees on hand in case the day starts wet.
- Rear tyre choice is most important. Front tread pattern is chosen to give a good balance to the rear. The narrower tyres (Rips) tend to be most stable, while a wider tyre like the Ellipse gives the most steering when the track is grooved.
- The insert is generally chosen to match the tyre carcass. The Sprinter and Ellipse have a thinner carcass and give more traction with closed cell inserts. The Flip Outs and DoubleDee carcass generally works better with open cell. At the front, closed cell will give more precise steering and more exit steering, whereas open cell will feel a little less responsive on turn-in but then feel more stable on exit. I usually match inserts front and rear.

Setup Changes

Each tyre/surface behaves differently, and you need to adjust your setup and driving to compensate. The most common changes we make to our Team Associated cars when we change tyres are weight bias (page *194*), rear toe (page *187*) and rear roll centre(page *177*).

JCONCEPTS 1/10 OUTDOOR TYRE GUIDE - RAY MUNDAY

August 2020

✓✓ Usually #1 choice
✓ Suitable alternative

STEP 1: COMPOUND CHOICE

Condition	Details	Black Mega Soft -07	Green Super Soft -02	Blue Soft -01	R2 (+A2) Medium Soft -R2 (-03)	O2 / Y2 Medium / Firm -O2 / -Y2	Treatment
Wet	Wet / Damp track, Some tyre pickup, Sandy surfaces		✓✓	✓			n/a
Cold / Very Low Abrasion	<10C/<50F, Surface cold to touch, Freshly oiled surfaces, Surface slightly soft to touch	✓✓	✓	✓			WD40 (goop on oiled tracks)
Cool / Dry	10-30C / 50-85F, Dry surface, hard base, Dusty to grooved			✓	✓✓		n/a
Hot / High Abrasion	>30C/>85F, High UV, Very abrasive surface, Surface treatment has dried			✓	✓✓	✓	n/a
Hot / Extreme Abrasion	>30C / >85F, Extremely abrasive surface (e.g. sugared tracks)				✓	✓✓	n/a

TIP: Compound is usually more important than tread pattern, especially for harder surfaces.
For treated (oiled) surfaces, if oil is fresh -> can use very soft compounds.
TIP: If tyre feels good for 2-3 laps then grip drops -> compound is too soft.
If can hear tyre spinning on surface -> compound is too hard.

STEP 2: TREAD PATTERN CHOICE (Rear Tyre / 4WD Front)

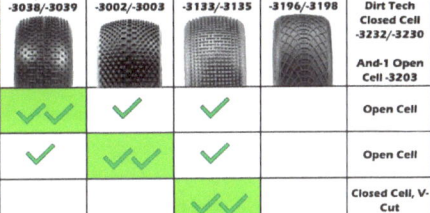

Condition	Details	Flip Out -3038/-3039	Double Dee -3002/-3003	Sprinter -3133/-3135	Ellipse -3196/-3198	Inserts Dirt Tech Closed Cell -3232/-3230 And-1 Open Cell -3203	Typical Direction of Sprinters and Ellipses
Soft / Sandy	Loamy, soft surface with 'roost' from tyres	✓✓	✓	✓		Open Cell	
Wet / Muddy	Wet / muddy track with heavy pickup on tyre	✓	✓✓	✓		Open Cell	
Hard base, Loose surface	Hard base, loose dust or loam on top, some tyre pickup			✓	✓✓	Closed Cell, V-Cut	
Grooved, Minimal dust	Hard base, minimal dust or tyre pickup			✓	✓✓	Closed Cell, V-Cut	

TIP: Usually match 4wd front tyre with rear tyre compound and tread pattern.
TIP: Sprinters work well in almost every condition. If unsure -> start with Sprinters.

STEP 3: TREAD PATTERN CHOICE (2wd Front Tyre)

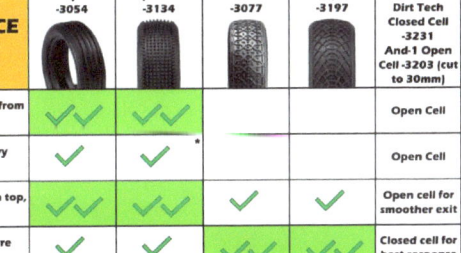

Condition	Details	Rips -3054	Sprinter -3134	Dirt Web -3077	Ellipse -3197	Inserts Dirt Tech Closed Cell -3231 And-1 Open Cell -3203 (cut to 30mm)
Soft / Sandy	Loamy, soft surface with 'roost' from tyres	✓✓	✓✓			Open Cell
Wet / Muddy	Wet / muddy track with heavy pickup on tyre	✓	✓	*		Open Cell
Hard base, loose surface	Hard base, loose dust or loam on top, some tyre pickup	✓		✓	✓	Open cell for smoother exit
Grooved, minimal dust	Hard base, minimal dust or tyre pickup	✓	✓	✓✓	✓✓	Closed cell for best response

* I use custom cut Double Dee 2wd fronts in very muddy conditions
Rips = smoother exit, Sprinters = more mid / exit steering
Dirt Web = Smoother mid, Ellipse = More mid/exit steering

STEP 4: SETUP DIRECTION

		Flip Out	Double Dee	Sprinter	Ellipse
Weight Bias	Softer tracks / pin tyre -> more weight at rear	Rear	Mid	Mid	Forward
Rear Toe-In	Pin tyres / open cell / softer tracks -> more rear toe-in.	3.5 - 4 deg	3.5-4deg	3.5 deg	3-3.5deg
Rear Camber	Bumpy track / softer surface -> more rear camber.	-2deg	-2deg	-1deg	-1 deg
Rear Roll Centre	Softer surface -> high rear roll centre for more traction.	High	High	Mid / Low	Low
Driving Style	More aggressive on softer surfaces	Aggressive	Aggressive	Smooth	Smooth

Tyre Tech

Ray Munday – Tech Talk

Tyres are possibly the most important part of your car. They are the only part of the car that should be touching the ground and they generate the grip to help your car accelerate, corner and brake. Working out how to get the most out of your tyres is critical to achieving racing success.

While they look simple, tyres are actually very complex and even in full-size racing no one can fully predict their behaviour. Just take a look at the changing fortunes of teams in F1 to see that even at the elite racing level, they are still a "black art"! F1 teams have literally dozens of people working on understanding tyre performance and have very complex equations to work out how much a tyre will wear depending on downforce, setup and other factors. This is obviously beyond our capabilities in RC, but what we will look at are the "fundamentals" of tyre behaviour and how we can get the most out of tyres with our driving style and setup.

How Does a Tyre Create Grip?

There are three mechanisms by which a tyre generates grip: adhesion, deformation and destruction.

- **Adhesion** is the surface of the tyre "sticking" to the surface and is a function of the compound and surface interaction.

- **Deformation** is where the tyre deforms around the ground (or deforms the ground) and is mainly a function of the tread pattern (for example, spikes digging into the ground).

- **Destruction** is where the tyre generates grip by literally ripping itself apart on the ground.

Depending on the surface type (soft/hard/abrasive) and temperature, a tyre will need to have a different chemical compound and different pattern to get the most grip. On very hard surfaces, the compound must do most of the work. On soft surfaces, the tread pattern is more important to dig into the ground. Generally, we don't want to rely on destruction (wear) to generate grip, but it is one of the reasons a soft tyre often generates more traction.

As rubber compounds get warmer, they get softer and provide more grip up to a point – but if a tyre is too soft, it will flex too much and lose grip. Therefore we choose harder compounds for hotter temperatures and softer compounds at lower temps.

Tyre Slip – How to get the maximum grip out of the tyre

You've probably all seen this situation: the car that looks super quick going around the track, spectacularly sliding through every corner, big drifts, the steering always moving. Then there is the car that looks slow – the car gently drifting through corners, taking neat lines but always looking in control. At the end of the race, it is usually the latter driver that is winning, and not only that, their tyres are usually in better shape! What is the difference? The smooth driver has learnt how to drive at the limit but not to go past it. To understand that, we need to understand tyre slip.

For a tyre to generate grip, it needs to have some "slip" relative to the ground. For cornering, this is called the "slip angle" and is the difference between the direction the tyre is pointing and the direction the tyre is moving. This doesn't necessarily mean a big slide – it is the tyre and tread squirming on the ground initially, then sliding as the slip angle increases. For acceleration/braking, it is the "slip ratio" which is the difference between how fast the tyre is spinning and how fast the car is going.

The most important thing we need to understand is that as slip increases, grip will increase up to a point – then it will actually start to drop back down again! So when we are driving, we need to try and feel the "limit" of the tyre but not to go past it, or we will actually start to lose grip. If we are too gentle on the car, you will maintain control but not be fast.

How can you improve your style to get the most out of the tyre? The number one tip I can give is to try not to use maximum steering lock everywhere. I see many people doing this, but for faster corners, this means you are using much more lock than you need, and you are generally losing grip. So try to practice using less lock for the faster corners and more lock for the slower ones. If you want to try this out, try backing off your steering travel EPA (page 167) and going through a fast corner to see just how little lock you actually need. A lot of the time, when people complain of high-speed understeer this is actually the cause!

For acceleration/braking, the key is to have a little bit of slip but not too much. Under power, try to feed the power on smoothly (especially in electric, where there is maximum torque at low RPM). It helps to get down to track level to hear the tyres – when you get it right, you can hear them working. If you are too aggressive, you will hear them "ripping". Under brakes, the tyres should never lock up – I try to set my brake EPA so that when I am braking in a straight line, they still rotate but are visibly turning a little slower than the car is moving. It's easy to spot this if you have spokes/markings on your wheels.

It's a delicate balance, and to make life difficult, the optimum slip will vary with tyre type, temperature and track conditions. Generally, I've found that when the surface is more abrasive, the less slip angle you want. As the surface becomes softer, you need a bit more slip. Dusty surfaces can be the trickiest – if the dust is deep, extra slip helps as you actually create grip by throwing the dust out. If there is a little bit of dust on top of a hard surface, you want less slip – too much, and the tyre tends to spin on the loose dust rather than gripping on the hard track.

Tyre Energy – Looking after Tyre Temperature

Something else to consider is the "energy" you put into the tyre and how this affects tyre temperature and wear. The greater the slip angle and the faster the speed, the more slip "energy" there is, and this is what creates tyre heating. The heating power is proportional to the square of speed – so if you go twice as fast you will generate four times as much heat in the tyre.

What does this mean? If you want to get some heat into the tyres, you can intentionally overdrive them a little in the higher speed corners or spin them under acceleration. If you want to try and prevent overheating, you should try and be gentler on them in the fast corners, but you can be aggressive in the slower stuff and the temps should still stay low. This is especially useful in control tyre events where the compound may be a little soft for the conditions, and it is easy to overheat them and lose performance at the end of the race/for subsequent races (or conversely if it is too hard for the conditions and needs some additional temp to work better).

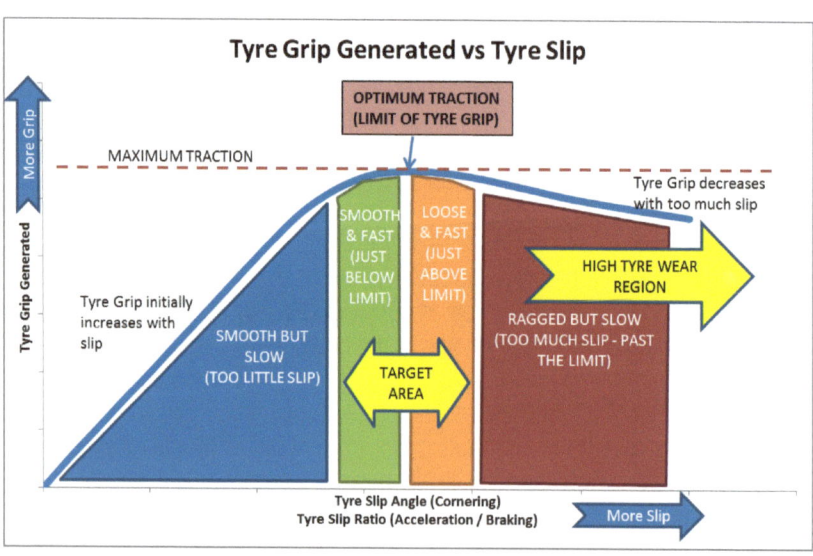

The Friction Circle – Getting the most out of the tyre at all times

Ok, so we have reviewed how to get the most out of the tyres under cornering and acceleration. What about when you have both, such as when you start accelerating out of a corner?

Pretty much all tyres follow the principle of the "Friction Circle". No, this has nothing to do with the tyre being round!

Rule 1 – The maximum cornering grip will come when you have no acceleration/braking force.

Rule 2 – Conversely, the maximum acceleration grip is when you are not cornering.

Rule 3 – If you have a combination of cornering and acceleration, the maximum combined grip of the cornering and acceleration grip is about the same as Rule 1 and Rule 2.

If you look at the top of the tyre and draw a line showing the maximum grip in any direction, it looks like a circle, hence the term "Friction Circle".

The Friction Circle is very important to understand as it is the key to getting the maximum grip out of your tyres at all points of the track. If you want to have the maximum cornering grip, make sure you aren't accelerating or braking. If you do, the car will start to slide. If you want maximum acceleration, you need to be pointing in a straight line. If you try to apply steering while you are at the limit of acceleration, the car will slide around and lose forward traction.

The really tricky part (and the biggest difference between the fast guys and the really fast guys) is combining cornering and acceleration/braking. Some of the traditional methods say to do all your braking in a straight line, then let off the brakes before you turn. Using this method, you aren't on the limit at all times – as you are changing from braking to cornering, there will be a period when you aren't using all of the tyres' available grip. The fastest method is the "blended" method or "transition" method, which is easiest to describe by breaking the corner up into five parts:

1. **Braking** – at the end of the straight, brake hard in a straight line.

2. **Transition from braking to cornering** – you can apply steering while you are braking, but you must release the brakes slightly first. Come off the brakes as you progressively apply the steering. Ideally, this should be a "blended" motion and is called trail braking. If you leave the brakes on too long in a 2WD, the car will spin out (you are asking too much of the rear

tyres), and a 4WD will understeer (you are asking too much of the front tyres). When you get it right, the car will tuck into the corner, and it will feel awesome!

3. **Mid-corner** – in the middle of the corner, you should be on the limit of the tyre's cornering traction and hence not be applying sudden brakes or throttle. If you try to apply the throttle, the car will push wide or spin out, depending on your setup.

4. **Transition from cornering to acceleration** – as the corner starts to open up, start to lessen the steering and simultaneously apply the power. If you get it right, the car will drift slightly but not change its line. Applying power too early will tend to make the car spin (2WD) or push wide (4WD); apply it too late and you will lose time, but the car will feel locked in.

5. **Straight** – once the wheels are straight and the car is pointed in a straight line, you should be at or close to full power. Your tyres now have maximum forward traction.

Get these five steps right, and you will find your lap times will definitely drop! The transition phases can be tough to get right, but once you have mastered it, you will find you can brake later, get on the power earlier and still be in control. The key to fast lap times is getting the most out of your tyres at all times – and the best thing is it costs nothing. It's best to try these techniques during practice to see how sensitive the car is to braking/accelerating during cornering, then start to use them during races.

I hope that this brief insight into the fascinating world of tyres helps you to enjoy your racing more!

If you want to read more, I can highly suggest the following book: "The Racing and High-Performance Tire" by Paul Haney. This has great information on rubber compounds, construction, how tyres grip and some good information on weight transfer.

– Ray Munday

Chapter 6

Car Setup Reference

Introduction

In this chapter, we cover the A–Z of setup settings, from Ackermann to Wings and everything in between. Where a term used in this chapter is not explained, refer to the *Glossary* on page *295*.

To make the information in this chapter easy to digest, I've given each setup heading a level: Basic, Intermediate or Advanced.

Basic – All racers should be familiar with these headings. They make the largest difference when setting up your car, and I encourage you to develop a thorough understanding of them.

Intermediate – Covers areas that are either more complicated than Basic items or changing them makes less of a difference to the car's handling. You should aim to develop a good understanding of these areas over time.

Advanced – These headings are the most complex areas. Developing some understanding of these settings over time is beneficial. However, treat them as optional. Many club racers will never change their car's Roll Centre or Ackermann. They are useful finetuning tools in order to maximise the car's handling.

Parts of the Cars

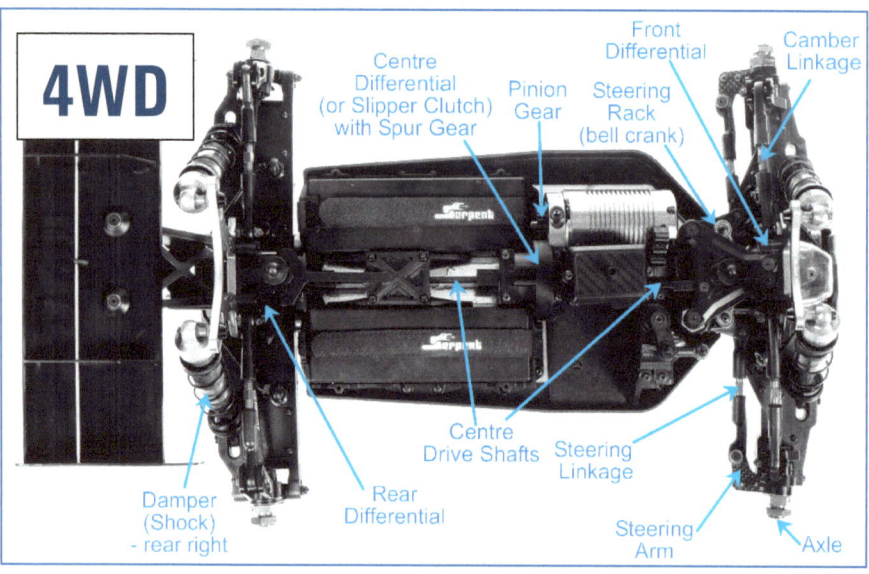

Car Setup Reference 6

2WD

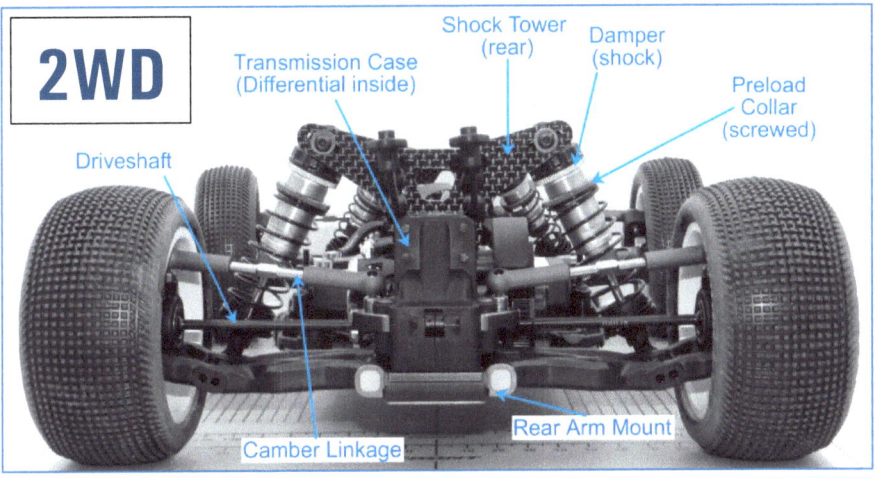

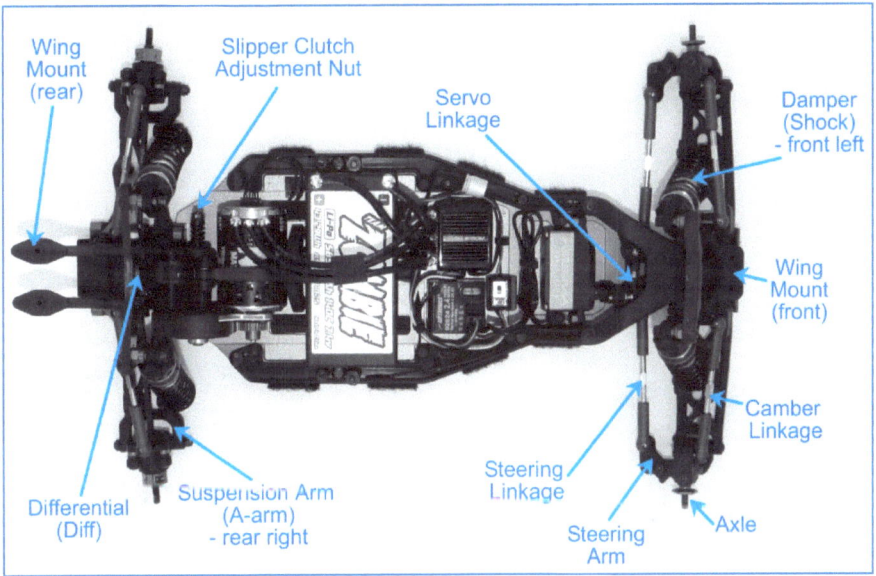

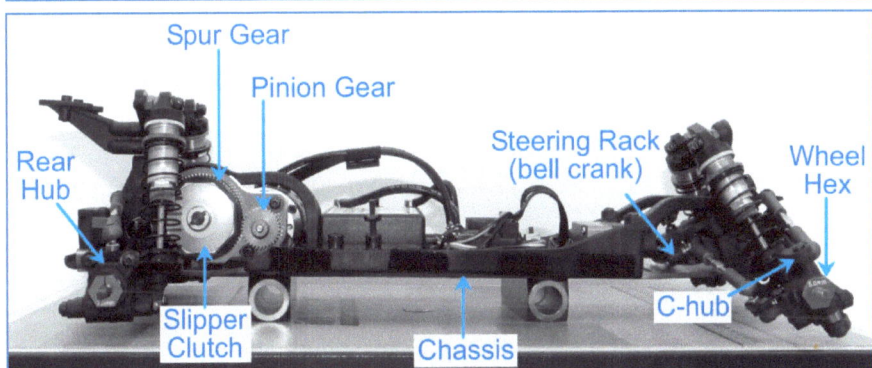

106

Ackermann

Level: Advanced (refer to page 105 for an explanation of each Level)

Ackermann (also called Steering Geometry or Dynamic Toe).

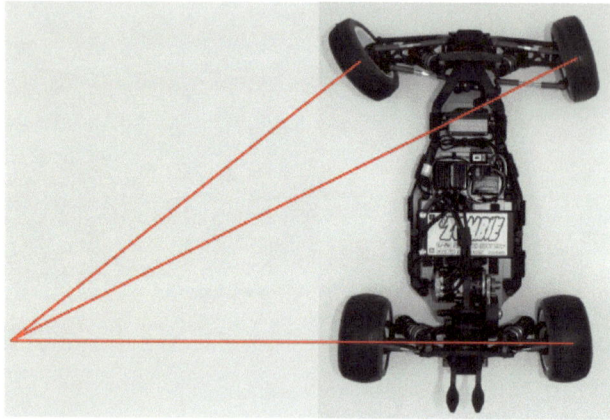

Put simply, the front inside wheel always has a tighter arc in any corner than the front outside wheel. Think of it in terms of the outside of the car has further to go than the inside of the car when turning.

There are many variables that affect the optimum turning angle for the inside and outside tyres (tyre, surface, corner angle, grip, weight, toe, etc.). However, let's say that at full lock, with the manufacturer's kit setup, our example car's inside tyre turns 22° (from straight ahead), and the outside tyre only turns 13°. The Ackermann angle is 22–13=9° at full lock. When wheels are straight ahead the Ackermann angle is 0° (assuming no Toe-out is set). The Ackermann angle from 0° (no steering) to 9° (full lock) is not a linear progression, i.e. when half steering lock is applied, the angle is unlikely to be 4.5°. The progression depends on the steering linkage angles and varies by manufacturer.

The Ackermann angle is changed by altering the geometry of the steering system (steering rack, linkages and arms). Usually this is done by changing the:

1. **Outer steering linkage ball stud location** (red dots below) – This makes a large difference to the Ackermann angle. This method often requires optional parts.

2. **Inner steering linkage ball stud location** (green dots below) – The most common type of steering rack is a dual bell crank system. You can change the shims between the steering rack and the steering link ball stud to change the distance from the pivot point to the steering link (which changes the Ackermann angle). The pivot points are usually at the rear of the rack but can also be in front of the rack (both options are shown below). Provides a finer adjustment to Ackermann than option 1 above.

Car Setup Reference

The photos below may not represent your car. Different cars will have different starting angles and different shimming/hole position options.

Pivot Points at Rear of Steering Rack

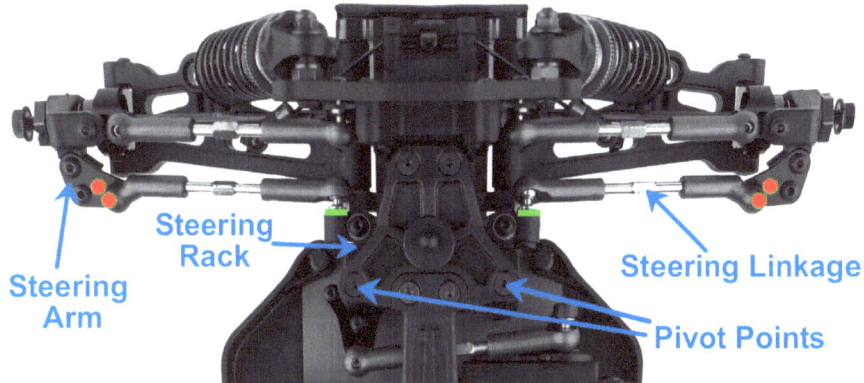

The above is the most common configuration

More Ackermann (for the example car above) – adding shims at the centreline location (green), or using a steering arm hole closer to the front of the car (red), increases the Ackermann angle (the difference between how far each tyre turns).

Less Ackermann (for the example car above) – removing shims from the centreline location (green), or using a steering arm hole (red) further away from the front of the car, reduces the Ackermann angle (the difference between how far each tyre turns).

Note: 1/8 scale cars normally use the above configuration. However, instead of adding or removing green shims, they often have three hole options for the inner steering link ball stud. Using the hole closest to the front of the car has the same effect as adding shims. Using the hole closest to the rear of the car is the same as removing shims.

108

Pivot Points in Front of Steering Rack

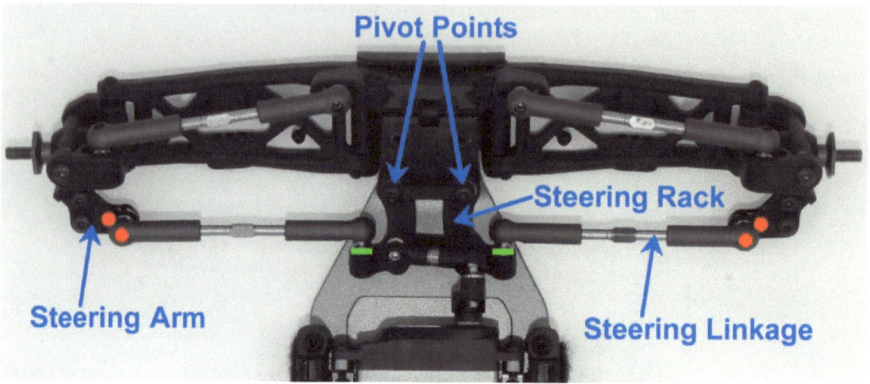

Front shock tower has been removed to expose steering system

More Ackermann (for the example car above) – removing shims at the centreline location (green), or using a steering arm hole closer to the front of the car (red), increases the Ackermann angle (the difference between how far each tyre turns).

Less Ackermann (for the example car above) – adding shims to the centreline location (green), or using a steering arm hole (red) further away from the front of the car, reduces the Ackermann angle (the difference between how far each tyre turns).

Setting	By Changing	Handling Impact
More Ackermann (difference between wheel angles is more)	Use a red steering arm hole closer to the front or change green shims: Pivot Point at **Rear** = add shims, or Pivot Point at **Front** = remove shims	• Smoother steering initially. • More steering mid-corner. • Less corner speed. • Less traction in the chicane. • Better for small and tight tracks.
Less Ackermann (difference between wheel angles is less)	Use a red steering arm hole further from the front or change green shims: Pivot Point at **Rear** = remove shims, or Pivot Point at **Front** = add shims	• Easier to drive. • Less initial steering into the corner. • Car reacts smoothly mid-corner. • More exit steering. • More corner speed. • More traction in the chicane. • Better for smooth flowing tracks with high-speed corners.

Generally, a more aggressive Ackermann setting (more Ackermann) is used in low-traction to increase the response and is not used to decrease lap times as much as it is to alter the "feeling" and "balance" of the car's steering characteristics.

A car's kit setup will usually suggest an Ackermann position where the car is easy to drive, with the best tyre wear (because increasing or decreasing Ackermann from this position changes the slip angle of the tyres).

Rather than shims, some cars use holes or optional parts. 1/8 cars will often use different holes for the steering link ball stud rather than shims.

Ackermann steering geometry changes as the steering input increases. It is a simple concept which can be complex in practice.

Ackermann and Tyres

Ackermann angles for a car in motion are very dependent on the tyres used (as slip angles vary for different tyres). So if the changes don't work as expected this is probably the reason.

Interaction

Front Toe angle (page *185*) affects Ackermann. The more front toe-out you have, the greater the Ackermann will be.

Anti-dive (front)

Refer to *Kick-up/Anti-dive* on page *165*.

Anti-squat/Pro-squat (Rear)

Level: Advanced

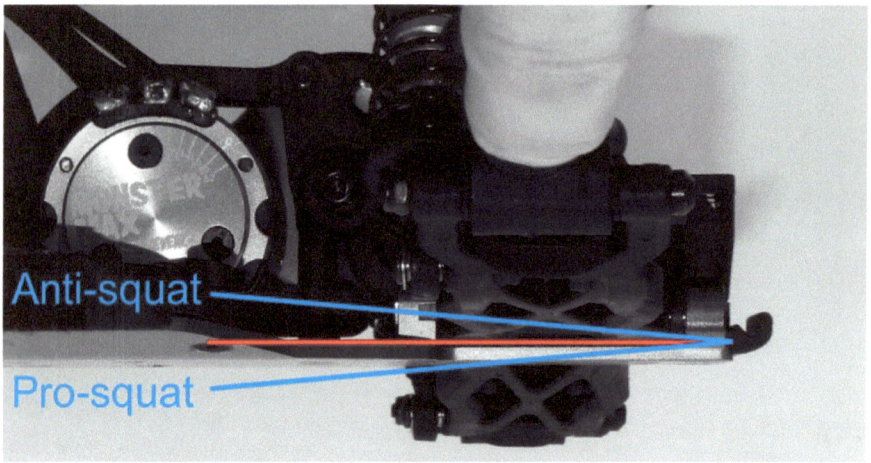

The left rear suspension arm has been pulled up so that the chassis is visible

Anti-squat affects how much the rear of the car "squats down" (settles into the suspension) on-throttle.

The anti-squat angle is often set by spacers under the rear suspension arm mounts or with eccentric arm mount inserts. Refer to your car's manual.

No spacers = arms horizontal to chassis = no anti-squat or pro-squat.

1–2 degrees of anti-squat is common for 1/10 and 1/8 scale.

A car with **anti-squat** will have the rear suspension arms tilted "backwards" so that the front of the arm is higher than the rear of the arm. Anti-squat is sometimes referred to as "positive anti-squat".

A car with **pro-squat** will have the rear suspension arms tilted "forwards" so that the front of the arm is lower than the rear of the arm. Pro-squat is sometimes referred to as "negative anti-squat".

Anti-squat	Effect
Anti-squat (front of rear arm is higher than rear of arm)	• Faster weight transfer to the rear of the chassis on-power. • Suspension compresses/chassis drops less on-power. • Car accelerates faster on smooth tracks. • Decreases steering response. • Increases rear traction during acceleration.
No anti-squat (rear arms level)	Compared to anti-squat, less or no anti-squat provides: • Slower weight transfer to the rear of the chassis on-power. • Suspension compresses/chassis drops more on-power. • Better on bumpy tracks. • Better rear grip on corner entry, more steering on corner exit.

Pro-squat (front of rear arm is lower than rear of arm) is not recommended.

On high-traction, we usually reduce anti-squat to prevent wheel standing (wheelie).

Interaction

Recheck your droop after changing anti-squat.

Arm Sweep

Level: Advanced

Some cars, primarily 4WDs, have the ability to change the front arm sweep.

Arm sweep is created by using wider suspension block/inserts on the front front suspension block (A block) compared to the front rear (B block). This angles the arm back (sweep) and will make the car smoother in all parts of the corner and provide slightly more on-power steering. It is good for high-traction tracks in order to smooth out an aggressive car, especially on initial turn-in.

Front Arm Sweep	Effect
More Arm Sweep	• More control entering the corner. • May make jump landing easier. • Better on smooth tracks or when traction is high.
Less Arm Sweep	• More off-power steering. • More weight transferred forward during braking. • Better on bumpy tracks.

Negative arm sweep (arm angled forward) is never used as it has no benefit. Rear arms are not typically swept.

Interaction

Changing the Arm Sweep changes the Toe (page *185*) and Ackermann (page *107*).

Axle Height
Level: Intermediate

Axle height adjustment allows you to maintain suspension geometry as you change ride height for different traction levels (arms stay level, roll centres remain constant).

Ray Munday produced the chart below for 1/10 Team Associated vehicles, showing how to adjust axle height for 2WD front, 4WD front and 2WD/4WD rear suspension configurations. A number of other manufacturer's vehicles have similar systems.

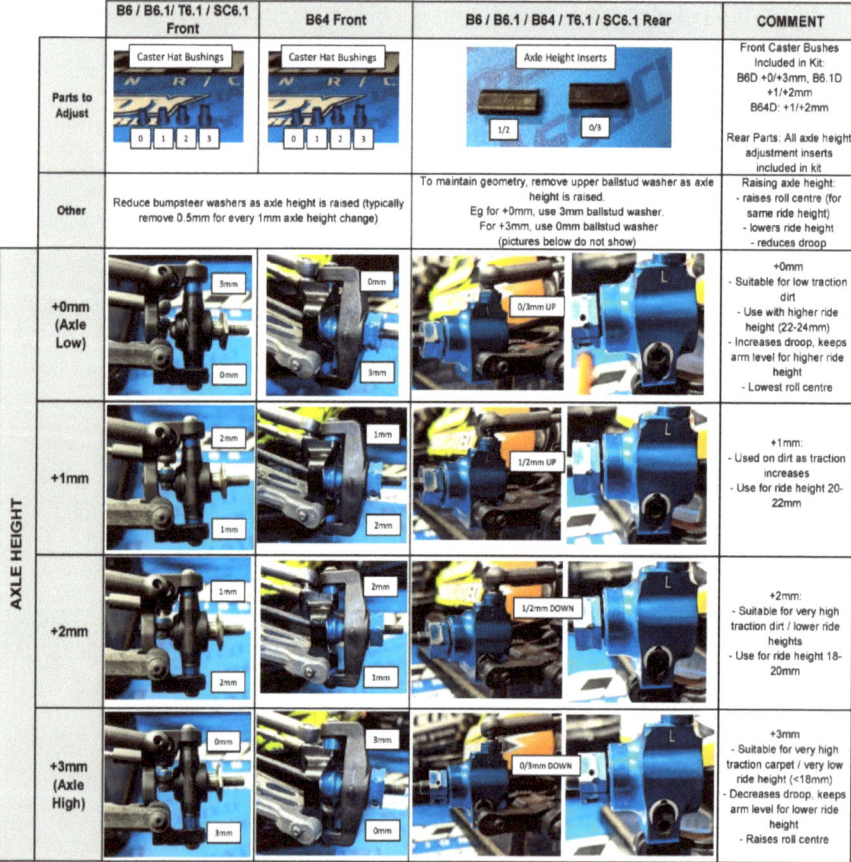

Axle height adjustment is a relatively new adjustment first used to win the 2015 IFMAR 1/10 world championships.

Interaction

Changing the Axle Height will change the Ride Height (page 168), Bump Steer (page 117), Roll Centre (page 177) and Droop (page 152). Refer to the chart above.

Battery Position

Level: Intermediate

If your chassis allows the battery to be moved forward or rearward on the chassis, then it can be used to tune handling:

Setting	Handling Impact
Forward battery position	• Car is more stable. • Less initial steering. • Less mid-corner rotation. • More steering on-power.
Rearward battery position	• Car is less stable. • More initial steering. • More mid-corner rotation. • Less steering on-power.

This is counterintuitive. But, adding weight at the rear does not add rear traction, it actually makes it easier for the car to spin out because of centrifugal force.

For further information, refer to page 194.

Bodies

Level: Basic

For all vehicles, it is best to keep the weight of the body to a minimum as much of the body is above the vehicle's Centre of Gravity (page 192).

For open-wheel vehicles, bodies make less difference to handling or performance, although you may find some bodies feel better than others. Such bodies are often designed to change the amount of front downforce and therefore steering.

Short Course Truck (SCT)

SCT bodies cover the wheels, and therefore, the choice of body can affect aerodynamics to a greater degree. The large surface area of the body also affects handling when jumping. Air can be trapped under the body, causing the front to pitch up in flight. Cutting a vent hole in the body near the rear window (check legality with your local rules) can assist the air to escape and your truck to jump more level.

SCT bodies often rub on the tyres when the suspension compresses, which reduces speed. Some bodies provide deeper wheel wells to reduce this.

Reducing vibration and body noise:

- Add bumper foam to any area the body can rub on the chassis.
- To stop the body hitting the chassis when landing a jump, Velcro the side of the body to the chassis or body side standoffs (also called Nerf Bars).
- To reduce body vibration, place an o-ring on each body mount for the body to rest on.

Painting

A how-to guide on painting good looking body shells would fill its own book. However, here are some errors to avoid:

- Always start with the darkest colour first.

- Don't use too many thick coats of colour. Thick coats will tend to chip off easily during a crash and add weight to the body.

- Use spray paint designed for Lexan RC body shells. Normal spray paint is not as flexible and will chip off easily in a crash. Your local hobby shop will be able to assist:

    o   Tamiya make a range of spray paints. Those with a part number starting with PS are for Lexan RC bodies.

    o   If air brushing then Faskolor, PROTOform or Auto-air work well.

If you would like a professionally painted shell, www.nicola670paint.com did a great job on my body (below):

Bump Steer

Level: Advanced

When the car goes over a bump, the front toe angle may be affected as the suspension compresses or rebounds (changing how parallel the wheels are). This is called "bump steer". The car is less susceptible to bump steer when the steering linkage turnbuckle is parallel to the lower suspension arm.

In the example photo, the thickness of the shims under the steering arm ball (shown in green) determines the angle of the steering linkage compared to the chassis. Bump steer may be adjusted differently on your car. Refer to your car's instruction manual.

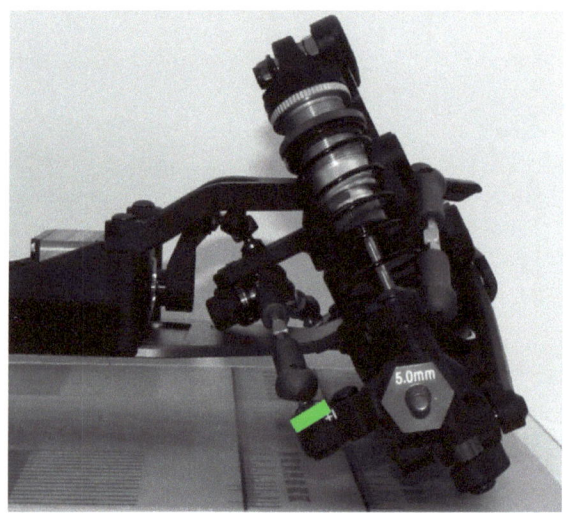

Bump Steer	Steering Linkage Angle	Shims	Effect
More Bump Steer (Toe-in)	Smaller angle (Linkage points down at outer end)	Usually less shims but check your car documentation	• Increased in-corner steering. • Car harder to drive. • Better for smooth track.
More Bump Steer (Toe-out)	Greater angle (Linkage points up at outer end)	Usually more shims but check your car documentation	• Decreased in-corner steering. • Car easier to drive. • Better for bumpy track.

Camber

Level: Basic

Camber angle is the angle at which the wheel leans in towards the chassis (negative camber) or away from the chassis (positive camber).

Zero degrees of camber (shown by the vertical blue line) means that the wheel is perpendicular to the track.

As a general rule, increasing negative camber improves grip on the outside wheel when cornering, thereby increasing steering (within limits, too much negative camber can reduce grip).

Visualise the car as it corners, transferring weight to the tyres on the outside of the corner, i.e. when taking a left-hand corner weight is transferred to the right-hand tyres, and when taking a right-hand corner weight is transferred to the left-hand tyres.

As the weight is transferred to the outside tyres, the car leans (rolls) towards those tyres. With the correct camber angle, the bottom of the outside front tyre will be flat, or close to it, as the car corners. This maximises the contact patch of the tyre with the racetrack, resulting in the most grip and, therefore, the most steering.

A rubber tyre tends to roll on itself when cornering. If the tyre had no camber, the inside edge of the tyre would begin to lift from the track, reducing the contact patch. With any negative camber, this effect is reduced, thereby maximising the contact patch.

With a 4WD car, there is a compromise between steering and maximising straight-line acceleration, as the greatest traction will be attained when the camber angle is zero and the tread is flat on the track.

Camber is normally adjusted by shortening or lengthening the upper turnbuckles. However, cars that have pillow ball front-ends (some 1/8 buggies) may use shims.

Off-road cars are less sensitive to camber than on-road vehicles.

Front Camber

Change	How	Effect
Increase Camber (wheel more angled)	By shortening the turnbuckle	More steering, smoother steering
Decrease Camber (wheel more upright)	By lengthening the turnbuckle	Less steering, car less sensitive to steering inputs

When you use more than about 1°, the steering actually becomes smoother.

Rear Camber

Change	How	Effect
Increase Camber (wheel more angled)	By shortening the turnbuckle	Decreases rear grip when cornering, but much smoother through bumpy corners
Decrease Camber (wheel more upright)	By lengthening the turnbuckle	Increases rear grip when cornering (to a point). Car is easier to drive.

If you have poor straight-line acceleration on a loose track, try 0° rear camber.

Initial Camber Setting

Initial Front	Initial Rear
–1°	–1°

You can use this initial setting as your base setup and normally only alter it around 0.5° either side of this. Never go outside the range of 0° to –3° (1/10 and 1/8 scale).

Normally, the left and right tyres at the front will both have the same camber setting, as will the left and right rears.

Ensure you reset the resting ride height by compressing and releasing the suspension before checking the measurement again after adjustments. Dropping the car onto a flat surface from a height of about 30cm (12") achieves this.

Ruts/Bumps

The more negative camber, the less side bite the tyres have, and therefore, the car is less likely to catch ruts (the edge of a bump) when cornering and flip over.

Wear

Check camber frequently:

Fronts – If the front tyre is wearing more on one side, usually the inside, decrease camber until the tyres wear evenly.

Rears – Adjust rear camber so that the rear tyres cone slightly to the inside (greater wear on the inside of the tyre).

Effect of More or Less Camber

More Camber
Increases the car's traction in the middle and exit of the corner but can cause the tyre to wear harshly on the inside. Adding more camber to one end of the car will cause that end of the car to have more traction in the middle to exit of the corner. Adding more camber to the front will give you better mid-exit steering while adding more camber to the rear will give you better mid-exit rear stability. Adding camber helps the tyres grip more smoothly in bumpy corners as the outside edge doesn't catch the ruts as much.

Less camber
Increases the car's traction initially and prevents "death rings". Removing camber from one end of the car will cause that end to have more traction initially but lose grip through the middle to exit of the corner. Removing camber from the front will make the car turn in hard initially but have less steering mid-corner and corner exit. It also helps to decrease traction roll problems substantially. Removing camber from the rear will allow it to grip initially when entering a corner. However, the car will lose traction and have decreased stability throughout the corner as it car.

Interaction

After you set the Camber, recheck the Ride Height and Toe settings. Conversely, after changing the Ride Height recheck the Camber.

The amount of front camber required to maintain the maximum contact patch also depends on the amount of caster. Higher degrees of caster require little or no camber, while lower degrees of caster require more negative camber.

Camber Gain

Level: Advanced

Camber gain is how much the camber angle changes as the suspension is compressed. Camber Gain is also referred to as "camber rise" or "camber intake".

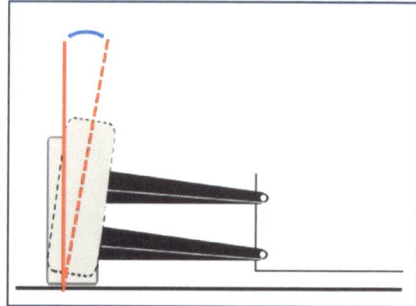

Camber gain is determined by the length of the top and bottom suspension arms (or turnbuckles) and the angle between them. If the top and bottom suspension arms are parallel and the same length, camber will not change as the suspension is compressed. If the angle between the arms is large, or the length of the top and bottom arms is different, the camber will increase as the suspension is compressed.

A certain amount of camber gain is desirable to maintain the face of the tyre parallel to the ground as the car rolls into a corner. Without sufficient camber gain, the outside rear tyre may end up with positive camber during the corner, reducing traction.

Measuring Camber Gain

To measure camber gain, first measure the camber angle (refer to page *118*). Next, push on the suspension in the centre of the shock tower, and measure the camber again. The difference between those two camber angles is the camber gain.

Setting Camber Gain

It can usually be adjusted by changing the upper link/arm mount location on the shock tower. However, not all cars offer this adjustment. Refer to your car's manual.

Camber gain occurs when the suspension compresses or rolls. Cars are designed to feed camber into the tyre as the car rolls to keep the maximum amount of tyre on the ground at all times. Adjusting how much the camber gains/changes can be a very important and useful tuning option and is changed via the camber link angle.

More camber gain
This occurs when the upper camber link increases in angle (bulkhead lower relative to hub). You can achieve this two ways, either lowering the link from the inner bulkhead or raising the link from the outer hub. It is best to work in 0.5mm increments which are noticeable. Increasing the camber gain will increase the car's

grip in the middle to exit of the corner and will decrease initial traction. It will also cause the tyre to wear more aggressively on the inside due to the extra camber gain, so you may experience "death rings". This change can often make the car more aggressive and difficult to drive.

A car with more camber gain will handle bumps in corners better.

Less camber gain
This occurs when the upper link decreases in angle (bulkhead higher relative to hub). You can achieve this by lowering the outside of the camber link near the hub or raising the inside on the bulkhead. Decreasing the camber gain will increase the car's initial grip but decrease traction in the middle and exit of the corner. It will improve the tyre wear in most instances, as the car won't be running as harshly on the inside of the tyre. This is often used to smooth the car out in high-traction.

As a general rule of thumb, more camber gain is better for low-traction in order to get the car to generate grip. Less camber gain is better for high-traction in order to smooth the car out and make it predictable.

Interaction

Higher caster angles will increase camber gain in cornering. Refer to Caster on page 124.

Camber gain interacts with roll centre. Lowering roll centre reduces camber gain; raising roll centre increases camber gain. Refer to Roll Centre on page 177. You could lessen this effect by changing static camber. For example, when lowering roll centre (which reduces camber gain), increase Camber (page 118) to prevent the outer tyres from having positive camber when cornering.

Chassis Stiffness (Flex)
Level: Advanced

Chassis stiffness is an important factor when setting up your car. Some cars have the option of using a thicker plastic or aluminium chassis to reduce flex.

Typically chassis that provide flex are better for low-grip tracks, as they generate more traction and increase in-corner steering, while chassis with less flex are better for high-grip surfaces. A stiff chassis may provide better steering and stability at high-grip tracks and are commonly used on carpet.

A stiff chassis also helps eliminate chassis flexing and twisting, which may introduce another factor that is difficult to measure or adjust.

Your car may have set up options that finetune the chassis stiffness by changing the mounting of components such as the servo, adding stiffener plates to suspension arms, or other components. Chassis stiffness can therefore be a setup tool, and you can make a car "softer" or "stiffer". Refer to your car's manual for options.

There is no right or wrong answer in regard to how much flex a car needs. It is very track dependant, so I would encourage you to test each track to find out what works best there. Most manufacturers will instruct you on the flex options of the car in the instruction manual.

More flex is generally better for lower traction tracks, as it makes the car generate more steering and corner speed due to the chassis flexing and making up for any lack of grip generated by the tyres. However, if the car is docile in high-traction, it can be useful to liven the car up and make it more responsive. Often adding more flex can work because it masks any problems in the car's geometry or suspension settings.

Less flex is generally better for high-traction tracks, as it helps maintain corner speed and stops the car binding up and over-gripping in corners. Too much flex can also make the car very twitchy and nosey on high-traction tracks, making it very difficult to drive. However, for some low-traction tracks, less flex can also work as instead of flexing, the car puts the force back into the suspension and tyres, making them work harder and thus, generating more traction. This is track dependant and should be tested to find the best flex combination.

Caster

Level: Advanced

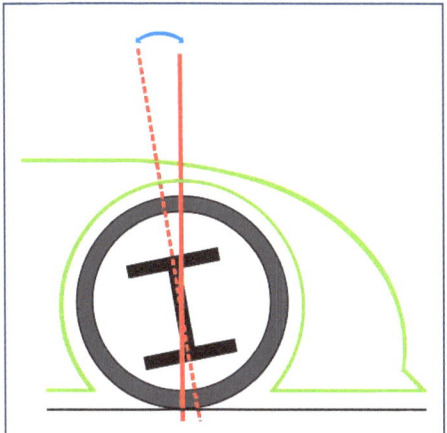
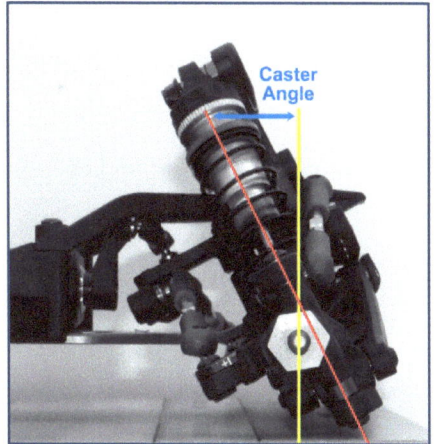

Caster is the angle that the front kingpin (or c-hub) leans to the rear of the car from the vertical (vertical being a line perpendicular to the ground). The Caster angle affects on and off-power steering, as it affects the amount the chassis tilts.

Technically, the pivot points of the steering are angled so that a line drawn through them intersects the track surface slightly ahead of the contact point of the tyre. The purpose of this is to provide a degree of self-centring for the steering (the wheel casters around so it trails behind the axis of steering, like a shopping trolley). This makes a car easier to drive and improves straight-line stability (reducing its tendency to wander). Excessive caster angle will make the steering heavier and less responsive.

Change	Effect
A lesser Caster angle (kingpin more upright)	• Decreases straight-line stability. • Increases off-power steering at corner entry. • Decreases on-power steering at mid-corner and corner exit. • Less stable in bumpy track conditions.
A greater Caster angle (greater kingpin angle from the vertical)	• Increases straight-line stability. • Decreases off-power steering at corner entry. • Increases on-power steering at mid-corner and corner exit. • More stable in bumpy track conditions. • More steering in sweepers driven on-power.

Caster is either set by changing the angle of the caster block or by changing the angle of the c-hub.

Caster Block Example	C-hub Example
2WD 1/10 buggy: 25° kick-up + a 5° caster block gives 30° caster.	*1/10 4WD and 1/8 buggy:* 8° kick-up + a 16° c-hub gives 24° caster.

Refer to your chassis manufacturer's manual for the kit setting and for instructions on changing Caster angle.

More caster will increase the camber to a **greater** degree as the steering lock is increased, which will provide more high-speed and sweeper steering, but less off-power, low-speed steering.

Less caster will increase the camber to a **lesser** degree as the steering lock is increased, which will provide more low-speed steering, but less high-speed sweeper steering. This will make the car more aggressive turning into corners.

Interaction

The Kick-up angle (page *165*) affects caster.

Centre of Gravity

Refer to page *192*.

Damping

Level: Intermediate

Damping controls the suspension's travel speed and resistance. An undamped car will oscillate up and down on its springs. With proper damping levels, the car will settle back to a normal state in the minimum time.

Damping	Effect
Softer	• Produces the most grip (both front and rear). • Greater chassis roll. • Decreases cornering speed.
Harder	• Produces the least grip (both front and rear). • Less chassis roll. • Increases cornering speed.

- Damping is controlled by the four shock absorbers.
- The front pair of shock absorbers should always be set the same (including length).
- The rear shock absorbers should always be set the same (including length).
- The front and rear shocks may have different settings.

Oil

The kit oil usually works well in most conditions, but thicker or thinner oil can be used for finetuning:

Lower viscosity oil (thinner)	Higher viscosity oil (thicker)
• Faster shock action. • Faster weight transfer. • Suspension works faster and smoothly keeps tyre in contact with track (more traction). • Absorbs the bumps better and therefore better at bumpy tracks. • Takes longer to accelerate out of the corner as the suspension compresses further. • More likely to become unsettled during sharp direction changes (chicanes).	• Slower shock action. • Slower weight transfer. • More stable at high-speed and more twitchy at low-speed. • Does not deal with bumps well and therefore better at smooth tracks. • Takes less time to accelerate out of the corner as the suspension compresses less. • Less likely to become unsettled during sharp direction changes (chicanes).

Damping oil and springs work together. If you use thinner oil, consider a softer spring. Similarly, thicker oil works better with a harder spring.

Air temperature can also be a factor, particularly outdoors. As the air temperature increases, the air in your shocks expands and you should bleed your shocks (refer to checklist on page *312*). Some drivers will increase the oil thickness as the temperature increases. If the oil/spring combination selected was working well and the air temperature increases by 10–15°C (18–27°F), then consider increasing the oil by 2.5 WT all around. Conversely, if the temperature drops by 10–15°C, consider reducing the oil by 2.5 WT all around.

Thinner shock oil will make the car softer and more reactive. It will decrease shock pack, which allows the piston to change direction faster and not load up. This generates more traction, but in hot weather can cause the tyres to overheat due to excess chassis roll and movement, making the tyres work overtime. This excess roll and movement also increase the chance of traction roll in high-traction.

Thicker shock oil will make the car stiffer and less reactive. It will increase shock pack, which causes the piston to lock up more when changing direction. Generates less traction but will make the car smoother and easier to drive. It will look after the tyres in hot weather due to the slowed reaction and less chassis movement. This slower response is generally better for high-traction as it makes the car less reactive and less prone to traction rolling.

Piston Holes

The kit number of holes in the shock piston usually works well in most conditions, but changing the number of holes in the piston (or keeping the same number of holes but changing the hole size) can be used for finetuning:

Change	Effect
Fewer holes or smaller holes	• Less oil can pass through the piston as it moves. • Provides harder damping – reacts like using thicker oil. • Greater resistance to fast shock movement (known as pack) and therefore greater damping off of jumps.
More holes or larger holes	• More oil can pass through the piston as it moves. • Provides softer damping – reacts like using thinner oil. • Less resistance to fast shock movement (known as pack) and therefore less damping off of jumps.

Less holes (one or two in 1/10) is less common and will increase the shock pack, which causes the piston to lock up when changing direction as there are fewer holes for the oil to travel through. It will make the chassis roll less and roll slower. However, due to the excess shock pack, it can make the car quite twitchy and aggressive initially.

More holes (three or four in 1/10) is a lot more common, especially in big bore shocks where the piston's surface area is increased due to the extra diameter. More holes reduce the shock pack, and can make the car less aggressive around centre, but overall generate more traction.

Position

Different shock positions change how the shock reacts to compression and how progressive the suspension is.

Change	Front	Rear
More Upright (stood up)	• Less progressive. • Improves on-power steering. • Increases high-speed steering.	• Less progressive. • Improves initial acceleration. • Increased rear stability.
More Inclined (laid down)	• More progressive. • Decreases high-speed steering.	• More progressive. • Improves in-corner steering.

Shock Position on Tower (in Red on Photo Above)

Higher shock position/more vertical (towards the outside of the chassis) will make the shocks harder, increasing initial traction and decreasing chassis roll. One negative of this is that the shocks put more pressure on the tyres and make them work harder, thus making them more prone to overheating. In super high-traction, it can also generate so much initial traction that it can cause the car to traction roll.

This setting is ideal for low-traction, where you are trying to generate grip and aggression.

Lower shock position/more inclined (towards the inside of the chassis) will generate less initial traction, increasing initial rotation and providing more traction in the middle and exit of the corner, and more side bite. It increases chassis roll but decreases the car's willingness to traction roll or overheat tyres due to the decreased pressure on the tyres. This is more appropriate in high-traction to smooth the car out and generate good corner speed.

Staggering shock positions is also common. Running the rear shock position higher than the front generates more forward traction, especially in low-grip. The higher rear shock position will increase initial traction at the rear on-power, and transfer more weight to the tyres, thus increasing the forward traction. However, this will increase steering into the corner as weight transfer to the front will be faster.

Shock Position on Arm (in Green on Photo Above)

Front: Moving the pivot point more inside on the front arm provides more steering but can be less predictable if grip increases. Moving the pivot more outside on the front arm smooths out the steering and allows you to attack harder but can push a little in low-grip. Generally, a position that is furthest out will be the easiest to drive.

Rear: Moving the pivot more inside on the rear arm gives more rear cornering grip in lower traction but can lose on-power traction. Moving it out increases corner speed in higher traction and gives better forward drive out of corners, but if too stiff can be skittish in lower grip.

Preload

Adjusting preload will change the Ride Height (refer to page 172).

Spring preload is normally set by screwing the collar above the spring so that the spring is more compressed or less compressed. Some cars use preload spacers instead.

Preload	Threaded Collar	Spacers	Ride Height
Increase	**Tighten** collar so it moves down the shock body	Use **thicker** spacer above the spring	Increases
Decrease	**Loosen** collar so it moves up the shock body	Use **thinner** spacer above the spring	Decreases

Front and rear are adjusted independently. Any preload applied to the left should also be applied to the right.

When using a threaded preload collar, marking the collar with a pen can make it easier to make the same change left-to-right. You can also measure the gap from the bottom of the shock cap to the top of the preload collar and ensure it is the same left-to-right.

Compressing the spring using the preload collar does not change the force applied by the spring.

Rebound

Remove the damper spring and push the shock shaft all the way into the shock body. When you let it go, the amount the shock shaft rebounds out of the shock body is the amount of rebound. If it doesn't move at all, then rebound is 0%, if it comes out halfway, it's 50%, and if it rebounds fully, then it's 100%. Rebound may be any percentage from 0–100%.

Rebound can finetune the feel of the car. 0% rebound is fairly common in off-road, especially if using an emulsification shock (no bladder).

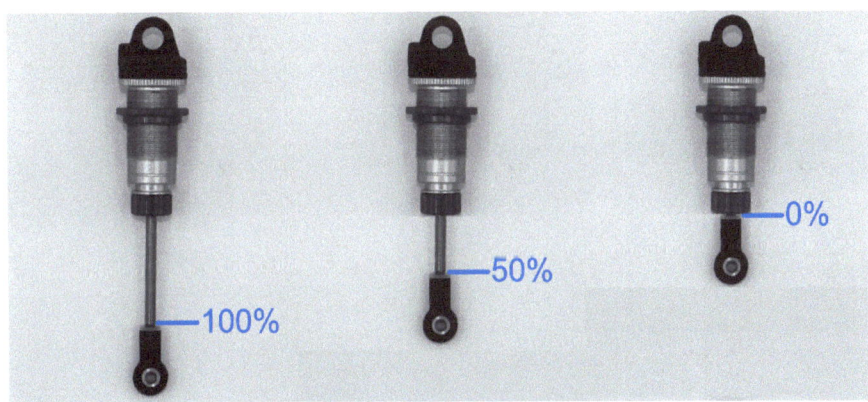

Change	Feel of the Car
More Rebound (higher %)	• Makes the car feel more responsive. • Car will be "bouncier" over bumps.
Less Rebound (lower %)	• Makes the car feel less responsive. • Car will be less "bouncy" over bumps and therefore easier to drive on a bumpy track.

More rebound will generate more traction, as it is constantly trying to force the tyre back onto the ground, like an extra spring. This makes the car more agile, increasing chassis movement. In low-grip, you can use more rebound to increase the car's aggression and ability to generate traction. Using more than 50% rebound can make the car snappy and aggressive.

In 1/10 scale, when using emulsification shocks, too much rebound can cause a hydraulic lock on compression

Less rebound will generate less traction, as there is no force pushing the tyre back to the ground. This makes the car smoother and decreases chassis movement. This can work well in high-traction when the car is already moving around due to the extra grip. Generally, you will decrease your rebound in high-traction in order to decrease the chance of traction roll and make the car easier to drive.

To Set Rebound

1. Assemble the shock as per the manufacturer's instructions..
2. Release the shock cap by 2–3 turns.
3. Push the shock shaft fully into the shock body. Depending on the design of the shock, oil will probably release through the overflow hole in the shock cap.
4. Tighten the shock cap. Oil will normally release through the overflow hole in the cap.
5. Test Rebound.
6. Repeat steps 2–5 until you obtain the rebound % you prefer.

Springs

The springs determine the amount of chassis roll and how quickly the chassis rolls.

If the car is rolling significantly, it will create a great deal of grip due to more weight being transferred onto the outside tyres in the turn. This is good for low-grip tracks. But on high-grip tracks, this will decrease the corner speed and slow the change of direction.

When do you know whether you have the best spring stiffness? Refer to the table below:

	Springs Too Soft	"Best" Spring Rate	Springs Too Hard/Stiff
Low-grip Track	This situation is the hardest to identify. Car will be slower in the corners than it could be.	Springs soft enough to generate sufficient grip without unduly slowing the car.	Car will grip initially, but part way into a corner, well before the apex, the rear end will break away suddenly and substantially.
High-grip Track	Decreases the corner speed and slows the "change of direction" responsiveness.	Harder springs while still generating sufficient grip without unduly slowing the car.	Car "hops" or "chatters" across the track when cornering.

In order to minimise lap times, aim to limit the chassis roll as much as possible by using harder springs without the car chattering or the rear end breaking away unexpectedly. Of course, you still need sufficient rear grip to accelerate as early as possible out of the corners and sufficient front grip to generate the steering you want. As with all car setups, it is about finding the best balance for your driving style at the current track.

The kit spring usually works well in most conditions, but a harder or softer spring can be used for finetuning:

Stiffness	Front	Rear
Softer spring	• More overall grip. • Decreased steering response. • Smoother steering. • Increased off-power steering. • Increased mid-corner steering. • Smoother under braking.	• More overall grip. • Increased in-corner steering. • Increased on-power steering. • Decreased mid-corner steering.
Harder spring	• Less overall grip. • Increased steering response. • Increased in-corner steering. • Increased on-power steering. • Decreased mid-corner steering. • The car may jump a little higher.	• Less overall grip. • Increased mid-corner steering. • Improved initial acceleration. • The car may jump a little higher.

The stiffness of the front springs and the stiffness of the rear springs are often different. However, the spring stiffness on the left and right must be the same.

Damping oil and springs work together. If you use thinner oil, consider a softer spring. Similarly, thicker oil works better with a harder spring.

Progressive vs Linear Springs

Linear	Progressive
• Distance between each coil of the spring is the same. • As the spring is compressed the force it takes to compress it further remains the same. • Therefore, the force required to compress the suspension, or the force it rebounds with, is the same (linear) at all points of compression.	• Distance between each coil of the spring is not the same. • Spring is initially soft. • Spring is progressively harder as it compresses more. • Can make the car more consistent with more traction and cornering speed.

Shock Length (Stroke)

The shock length, also called stroke, determines the droop (refer to page 152).

Damper Theory

Ray Munday – Tech Talk

Dampers – also known as shocks, shockers, or shock absorbers – are probably the most critical part of the suspension of your car, whether it be on-road or off-road. Here I'll cover why we need dampers, how they work and how to tune them.

Before I start, I want to highlight that the interaction of dampers, springs, masses and suspension geometry is a huge field, and many smart people spend their entire lives just working on dampers! Obviously, I can't give a full description of dampers in this space but hopefully will provide you with a better fundamental understanding of how they work and why to tune them.

Why do we need dampers?

All suspensions systems have springs. Springs support the mass of the chassis (called the "sprung" mass), and the further you compress them, the more force they provide. The problem is that they store energy then release it – if you just have springs, your car will bounce around like a pogo stick as the springs compress then release, and bottom out terribly off jumps.

Dampers are devices that dissipate or "damp out" this pogo motion. The force of a damper is related to how fast the damper moves. Instead of the chassis bouncing up and down on the spring, the damper settles out the motion, and it returns to a stable condition. The dampers are effectively taking out the energy that the springs store.

For any given mass/spring combination, there is an optimal rate of damping to dissipate this motion. If there isn't enough damping, the mass will take many cycles of bouncing before stopping. If there is too much damping, the response will be very slow as the mass "oozes" back to its natural position.

When you have a sudden input (such as turning into a corner or landing off a jump), the damper also plays a huge role in controlling how fast the sprung mass moves and how quickly it slows down. In the case of off-road, if the mass isn't slowed down quickly enough, it will bottom out heavily.

When thinking of a car, the easiest motion to think about is the sprung mass bouncing up and down on the springs. There is another important mass we need to consider – the "unsprung mass". This is the mass of the wheel and suspension assembly at each corner. The tyre is actually a spring, and this unsprung mass can "bounce" between the tyre and the suspension spring. This is a much faster movement than the chassis sprung mass and is critical to controlling traction. If this is not properly damped, the tyre will chatter over bumps. If you've ever driven down the road next to a car with worn dampers, you will see that not only is the whole chassis slowly moving up and down, but the wheel will also be bouncing up and down quickly.

The Requirements of the Damper

On a race vehicle, the damper has to do many tasks, and these are often conflicting. This is what makes damper tuning tricky and full of compromise. When talking about damper characteristics, we talk about the force it resists at each speed you push or pull the shaft.

The main tasks are:

1. Controlling the sprung mass after bumps. This is heavy, so the movement is quite slow but needs a lot of force to control it at low-speed.
2. Controlling the rate of chassis roll and pitch during cornering/braking/accelerating (refer to Weight Transfer on page 27). These movements are relatively slow.
3. Controlling the unsprung mass after bumps. This is light, so the movement is fast, but the mass is lower, so less force is required.
4. Allowing the suspension to absorb bumps in the road. These can be very fast. If the damper is too hard, the car will bounce over the bump and lose tyre contact. Too soft and the suspension will bottom out, launching the car.
5. Preventing bottoming out after jumps. The speed of these inputs can be very fast and we want a high force to stop the chassis from hitting the ground. Too stiff and the car will bounce instead of soaking up the landings.

Low-speed and High-speed Damping

The requirements of a damper can generally be split into low-speed and high-speed (in RC terms these are often called static damping and pack, respectively). It's important to understand that **every** input goes through the low-speed range – any input, no matter how fast, must start off slower and then become faster – but the low-speed tasks don't go into the high-speed range. Therefore any adjustment in the low-speed range will affect every input, but adjustments to high-speed damping will only affect the high-speed inputs.

You will see that tasks 1 and 2 above happen at low-speed. Damping at low-speed controls the basic handling of the vehicle and the movements of the chassis. The rate of damping we want will depend on the response we want out of the vehicle.

Tasks 3–5 happen at much higher speed and have conflicting requirements. We want the damper soft enough to absorb bumps but stiff enough not to bottom out. To understand how we can tune these parameters, we will look at how a damper actually works.

How does a Damper work?

Almost all RC cars use hydraulic piston style dampers. (The main exceptions are F1 and 1/12 scale cars which use thick grease on a sliding pin on the front and side suspension, the Awesomatix touring car which uses rotary dampers, and some cheaper cars which have friction dampers). A hydraulic piston damper has the following main components:

1. Outer cylinder.

2. Piston which fits inside the cylinder and is connected to a rod which extends out one end of the cylinder. The piston will have one or more holes in it (page 127).

3. Hydraulic oil (of a particular viscosity – the viscosity is a measure of how "thick" the oil is). Page 126.

4. A top cap to hold the oil in, and a bottom cap with a seal around the rod.

5. Some method of holding some air in the cylinder to allow for the volume of the rod to go in and out of the cylinder.

The key parts of the damper are the piston (with hole/holes) and the oil. As the piston is pushed through the cylinder by the rod, the oil is forced through the holes in the piston. The smaller the holes (or thicker the oil), the more resistance there is to the flow. The fluid resistance is seen as a pressure build-up in the oil on top of the piston, which creates a force acting over the piston. The faster the piston is pushed through the oil, the greater the resistance and the greater the force.

This resistance within the fluid actually causes heating of the oil. It takes energy to create heat, which is how the damper is dissipating energy. If you feel a shock after a run on a rough track, you will notice that it has become warmer than at the start of a race (don't try touching a full-size car shock after driving on a rough road – you will burn your hands!)

Physics of Low-speed and High-speed Damping

As mentioned above, thicker oil and smaller piston holes both give increased damping force for a given damper speed. To understand how to tune this, I will briefly explain the basic fluid dynamics that occur.

1. **Laminar flow (low-speed)** – When the piston is slowly pushed through the oil, the oil smoothly flows through the piston hole. In this range, the pressure drop is linear with speed (i.e. push it twice as fast and you get twice the force). The viscosity of the oil is causing this pressure drop. In RC, we call this laminar flow "static damping".

2. **Turbulent flow (high-speed)** – When the piston is pushed quickly through the oil, the flow of the oil becomes turbulent instead of being smooth. This turbulence has a lot more energy, and it is the density of the fluid which is more important than viscosity. In this range, the pressure drop is a function of speed squared (i.e. push the piston twice as fast and you get four times the force). An important factor here is that smaller holes and thinner oil become turbulent more easily than thicker oil and bigger holes. In RC, we call this turbulent flow "pack".

How to adjust Low-speed and High-speed Damping?

Using the above description, I will use two examples to show how to adjust the damping characteristics:

- Example 1: Heavy oil, large piston holes.
- Example 2: Thin oil, small piston holes.

Low-speed (Static) Damping: We will assume that Example 1 and Example 2 have the correct combination of damper oil and piston holes to have exactly the same damping at low-speed. If you push the shaft in and out slowly by hand, they will feel the same. Both are still in the laminar range.

High-speed Damping (Pack): If the oil is thick enough and the hole is large enough in Example 1, the flow will still be laminar (smooth). However, Example 2 will have become turbulent earlier, and therefore the force will be much higher.

So with this example, both Example 1 and Example 2 have the same low-speed damping, but Example 2 will have a much higher force at high-speed. Generally, both will feel the same for handling inputs (low-speed), but Example 1 will ride the bumps better and Example 2 will not have as much traction over bumps and may skip over them instead. Off big jumps, Example 1 may bottom out easily while Example 2 will land better.

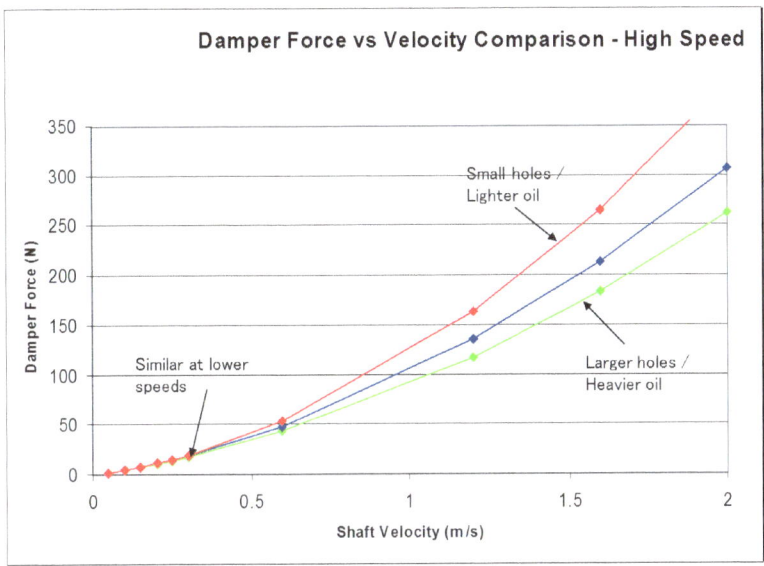

Obviously, there is an almost infinite number of combinations of pistons and oils that you can create, but hopefully, these two examples will help you to understand *why* we adjust oils and pistons.

Rod Volume (Emulsification vs Bladder Dampers)

As the piston rod goes in and out of the cylinder, there needs to be room for the volume of the rod to be absorbed. Without that, the damper would have a "hydraulic lock" and would not be able to operate. There are two ways of doing this: emulsion and bladder style.

Emulsion dampers have a small amount of air mixed in with the oil. As the rod enters the damper, the air is compressed and expands as the rod extends out. While air in oil isn't always desirable, once you have pumped the damper a few times, the air becomes thousands of tiny bubbles within the shock. There is a small delay in an emulsion damper – when the piston is first moved, the bubbles have some "give" before the oil is forced through the piston. This gives a traction improvement over small bumps but takes away some initial response. They are most common on 1/10 off-road cars.

Bladder dampers use a small rubber bladder at the top of the oil. The air is held on the other side of the bladder (between the bladder and the cap) with ideally no air in the damper fluid. As the piston rod enters the damper, the extra volume in the oil pushes the bladder, which can move against the air behind it. Bladder dampers are typically more responsive than emulsion style and have less fade but can lose some traction on small bumps. They are typically used in touring car and 1/8 scale off-road. There are vacuum pumps available to suck all the air out of dampers before assembling them.

Big Bore Dampers

There has been a trend in RC to move towards bigger dampers (it's not a new trend – the original RC10 had much larger shocks than its competitors when it was released in the 80s). There are a couple of potential advantages to big bore shocks, but the main one is to get more response and more control with less heat build-up.

When talking about dampers, the performance is usually a function of piston area squared. Therefore a small change in piston size can have a dramatic effect on the force:

1. Piston force = pressure drop x piston area.
2. Flow through piston holes = piston area x piston speed.
3. Pressure drop through piston holes is proportional to flow through the holes.
4. Therefore damper force is proportional to piston area x piston area or written another way (piston area)^2.

Let's compare dampers with a 10mm diameter to those with a 12mm diameter. If we use the same oil and the same size/number of holes, the force of the 12mm damper would be over double the 10mm damper. Therefore we need to use bigger holes (which are more precise to make and easier to adjust in fine increments).

In addition, the heat generated in the damper is less. There is less pressure drop required in the first place, and the volume of the oil is larger, so it takes longer to heat up. Damper fade isn't necessarily noticeable in a five minute race, but it is noticeable on some tracks with big jumps and high temperatures.

Calculating the force of a damper is quite complex. The graph below shows the force of dampers at different velocities for different piston and oil combinations. This is based on actual university measurements of pressure drop of oil through small holes at different speeds, and I have found it to be handy to work out what oil to start with if I am changing from one piston to another.

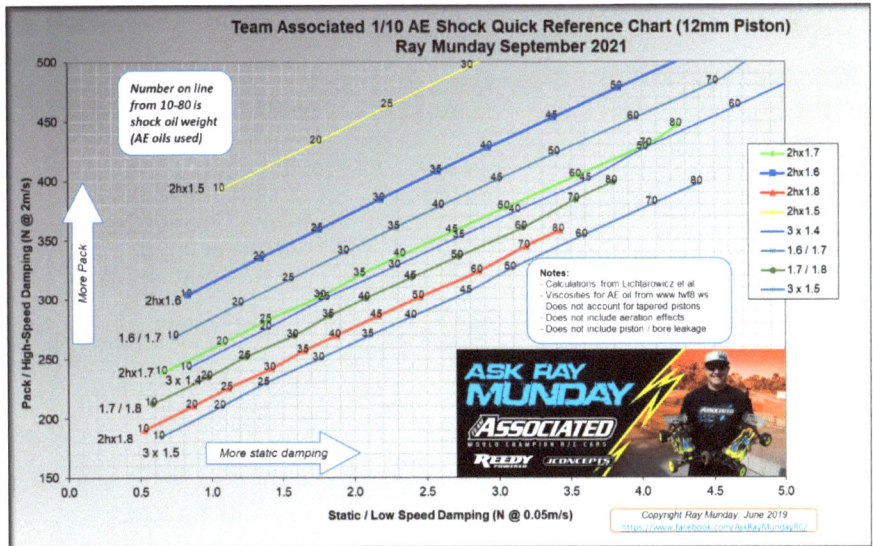

Each line represents a different piston. E.g. "2hx1.6" is a two hole piston where each hole is 1.6mm diameter and "1.6/1.7" is a two hole piston with one 1.6mm hole and one 1.7mm hole

Tuning Dampers

This is a very lengthy subject in itself, but I try to follow these principles with my off-road cars:

- **Low-speed damping** – reducing low-speed damping makes the car react faster. Increasing the damping makes the car smoother to drive, but too much can make it unresponsive. In low-grip/tight tracks reduce low-speed damping. For flowing/high-grip tracks increase it. Less damping at the front tends to make the car "square off" the corner more.

- **High-speed damping** – our tracks in Australia are generally bumpy so I try to run as little high-speed damping (pack) as I can for the jumps on the track. If the track has big jumps with flat landings, you may need to increase the pack. If the track is smooth with high-grip, increasing pack can also make the car feel more stable and easier to drive.

- You should try and match your low-speed damping with the spring rate. Stiffer springs need firmer damping. The spring and the damper need to work together as a team for best performance.

– *Ray Munday*

Differential

Level: Basic

The wheel on the outside of a turn always has to travel farther than the inside wheel. The front wheels turn at different angles to allow for this (refer to Ackermann on page *107*). The rear wheels on a 2WD, and both the front and rear wheels on a 4WD, use a differential (or diff) to allow the wheels to turn at different speeds and this assists the car to rotate into corners.

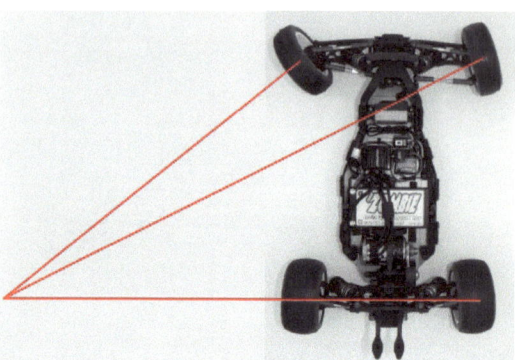

In 4WD, gear diffs have largely replaced ball diffs due to their consistency and lack of maintenance. 2WD tend to use ball diffs for reasons explained on page *149*.

Rear – A diff is always used at the rear.
Centre – 4WD cars usually have a centre diff or a centre Slipper Clutch (page *180*).
Front – 4WD cars usually have a front diff.

Checking the Diff Action

Put the car on the stand and turn the right wheel clockwise. The left wheel should turn anticlockwise. If it doesn't, then check you have assembled your diff as per the manufacturer's instructions. The diff should feel reasonably smooth. It is unnecessary for the diff to be perfectly smooth with no gritty feel at all, but the smoother the diff feels, the better it will perform.

The "Diffing Out" Problem

Put your car on a stand so that all the wheels are off the ground. Hold one of the rear wheels and apply some throttle. You should notice that the wheel you are not holding spins twice as fast as it normally would for that amount of throttle.

Imagine that the wheel you are holding is the wheel on the outside of the corner and your car is leaning on this wheel. This outside wheel has most of the weight of the car, giving it more traction, and the inside wheel will have less weight on it and therefore less traction, allowing it to possibly break traction and start spinning. This is a "diff out" and will cause your back end to oversteer.

A tighter ball diff will assist to prevent "diffing out". For a gear diff try a thicker diff oil.

Gear Diff

Most modern 4WD kits come with a gear differential. They are also available from third party suppliers. They increase on-power steering compared to ball diffs.

Gear diffs require significantly less maintenance than ball diffs but use oil viscosity for adjustments rather than a simple nut. Modified cars tend to use thicker oil. The manufacturer should provide a recommended starting point for oil viscosity.

As a general rule, thinner oil increases traction and thicker oil increases on-power steering and stability. Use thinner oils on low-grip tracks and thicker oils for high-grip.

Diff oils are measured in thousands of cSt. A 5,000 cSt oil is also referred to as 5K. In a 4WD with a front, centre and rear diff you might see oil settings written like this 10K–7K–5K or even 10–7–5. This shows a 10K front diff oil, 7K centre and 5K rear.

Rear Diff

For the starting oil to use, refer to the manufacturer's manual for your kit. If no oil is specified, then use the following as a guide for a dirt track:

	2WD	4WD (1/10)	4WD (1/8)
Starting Setting	N/A (Ball Diff is typical)	TLR* 5,000 cSt AE** 10,000 cSt	5,000 cSt (Typical range: 3,000–10,000 cSt)

*Team Losi Racing (TLR)   ** Team Associated (AE)*

Setting	Rear Diff
Higher viscosity oil (thicker)	• Less traction. Used for higher traction conditions. • Better acceleration. • Less stability. • More on-power steering. • Harder for the car to rotate into the corner. • Less off-power steering.
Lower viscosity oil (thinner)	• More traction. Used for lower traction conditions. • Less acceleration. • Greater stability. • Less on-power steering. • Easier for the car to rotate into the corner. • More off-power steering.

A diff is always used at the rear.

Front Diff (4WD)

Some drivers use a locked diff (spool) at the front of a 4WD car. However, it is more common to use a diff. A diff in the front increases on-power steering and cornering speed.

For the starting oil to use, refer to the manufacturer's manual for your kit. If no oil is specified, then use the following as a guide for a dirt track:

	2WD	4WD (1/10)	4WD (1/8)
Starting Setting	No Front Diff	TLR * 7,000 cSt AE ** 10,000 cSt	10,000 cSt (Typical range: 5,000–20,000 cSt)

*Team Losi Racing (TLR) ** Team Associated (AE)*

Setting	Front Diff
Higher viscosity oil (thicker)	• Smoother steering response. • More forward traction. • More on-power steering. • Less off-power steering. • Better stability when braking. • Lower cornering speed.
Lower viscosity oil (thinner)	• More aggressive steering response. • Less forward traction. • Less on-power steering. • More off-power steering. • Less stability when braking. • Higher cornering speed.

Front diffs tend to benefit from thicker oils. The thicker the oil, the closer the driving feel is to that of a solid axle (spool). For more information on solid axles (spools), refer to page *182*.

Centre Diff (4WD)

For the starting oil to use, refer to the manufacturer's manual for your kit. If no oil is specified, then use the following as a guide for a dirt track:

	2WD	4WD (1/10)	4WD (1/8)
Starting Setting	No Centre Diff	1/10 often uses a centre Slipper Clutch instead of a diff. A Centre Diff may be an optional part: TLR * 200,000 cSt (such a thick oil provides spool like performance).	7,000 cSt (Typical range: 5,000–20,000 cSt)

Team Losi Racing (TLR)

Setting	Centre Diff
Higher viscosity oil (thicker)	• Greater acceleration from all four wheels. • Most stable off-power. • Harder to drive on a low-grip track. • Better for smooth tracks.
Lower viscosity oil (thinner)	• Easier to drive on-power. • Acceleration will be less and more controllable. • Assists the car to rotate into corners. • Better for bumpy tracks. • Harder to drive on high-grip tracks. • Can cause diffing out on high-grip tracks.

In the centre diff, you can keep increasing the diff oil thickness until the car oversteers on acceleration, and then you have gone too far.

Ball Diff

Setting	Handling Impact
Tighter diff	Better acceleration, harder for the car to rotate into the corner.
Looser diff	Less acceleration, easier for the car to rotate into the corner.

How Tight Should the Diff Be?

For off-road, I tighten the diff with a wrench so it is tight (without cranking down), then let off 1/8 of a turn. For a tighter diff, let off less than 1/8 of a turn; for a looser diff, let off more than 1/8 of a turn. A tight diff may turn the motor over when you check the diff action (see above).

Running in the Diff

After rebuilding the diff, and before checking the diff tightness, run the diff in by holding one of the rear wheels and providing a little throttle to spin the other wheel. Don't run at full throttle, and don't run for more than a couple of seconds. Then hold the other wheel and do the same thing.

Checking the Diff Tightness

Hold the right wheel and the spur gear with your right hand and use your left hand to try and turn the left wheel. The left wheel should be very difficult to rotate. If it is not, then tighten or loosen the diff nut slightly and retest until the desired result is achieved. Note: if the slipper clutch is set to be very loose then this may not work.

Ball Diff Rebuild

The ball diff should be rebuilt periodically, typically when it feels "gritty" when rotating one rear tyre by hand or if it is no longer smooth, indicating it may need regreasing.

Rebuild by disassembling and thoroughly cleaning the various parts of the diff. Check the diff rings. If they have a line scored into them by the diff balls, then replace, or remove the line by sanding the diff rings using 600 grit wet and dry sandpaper. Wet the sandpaper with brake cleaner and sand the rings in circles until the groove is removed. Clean the rings with brake cleaner and a rag after sanding.

Diff Height

Diff height adjusts the driveshaft angle into the outdrives. It is a useful tuning tool for tuning for the grip level.

Setting	Affect
Higher Diff	Use on higher grip tracks where ride height is lower.
Lower Diff	Use on lower grip tracks where ride height is higher.

High diffs will smooth the car out and make it easier to drive as there is less "binding" in the driveshafts. This is often better for higher traction tracks to help the car maintain corner speed and make it easier to drive.

Low diffs will make the car more aggressive and generate more initial traction as there is more "binding" in the driveshafts. This is often better for low-traction tracks in order to generate grip and aggression.

Diff Tech

Ray Munday – Tech Talk

The differential is commonly misunderstood, and in this section I talk about how they affect the handling of the vehicle.

What is a differential?

The differential (or diff) is the part of the drivetrain that connects the left and right-hand wheels together. In a 4WD, there is also a differential between the front and rear diffs. The name implies that it allows a differential in speed between the left and right-hand wheels (or front and rear). This is very important for road cars as when you are turning tight corners (such as in a car park), the inner and outer wheels travel very different distances. Without a differential in a road car, it would be almost impossible to turn the car in this situation.

Race vehicles are very different to road cars. In a race car, there is almost always some sliding during corners, so the distance the inner and outer wheels travel is not so different. It is possible to have a race car with a locked differential (often called a spool). In a race car, it is not the speed difference that is important but the torque distribution. Different types of differentials give different torque distribution, and that is what we will discuss here.

How do diffs work?

There are three types of diffs we will discuss. The first is the gear diff (which is used in most on-road cars, 1/8 cars, and 4WD 1/10 cars). The left and right-hand driveshafts are each connected to a gear, and another gear sits in between these two connected to the crown wheel. The two wheels can turn in opposite directions, but when the crown wheel turns, the centre gear tries to rotate both the wheels forward. The average speed of the two wheels will be the same as the crown wheel, but one may be going faster than the other.

The ball diff (unique to RC cars) has balls sitting in the crown wheel, and each axle has a ring that runs on these balls. There is a thrust screw that pulls the two halves together, creating pressure between the diff rings and diff balls. The diff balls drive the rings, and differential motion is created by the balls rotating in their recess. The ball diff is very smooth and adjustable, but it can slip if not set correctly, creating wear.

The spool is literally a solid piece connecting the crown wheel and two axles together. The two axles will always be turning at the same speed as the crown wheel.

Torque Distribution – Why is it important?

Torque distribution refers to how much torque each axle receives. Torque in the driveshaft becomes the force at the tyre trying to accelerate the car. Torque distribution can significantly influence the handling of the car. If you look at the car from above – imagine that both left and right tyres are pushing with the same force. In this case, the car will accelerate straight. If the right-hand tyre has a greater force than the left under acceleration, it will try and steer the car to the left (think of it like a tank). If the right-hand tyre has a greater force than the left under braking, it will try and steer the car to the right.

Note that all of this relates to when you are either on the power or on the brakes, and this is when the effects of differentials are most important.

We will now review the torque distribution for different differential settings. For this part, if you have a differential in your hand, hold one axle with one hand, and turn the crown wheel with the other hand to feel how much torque is being transferred.

Case 1: Open Differential

An "open" differential is one in which the differential action is completely free (if you spin the left wheel, you will see the right wheel spin freely in the opposite direction). This is the case for a gear differential with no grease or a ball differential set very loose.

With an open diff, the torque is always the same for the left and right wheels. This means that under power, the car will be the most stable as the left and right wheels have the same torque. The downside is that if one wheel loses traction (for instance, during cornering, there is weight transfer to the outside wheel, reducing the grip available from the inside wheel), the diff will make that wheel spin faster and provide less torque to the wheel with traction. This is often referred to as "diffing out" and is obvious when the inside tyre balloons up under power. It can also happen under brakes on a 2WD if a rear wheel is in the air – there is no braking effect at all, and the car will suddenly lose brakes.

Case 2: Locked Differential (Spool)

A spool allows no speed difference between the left and right wheels. In this case, the amount of torque in the left and right wheels depends on how much traction is at the tyre. In the extreme case, if you have one wheel completely off the ground (no traction), it will still drive the other wheel, and 100% of the torque will go to that wheel.

With a locked differential, you get maximum traction, but it can come at the expense of stability. On a rough track, the tyre force is always changing, so the car may change direction very quickly and unpredictably.

When cornering, a spool will make the car behave very differently from on-power to off-power. With weight transfer to the outer wheels, there is more traction available at the outer wheels, so more torque is transferred to these wheels. This means that under power, the car will be pulled in the direction of the corner (lots of on-power steering), but under brakes, it will be pulled away from the corner (feels like strong understeer off-power).

148

Case 3: Limited Slip Differential

A Limited Slip Differential (LSD) is one that allows some differential action, but there is some resistance. This can come in the form of tightening up a ball differential, adding thick grease inside a gear diff, or using small friction plates within the diff.

With an LSD, there will be some torque difference between the left and right-hand axles, but it will not be as much as with a spool. The more the resistance, the more it will act like a spool (improved steering on-power, less steering off-power, more traction but less straight stability). In most off-road RC racing situations, we use an LSD setting.

2WD Differential Setting

Typically in a rear-motor 2WD buggy, we run the diff as free and smooth as possible. This gives the most stability (which is critical in a 2WD) as the left and right wheels will get equal torque and try to push the car ahead in a straight line. Usually, there is a large proportion of the vehicle weight over the rear wheels and, under acceleration, there is additional weight transfer to the wheels, so usually both rear tyres have good traction available and it isn't common to "diff out".

With mid-motor cars, we have found you need to run the diff a little tighter to keep good drive out of the corners (it's easier to "diff-out" as there is less weight over the rear tyres). Mid-motor cars also turn in faster, so a slightly tighter diff will smooth this out. It's important to ensure that the diff is smooth and not gritty.

A spool diff in the rear of a 2WD buggy is almost undrivable! Generally ball diffs are used as they are very smooth and easy to adjust. Gear diffs are used in some 2WD cars, but they tend to not be as smooth as a ball diff which works better on higher grip surfaces such as carpet.

4WD Front Differential Setting

With a 4WD (off-road and on-road), stability isn't such a big issue, but it is important to have a vehicle that lets you put maximum power down out of corners. Under acceleration, there is weight transfer from front-to-rear, so it is easy to "diff out" the inner front wheel under acceleration out of corners. If this happens, the car basically turns into a rear-wheel drive and can become suddenly unstable and lose traction. To avoid this, the front differential is usually run tighter than the rear. This has the added advantage of giving lots of on-power steering but can take away off-power steering. If the track has lots of tight hairpins, it is better to run the front diff a little loose. If the track has lots of sweeping corners requiring acceleration when exiting turns, it is better to have the diff tighter.

With a tight front diff, a 4WD likes to be driven on-power through all corners or it will understeer.

I find that a change to the front differential setting is one of the most sensitive adjustments on 4WDs.

4WD Centre Differential Setting

Most modern 1/10 and 1/8 4WD buggies use a centre differential when driving on dirt/clay surfaces. These balance the torque between the front and rear axles, which makes the car easier to drive on-power, and also allows the car to steer much better into tight corners. The downside is that under power, as the weight transfers to the rear, the front tyres have less traction available, but the diff will still send power to the front creating front wheelspin and less drive to the rear tyres. To counter this, we generally use a thicker oil in the centre diff (especially in 1/10, where we often use 100,000 to 500,000 cSt oil).

On very high-traction surfaces (carpet/astroturf), 1/10 buggies use a slipper clutch which is a spool type "locked" diff (the slipper protects the motor during peak torque loads while the spool connects the front and rear). This gives maximum drive on-power and maximum braking but slows the turn-in (which is fine in very high-grip as the cars already have a lot of steering). Both centre diff and spool stop all four wheels in the air giving good jump control.

A few years ago, it was common to run a one-way centre diff which locked under power, but under brakes allowed the front wheels to freewheel (i.e. braking was to the rear only). This gave maximum steering off-power but gave longer braking distances and less control in the air (under brakes, only the rear wheels slowed down, so there was less pitch control). As motor and battery tech have improved and the jumps have become bigger, these have become less common.

Interaction Between Diff and Suspension Settings

The suspension and diffs interact with each other, which can sometimes make setup changes confusing. When you run a tight front diff on a 4WD, sometimes changes to the suspension setup can have some unusual effects. For example, if you want to increase steering, you typically make the rear stiffer, which increases weight transfer at the rear and reduces it at the front. However, this reduced weight transfer at the front means that there is less torque transfer at the front diff, giving less on-power steering. The stiffer rear suspension may therefore give you more mid-corner steering, but less on exit, due to the interaction with the diffs. So if some changes work backwards to what you'd expect, first ask yourself if the diffs are tight. If they are, they could be part of the issue.

Conclusion

The differential is a critical tool in setting up your car. Race car differentials control how the torque is distributed to the driving wheels under acceleration and braking and have a large effect on the handling response of the car. The next time you hit the track, have a play with these settings so you can understand their effect – you never know, it may unlock that extra 0.1s you have been chasing!

– Ray Munday

Droop (Down Travel)

Level: Basic

On-road racing generally makes no distinction between shock Down Travel (shock is fully extended) and Up Travel (shock is fully compressed) and refers to both as Droop. However, only the Down Travel is actually Droop and in off-road racing it can be an important distinction.

This section discusses Droop (also called Down Travel). Up Travel is discussed on page *191*.

With the body off, place your car on a level surface and settle the suspension so the car is sitting at ride height. Take hold of the front shock tower and slowly lift until the front wheels just start to come off the ground. As the car lifts the front shocks extend and the shock piston travels downwards within the shock body (Down Travel). This is droop.

Droop is normally different at the front and rear of the car and you'll see this if you repeat the above experiment for the rear.

Droop is an important tuning option as it is the amount of suspension travel the car has available to transfer weight when the car accelerates or brakes.

The more droop the car has:

- The further the car can lean into a corner without lifting the inside wheel.
- When landing a jump, the wheels will touch the ground sooner, and there is more suspension travel to absorb the landing.
- When going over a bump, the wheel can stay in contact with the ground longer.
- Too much droop can make the car roll too much, make it respond slowly and may make it oversteer.

Measuring Droop

There are three methods of measuring droop. Whichever method you choose, make sure you are consistent in your measuring technique so that you can keep track of any changes.

If discussing Droop with another racer, ask them which method they use. If they have the same chassis as you, then you can compare droop settings using any of these methods. However, if they have a different chassis, then you can only compare droop measurements using the Ruler or Droop Gauge methods.

A. Ruler Method

1. Put the tyres on the car. Car should be race ready.
2. Place the car on a flat surface, on its wheels.
3. Push down and release the front and rear of the car so that the suspension settles.
4. Use a ruler to measure the **starting ride height** at the bottom of the chassis in the centre (front or rear). Below, the rear ride height is 23mm.

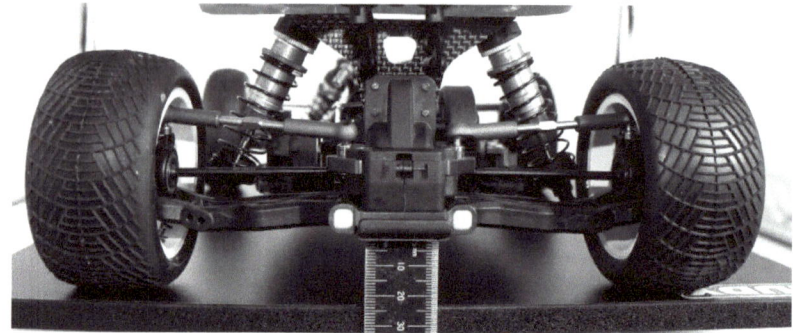

5. Use the ruler to lift the car until the wheels just leave the ground. Now measure the **ending ride height**. The difference in the starting and ending ride heights is the droop. Below ending rear ride height is 41mm. 41mm – 23mm = 18mm of droop.

6. Repeat steps 3–5 for the other end of the car.

Note: Using a ruler is less accurate and less repeatable than other methods. It requires a steady hand. It also requires that you judge the moment the tyres leave the ground (and of course the rubber tyres make this judgement difficult as the tyres will have some sag). The Ruler Method can be compared between different manufacturer's kits.

B. Droop Gauge Method

This is the most accurate method, and can be compared between different car brands. You are actually measuring the height difference between the chassis and the wheel axles (and therefore, the numbers tend to be only a few mm and are quite different to those of the Ruler Method).

You will need droop blocks and a droop gauge. These can be confusing to buy. Generally, on-road cars use 10mm droop blocks (which are too small for off-road cars), 1/8 off-road cars use 30mm droop blocks, and 1/10 off-road cars can use 20mm or 30mm droop blocks. Make sure you buy a droop gauge designed to work with the size of droop blocks that you buy. The photo below shows a 1/10 buggy on 30mm droop blocks:

1. Remove the tyres. Shocks and roll bars should be attached.

2. Place the chassis on the droop blocks on a flat surface. The chassis should be parallel to the table and the blocks must not interfere with the suspension arms.

3. Check that the suspension is settled by tapping the camber link of the suspension arm that you're checking.

4. Place the droop gauge under the stub axle hex. This is the droop measurement. Always measure in the same place. In the example photo, the gauge shows 5mm. On this particular gauge the bottom of the chassis is level with the 10mm mark. So 10mm – 5mm = 5mm difference between chassis and bottom of the stub axle = 5mm droop.

5. Repeat step 4 on the other side of the car.
6. Repeat steps 3–5 for the other end of the car.

C. Shock Length Method

This method can't be compared between different car brands. It is the least accurate as shock length is not the only setup factor which impacts droop (for example, changing ride height or laying the shocks down will also change droop):

1. Remove the tyres. Shocks and roll bars should be attached.

2. Place the chassis on droop blocks on a flat surface. The chassis should be parallel to the table.

3. Check that the suspension is settled by tapping the camber link on the same side as the shock that you're checking.

4. Measure the shock length from the top centre of the shock to the bottom centre (as pictured). NB: 1/8 car manuals usually measure from the centre of the screw in the shock tower to the centre of the screw in the suspension arm. This is harder to measure accurately and consistently.

Adjusting Droop

- Some buggies (mostly 1/8 scale) use droop screws in the suspension arms. This is a very easy way to adjust droop. Tightening the screw reduces the droop and loosening the screw increases droop.

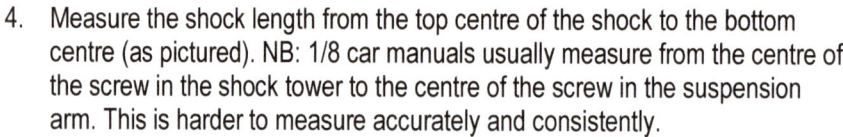

- You can change the Axle Height (page *113*) to change droop.

- On any vehicle, changing the length of the shock (also called stroke) will change the droop. Refer to your car's manual for the starting shock length.

- If you wish to shorten the shock length but run out of adjustment, you can insert a shock limiter (also called droop limiters and down travel limiters) inside the bottom of the shock body to further limit the shock length. A shock limiter is a bushing or washer that sits on the shock shaft between the shock piston and the bottom of the shock body.
- Using a longer or shorter lower shock eyelet will change droop.
- Left side droop must equal right side droop (left shock length equals right shock length).
- Front droop and rear droop are set independently.

Setting	Shock Length/Stroke	Shock Limiter	Lower Eyelet	Droop Screw
More Droop	Increase	None	Longer	Loosen
Less Droop	Decrease	Add	Shorter	Tighten

Regardless of how you measured your droop, a 0.5–1.0mm change to droop should make a noticeable difference to the car's handling.

Excessive droop can affect driveshaft engagement (check that the dog bones of the driveshaft are still engaging in the diff outdrives at full droop). Longer driveshafts are often available as optional parts.

Rear Droop

Setting	Handling Impact
Increase Droop	• Increases rear chassis upward travel off-power and under braking. • Increases forward weight transfer. • More steering. • Less stable and harder to drive, especially in high-grip. • Better on bumpy tracks. • Jumping and landing is easier.
Decrease Droop	• Decreases rear chassis upward travel off-throttle and under braking. • Decreases forward weight transfer. • More stable under braking. • More stable on-power. • Better on smooth tracks. • More rear traction. • Jumping and landing is more difficult. • May increase corner speed in sweepers.

Increasing rear droop will increase the weight transfer to the front, especially off-power. This will give the car more steering and rotation off-power and on-power. It gives the car more overall steering and generally makes it harder to drive. Usually, you will add rear droop when looking for more steering and rotation. Too much rear droop in high-traction can make the car very difficult to drive. In 2WD we often use more rear droop in low-traction to keep the tyre connected with the ground.

Decreasing rear droop will decrease the weight transfer to the front, especially off-power. This will give the car more stability off-power, and more on-power stability. It gives the car more overall rear traction and makes it easier to drive. Not enough rear droop can make the car "bind up" in the corner and lead it to lack rotation and steering.

Front Droop

Setting	Handling Impact
Increase Droop	• Increases upward chassis travel on-power. • Increases rearward weight transfer. • More responsive, less stable. • Better on bumpy tracks. • More rear traction. • Jumping and landing is easier.
Decrease Droop	• Decreases front chassis upward travel on-power. • Less rearward weight transfer. • Less responsive, more stable. • Better on smooth tracks. • Jumping and landing is more difficult.

Front droop is a good tuning option to adjust the aggressiveness of the car. If the car is too aggressive, add front droop. If it is not aggressive enough, remove front droop.

Increasing front droop will increase weight transfer to the rear, especially on-power. This can increase rear traction on-power and increase high-speed steering due to centrifugal forces acting on the rear of the car while it is loaded up. It will, however, decrease initial turn-in and low-speed steering.

Decreasing front droop will increase initial turn-in and low-speed steering. It decreases rear stability on-power and makes the car more stable at high-speed.

Tyres and Droop

Some brands of tyres may have a different diameter. If changing tyres changes the tyre diameter, then you will need to check and adjust your ride height and droop in order to maintain your setup. For a bigger diameter tyre, we need to lessen the amount of droop. For a smaller diameter tyre, we need to increase the amount of droop.

Interaction

If changing droop via droop screws, unscrewing the lower shock eyelets or adding internal travel limiters, ride height will remain unaltered. If swapping out the lower shock eyelets for shorter or longer length eyelets, recheck ride height (page 172).

Increasing the ride height will decrease the droop value. Decreasing the ride height will increase the droop value.

ESC Settings

Level: Basic

Blinky (non-timing mode) – Stock classes normally require the ESC to be in "Blinky" mode. "Blinky" denotes a mode of the ESC with no dynamic timing. This is often shown by a blinking light on the ESC – hence "Blinky". It is also referred to as "non-timing mode". There are no such restrictions for the Modified class or in 1/8.

Brake Strength – set brake strength to 100% and then reduce the brake EPA on the radio until you are comfortable with the brake force.

Brake Frequency – this is the frequency of the "pulsing" of the electronic signal to the motor under braking. Higher brake frequencies tend to provide stronger brakes at high-speed with less at low-speed. They work well on more open tracks. In comparison, lower brake frequencies give more braking at low-speed and feel more aggressive. Lower frequencies can help on tighter tracks.

Drag Brake – drag brake is the amount of brake applied when the throttle is in neutral. Some drivers swear by it, while others prefer not to use it. It can be a useful tuning aid and changes the feel of the car when entering a corner.

Drag brake helps slow the car down for each corner and tends to add more steering to the car (more weight transfer). Compared to using the trigger, it is more consistent, especially important in 2WD vehicles. Good starting points are 18% for 2WD buggy and 12% for 4WD and SCT. If the grip comes up, reduce the drag brake. On a very slippery track, extra drag brake on a 2WD buggy usually adds steering.

Drive Frequency – this is the frequency of the "pulsing" of the electronic signal to the motor under throttle. Lower frequencies give more punch (good for Stock), while higher frequencies make the throttle smoother (good for lower traction tracks and in Modified).

Minimum Drive/Deadband – these two adjustments control the sensitivity of the ESC to small throttle movements. Minimum drive is the minimum signal that the ESC will send the motor when you first pull the trigger. A lower minimum drive setting means that micro-movements of the trigger will be less sensitive but more controllable. A good starting point is 0% in Modified, but some Stock racers may like a higher setting as this can give a stronger punch feel. Deadband is the amount of free play the trigger has before the ESC will send a signal to the motor. 6% is a typical setting to balance response and "edginess".

Reverse – is illegal for racing, so disable it.

Throttle – in Stock classes this will normally be set to maximum. In Modified, set the aggressiveness of the throttle on the ESC to a medium or midway setting initially and tune from there.

Turbo and Boost – you can set most 1/10 ESCs, and some 1/8 ESCs, to advance the motor timing electronically to provide higher top-end RPM using the Turbo and Boost settings. Refer to your ESC manual for instructions. Turbo and Boost are not usually legal in Stock classes. Refer to your local rules.

Turbo Example in Modified	2WD (1/10)	4WD (1/10)
In the example Reedy motors and ESC were used on AE buggies	• 8.5T motor • 30° end bell timing • 8.13:1 Final Drive Ratio * For a long straight, add 10° Turbo timing. For a tight/low-grip track, drop end bell timing to 20°.	• 6.5T motor • 20° end bell timing • 9.64:1 Final Drive Ratio * • 15° Turbo timing.

* The example above is based on Australian tracks. Australian and European tracks tend to be larger than US indoor tracks. In general, a pinion 2 teeth larger might be used on an Australian/European track versus a US track.

Boost is where the timing ramps up as RPM increases. Generally, boost is used on a bigger track with good traction when more power is beneficial.

Turbo (also called Top Speed Timing) is a progressive timing ramp up which commences at full throttle.

Flex

Refer to Chassis Stiffness (Flex) on page 122.

Gearing and Rollout

Level: Basic

The correct gearing is essential to minimise your lap times. Gearing determines both acceleration and top speed.

The "best" gearing for you depends on your driving style, the track environment, and the motor/chassis setup. Therefore, it is likely that you will change your gearing for different tracks. A large flowing track might benefit from higher top speed, while a smaller and tighter track might benefit from better acceleration out of the corners.

Gearing for Final Drive Ratio or Rollout?

Off-road cars have a Final Drive Ratio (FDR) often called "gear ratio" or "ratio" or "gearing". FDR is the number of times the motor must turn so that the wheels turn once. Expressed as a ratio, e.g. 4.0:1 means the motor turns four times to rotate the wheels once.

Rollout tends to be used in on-road when using foam tyres. Rollout is how far the car will move forward with one revolution of the motor. This depends on your FDR and the diameter of the tyres. As tyre diameter reduces, the work the motor does changes. TQ RC Racing has an excellent Rollout Calculator (www.tqrcracing.com).

Tyres	Wear	FDR or Rollout
Rubber	Minimal	FDR
Foam (not used in off-road)	Significant reduction of tyre diameter (by mm per race meeting)	Rollout

160

Final Drive Ratios

Lower FDRs provide higher RPM, and therefore faster top speed, but less torque and consequently slower acceleration. Lower means "less than" so 3.0:1 is lower than 4.0:1.

Higher FDRs provide lower RPM, and therefore slower top speed, but more torque and consequently greater acceleration. Higher means "greater than" so 4.0:1 is higher than 3.0:1.

Calculating the Final Drive Ratio (FDR)
FDR = (Spur / Pinion) x Internal Ratio

The internal ratio will be specified in your car's manual.

For example, a 72 tooth spur gear with a 33 tooth pinion and an internal ratio of 2.6 provides an FDR of 72/33 x 2.6 = 5.67. This means 5.67:1, or the motor turns 5.67 times for every 1 time that the wheels turn.

Gear Ratio Charts

It can be handy to make your own gear ratio charts to refer to. There are many websites that will create a chart based on a range of spur and pinions you specify. For example, TQ RC Racing's Gear Chart (www.tqrcracing.com).

So What FDR Should You Start With?

Where your motor's manufacturer does not provide recommended starting gearing, you can use the following table as a starting point. Always check the temperature carefully when gearing a new motor for the first time (refer to Motor Temperature on page *164*).

1/10 Brushless Motor	Starting FDR (Medium Sized Track, 2S Lipo)		
	4WD Buggy	2WD Buggy	Stadium Truck
6.5 turns	10.0:1	10.1:1	12.5:1
7.5 turns	9.5:1	9.7:1	11.7:1
8.5 turns	9.1:1	9.2:1	11.0:1
9.5 turns	8.7:1	8.8:1	10.5:1
10.5 turns	8.3:1	8.5:1	9.5:1
13.5 turns	6.9:1	7.2:1	8.3:1
17.5 turns	6.2:1	6.5:1	7.6:1
21.5 turns		5.7:1	

1/8 Brushless Motor	Starting FDR (Medium Sized Track, 4S Lipo)
1700 Kv	10.4:1
1900 Kv	10.9:1
2100 Kv	11.4:1
2200 Kv	11.9:1

In 1/8, it is less common to talk about FDR. It is common to simply specify a spur/pinion combination. This makes it difficult to compare FDR between drivers running different brands.

Many racers will use a lower FDR than shown above. However, the above is a good starting point.

Things you should consider when setting your FDR:

- All motors are not created equal. Always follow the motor manufacturer's gearing recommendation.
- Track (open with long straight = lower, or short and tight = higher).
- Whether you have advanced the end bell motor timing (see below).
- Air temperature (see Motor Temperature below).

What Rollout Should You Start With?

Rollout is not normally used in off-road. However, it is how far the car will move forward with one revolution of the motor.

Calculating the Rollout

(Tyre Diameter x 3.14) / ((spur gear / pinion gear) x internal ratio)

For example, a car with 64mm diameter tyres with an 80 tooth spur gear, 35 tooth pinion and an internal ratio of 1.8 provides:

(64mm x 3.14) / ((80 / 35) x 1.8) = a 50.29mm rollout, i.e. the car will move forward approximately 50mm every time the motor rotates once.

Gear Mesh

Setting the correct gap between the pinion gear and the spur gear is vital. If the gap is too large, the spur gear will strip; if the gap is too small, the spur will cause drag on the pinion (often accompanied by excessive gear noise and motor overheating). Some sources suggest 0.3mm of play between the spur and pinion gear teeth. However, this is difficult to measure. If you shine a torch on the mesh, you should see a very small gap. Another option is to run a small piece of paper between the gears by turning the spur gear. It should feed all the way through and drop out. If it won't, then the mesh is too tight. Lastly, you can hold the pinion and rock the spur back and forth; there should be a little play. Modified mesh has slightly less play than Stock to prevent stripping the spur gear with the greater torque. For photo examples of correct gear mesh refer to page 305.

End Bell Timing

You can increase the RPM of a brushless motor by advancing the motor timing. This is often done by loosening the end bell screws and rotating the end bell. You can see in the photo that the example motor is set to 30° of end bell timing. To increase RPM, increase the timing, e.g. to 31° or more. Some notes of caution:

1. Increasing the end bell timing will increase your motor temperature (see Motor Temperature below).

2. Increasing end bell timing will reduce motor torque, i.e. the motor will have a faster top speed (RPM) but will accelerate slower (torque).

3. Never increase motor timing past the last timing mark by the manufacturer.

4. To increase motor timing, loosen (but don't remove) the end bell screws and rotate the end bell. Most motors use a similar system for changing timing.

Tuning Gearing for the Lowest Lap Times

Electric motors generate maximum torque at 1 RPM and the torque declines as the RPM increases. It is possible to lose too much low-end torque to effectively accelerate the weight of the car from a slow corner.

Track	Gearing	By Using	Result
Small, tight track	Higher	Smaller pinion	More torque, less top-end RPM
Large, open track	Lower	Larger pinion	Less torque, higher top-end RPM

Caution: changing gearing will affect Motor Temperature (see below).

Selecting the "best" gearing for a particular track is a compromise and often involves trial and error by changing the gearing and watching the lap times to see if they are faster or slower.

To speed up this process when you race at a new track, ask other drivers who are using the same brand and model of motor for their FDR recommendation.

Motor Temperature

Take the temperature of the motor using an infra-red temperature gauge. Some motors are more susceptible to heat than others, but as a rule of thumb, we want to make sure that our motor is 72°C (162°F) or less at the end of a race. If it is between 72°C and 80°C (176°F), then decrease the size of the pinion by 1 tooth or decrease the end bell timing by a couple of degrees. The motor can handle 80°C occasionally, but the motor life will not be as long as motors that operate at 72°C. If it is over 80°C, then unfortunately, the motor may have been damaged.

If it is under 65°C (149°F) at the end of the race, then you can risk lowering the FDR by increasing the size of the pinion by 1 tooth, or increasing the end bell timing by a couple of degrees.

Wait until your motor has cooled down and drive some more laps, this time stopping every 1 minute and taking the temperature.

Repeat the process until the car is as fast as you can make it while coming off the track at 72°C (162°F) or less.

If on race day the air temperature is hotter than when you carried out your testing, consider raising the FDR or lowering the end bell timing, so you don't overheat the motor.

Overheating melts the solder inside the motor, and soon afterwards, the motor will probably stop working. It might just go slowly, or it might grind to a halt in the middle of a race and start smoking! Motors that have overheated tend to smell (forever).

The first time you run a new motor, stop and take the temperature every couple of minutes.

Motor Cooling Fan

A fan and/or motor heat sink will assist in dissipating heat.

On a 1/10 car, if you are able to solder your fan wires direct to the + and – outputs on the ESC, then the fan will receive an additional 2.4V (and therefore spin faster and provide more cooling) compared to plugging into the receiver. Don't do this on a 1/8 vehicle, as the additional voltage will probably damage the fan.

Kick-up/Anti-dive (Front)

Level: Advanced

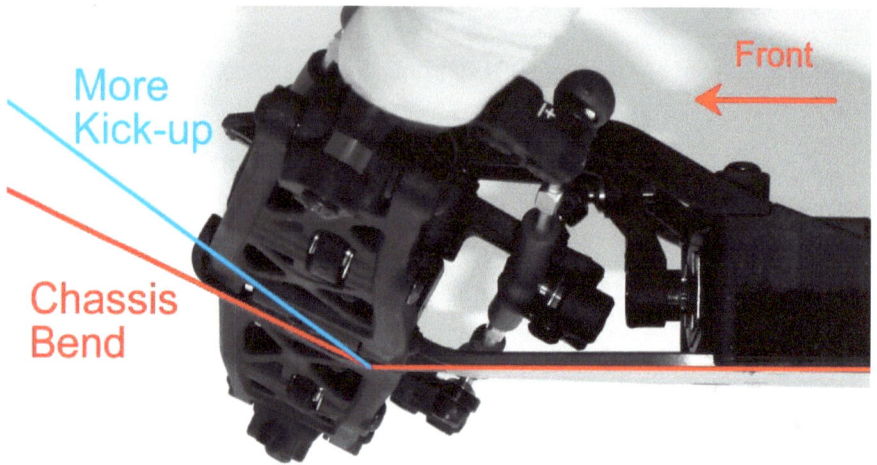

The left front suspension arm has been pulled up for the photo so that the chassis is visible

Kick-up affects how much the front of the car dives down (settles into the suspension) off-throttle and under braking.

A car with **kick-up** will have the front suspension arms tilted "backwards" so that the front of the arm is higher than the rear of the arm. Kick-up is sometimes referred to as "negative anti-dive".

A car with **anti-dive** will have the front suspension arms tilted "forwards" so that the front of the arm is lower than the rear of the arm. Anti-dive is sometimes referred to as "positive anti-dive".

Off-road cars usually have the front of the chassis bent up to provide a substantial amount of kick-up. You can add more kick-up using spacers under the front suspension arm mounts, inserts for the hinge pin or via optional parts. Refer to your car's manual. Anti-dive is not used on off-road cars.

Total Kick-up (the chassis angle plus any spacers) of 20–30° is common in 1/10 2WD and 8–12° in 1/10 4WD and 1/8 scale.

Kick-Up	Effect
More Kick-Up	• More weight transfer to the front of the chassis off-power and under braking. • Suspension compresses/chassis drops more off-power and under braking. • Better on bumpy tracks. • Decreases steering response.
Less Kick-up	• Less weight transfer to the front of the chassis off-power and under braking. • Suspension compresses/chassis drops less off-power and under braking. • Better on smooth tracks. • Increases steering response.
Anti-dive (front of front arm is lower than rear of arm)	Not used in off-road vehicles.

Interaction

Adding kick-up increases Caster (refer page 124).

Recheck your droop, ride height, toe and bump steer after changing kick-up.

Pro-squat

Refer to Anti-squat/Pro-squat (Rear) on page 111.

Radio Settings

Level: Basic

Modern radios (also called transmitters or remotes) have a wide range of adjustments, but there are a few key ones that can make a big difference. On high-end radios, you can assign a button to these settings, so you don't need to go through menus to find them.

The following are general guidelines for use as a starting point:

Too Much Steering

If your car has a lot of steering, you can change radio settings to reduce it. This might be useful when you have limited practice time (such as at an event), and there is insufficient time to return to the pits and change the setup:

- **End Point Adjustment (EPA) Servo setting** – reducing the EPA to less than 100% will reduce the amount of steering. However, it is recommended that you use Expo or Dual Rate rather than EPA to reduce steering. Once your EPA is set, you shouldn't need to adjust it unless you change your toe-out setting. Refer to steering throw on page *182* for how to set your EPA.

- **Dual Rate** – Dual Rate is similar to EPA, but it adjusts both the left and right side by the same amount, and therefore should be used to decrease the overall steering lock. Doing it this way allows you to always have a perfect steering balance left-to-right, with no guessing. If a track is flowing with high-traction, sometimes the full steering angle is too much and overpowers the tyres, causing an unstable feeling vehicle. In this case, try taking the Dual Rate down to 85% or so.

- **Steering Curve (Expo)** – refer to Exponential below.

Too Much Power for the Conditions

Throttle EPA – it's rare, but sometimes you can have too much power for a track. In this case, use the throttle EPA setting to limit the power output. This is most useful if a track becomes very slippery or if you are racing on a very small track.

Brake EPA – this determines the strength of your braking at full brake on the trigger. For example, 80% EPA means your radio will only send a signal of 80% brake to your ESC when you push the trigger to full brake. A good way to set up your car is that at full speed in a straight line, when you hit the brakes the wheels don't just lock up. Locked wheels lose traction and control. Check this on the warm-up lap, and if the grip level has changed, you can adjust it before the race start.

Throttle Expo – refer to Exponential below.

Exponential (Expo)

Exponential refers to how linear the signal is from your input (via the wheel or trigger) to the output (what the receiver sees). 0% Expo means that the movement is totally linear. Negative Expo (for example, –15%) means that when you first pull the trigger/move the steering, the output to the receiver is smaller. This means it is less sensitive to small movements. As you turn the steering/pull the trigger further, it becomes more sensitive. Positive Expo makes the output more sensitive for small inputs. Expo does not change the overall steering/power available, only how much is delivered at a particular point on the wheel/trigger.

Throttle Expo – you can use negative expo to mellow out the throttle input if there is low-traction. Running a small amount of negative expo on the throttle (–15%) on off-road buggies allows finer control of the initial response. Electric motors are most sensitive at low RPM, and this setting allows you to tune the response to your own preference.

Brake Expo – a small amount of positive Expo on the brakes makes the initial response a bit stronger. This comes down to personal preference.

Steering Curve (Expo) – on carpet/astroturf, where the slightest steering input may give a lot of steering, you can slow this down by using negative steering expo. –15% to –20% is a good starting point that will soften the initial steering input and allow the car to react gradually without changing the total steering available. On dirt tracks, 4WD steering tends to be more responsive than 2WD, and some negative expo can assist with this. It is normally easier to drive 2WD on a dirt track when the steering is linear (no Expo).

Ride Height

Level: Basic

Overview

Ride height is measured with the wheels on the car and the car ready-to-race. Ride height affects the car's traction (as it alters the centre of gravity and roll centre). Generally, a lower car is better on smooth, fast tracks and a higher car is better on a bumpy track or one with lots of jumps.

Setting	Effect
Decreasing Ride Height (lowering the car)	• Smoother steering response. • Reduces chassis roll. • Increases cornering grip but decreases forward traction. • Better on smoother high-grip tracks and on these may corner faster. • Reduces likelihood of traction rolling.
Increasing Ride Height (raising the car)	• Steering response more reactive. • Increases chassis roll. • Increases overall grip. • Better on bumpy and dirt tracks. • Increases likelihood of traction rolling.

Ride height can be altered to change the balance of the car and its ability to absorb bumps.

Increasing ride height

Increasing the front and rear ride height will make the car more stable, and increase its ability to handle bumps. However, on high-traction tracks, it can cause the car to traction roll.

Decreasing ride height

Decreasing the front and rear ride height will make the car more aggressive, and decrease the ability of the car to soak up bumps. This is also suitable for high-traction tracks, as the lower centre of gravity can minimise the chances of traction rolling.

Ride Height Split

In 1/8 a Ride Height Split (also called Rake) is common, with the front ride height lower than the rear by 1–2mm. In 1/10 off-road, front and rear ride height are more often set the same.

Front Lower than Rear (more common)	Front Higher than Rear
• Increased corner entry steering. • Increased stability in corners. • Increased on-power oversteer.	• More stable. • Smoother steering. • In very low-traction or very bumpy conditions may handle bumps and jumps better.

Increasing ride height split
Increasing the difference between front and rear ride height can have noticeable balance effects on the car. Lowering the front or raising the rear will cause the car to be more aggressive, especially entering corners and at high-speed. This will give the car more steering and is generally more suitable on low-traction tracks.

Decreasing ride height split
Decreasing the difference between front and rear ride height can smooth out an aggressive car, especially entering corners and at high-speed. This will keep the car more stable and is generally suited to higher traction tracks, as it can reduce the chance of traction roll.

Starting Ride Height

Check your car's manual for the starting ride height. If it is not specified then the following are reasonable starting ride heights for buggies.

Track	2WD 1/10 (front & rear)	4WD 1/10 (front & rear)	1/8 Buggy
Carpet*	18mm	16-18mm	
Dirt	22mm	20mm	Front 25mm/Rear 27mm

* Carpet tracks may specify a minimum ride height to protect the carpet surface. Check the local rules.

Important: Measure ride height when the car is race ready, including battery.

If your Stadium Truck manual doesn't specify a starting ride height, refer to the Case Studies chapter for ideas (page 245).

Measuring Ride Height

Ride height refers to the height of the chassis off the ground and is measured with a ride height gauge:

1. Drop the car onto a flat surface from about 30cm (12"). This will settle the suspension.
2. Measure the ride height at the front and rear of the car at the lowest points of the chassis.

Front Ride Height

Rear Ride Height

Chassis on dirt tracks tend to wear in the locations we use to measure ride height. If your chassis is badly worn, then measure in a different location (I suggest behind the front suspension arm and in front of the rear suspension arm).

Left vs Right Side Ride Height

It is possible for the ride height on the left and right of the car to be different. Therefore we ideally measure in the centre of the chassis. However, if the difference between the sides is greater than 0.2mm, it can cause handling issues.

Possible causes:

- The left-to-right weight balance of the car may be different (page 192).
- The shock springs may no longer be the same length and therefore need replacing.
- The shock preload may not be the same left-to-right (page 129).
- The car's suspension may be Tweaked (page 201).

Changing the Ride Height

Ride height is changed using shock preload. Refer to page 129. Do not change ride height with the droop screws if your car has them (refer to Droop on page 152).

Ride Height Interactions

Recheck the ride height whenever you:

- Change tyres.
- Change Droop (page 172).
- Change Camber (page 118).
- After a crash.

Ride Heights interact. As you increase the front ride height, the rear ride height will reduce slightly and vice versa. After changing one end of the car, always recheck the other end.

When ride height is changed, the following may be affected and should be checked:

- Camber.
- Toe.
- Droop. For instructions on changing Droop refer to page 146.

When you do this to Ride Height	Also do this to Droop	Notes
Increase	Increase	Increasing ride height will decrease droop
Decrease	Decrease	Decreasing ride height will increase droop

Roll Bars

Level: Intermediate

Roll Bars are also called Anti-roll Bars, Swaybars and Torsion Bars.

Roll bars can limit the chassis roll while running slightly softer springs than would otherwise be possible, giving more steering going into a corner, more rear grip coming out of the corner and better stability and directional responsiveness. Running roll bars increases roll resistance when cornering while having minimal effect on bumps and jumps. However, stiff roll bars can affect bump handling on bumpy tracks and you may need to choose between roll stiffness or bump handling.

While overall traction cannot be changed, roll bars allow the traction to be balanced. Increasing the stiffness of a roll bar on one axle decreases its traction and increases the traction of the axle at the other end of the car.

Roll Bar	Setting	Effect
Front	Thicker (stiffer)	• Better on a higher grip track. • Reduces chassis roll. • Decreases front grip. • Increases rear grip. • Reduces off-power steering at corner entry, increasing understeer. • Faster steering response.
	Thinner (softer)	• Better on a lower grip track. • Increases chassis roll. • Increases front grip. • Reduces rear grip. • Increases off-power steering at corner entry. • Slower steering response.
Rear	Thicker (stiffer)	• Better on a higher grip track. • Reduces chassis roll. • Decreases rear grip. • Increases front grip. • Increases on-power steering. • Faster steering response in high-speed chicanes.
	Thinner (softer)	• Better on a lower grip track. • Increases chassis roll. • Increases rear grip. • Reduces front grip. • Decreases on-power steering.

Roll bars are a good tuning option for changing the front-to-rear balance of the car. Usually, you should adjust them independently, not both at the same time. Adjusting independently allows you to finetune the balance.

Front Roll Bar

Thicker will increase overall steering, most noticeably turn-in and high-speed. It makes the car edgy and more difficult to drive.

Thinner will decrease steering and make the car easier to drive. The front will be less twitchy and more stable at high-speed.

Rear Roll Bar

Thicker will decrease on-power rear traction and off-power rotation.

Thinner will increase on-power rear traction and off-power rotation.

Roll Bar Installation

First, check that the roll bar wire is flat; you can do this by putting it on a flat surface, checking there are no twists or bends. If it is not perfectly flat the entire way along the bar, then you may need to lightly bend the wire in order to straighten it. You must do this for both the front and rear bars first before assembling anything.

Depending on your brand of car, your roll bar system will pivot on bearings, or rotate inside a plastic holder with a grub screw that adjusts the play.

- With the **bearing system**, installing the roll bar is fairly straightforward; the biggest thing here is to ensure that the roll bar is located in the centre of the car.

- With a **holder and grub screw**, you need to tighten the grub screws until they just restrict the roll bars movement. Then you can back both of them off to ensure the roll bar has perfectly free movement with zero slop. To achieve this, you will need to back each grub screw off in 1/16 of a turn increments to get it absolutely spot on. At the end of this process, your roll bar should rotate up and down with no resistance and have no slop between the wire and the grub screws.

Next comes the installation of the roll bar linkages, the crucial element in having a perfectly functioning roll bar system. When you assemble the linkages, ensure they are the same length. If your car's manual does not specify a linkage length, then set them so that the wire is parallel with the ground when the car is on droop blocks. Make sure your droop is correct before you check this (you can set it now by referring to page *152*), and you should come up with a measurement that you can always replicate.

Next, ensure that the ball cups are perfectly free on the balls connecting to both the arm and the roll bar end. You can check by individually popping the top and bottom ball on, checking that the linkage pivots with no binding. If there is binding, sometimes squeezing the ball cup with pliers or heating it up quickly with a heat gun or cigarette lighter is all it takes to free it up.

De-tweaking Roll Bar Linkages

Roll bar tweaks are common in over 90% of RC cars and occur when the roll bar does not affect both sides of the car in the same way.

In off-road, with rough, bumpy tracks, it is not crucial that the roll bars work identically to the left and right. However, they should be close, and on smooth tracks it can make a noticeable difference if they are not exactly the same.

To correct this tweak, we need to alter the length of the roll bar links to counteract any minute imperfection in the roll bar.

Disconnect your shocks. With the shocks connected it may be too difficult to tell the exact point that the roll bar starts working.

The car must be on droop blocks, on a flat surface. Use your 1mm increment droop gauge or ride height gauge, whichever suits. You can start on the left or the right side; it doesn't matter. Slide your gauge under the outside of the suspension arm, lifting the arm until the arm on the other side of the car starts to lift. Make a note of that number.

The rear right suspension arm at the point that the roll bar begins to lift the rear left suspension arm

Let's say it's the right side, and the opposite side is lifting up at 2. Now check the left side, and let's say it starts lifting up the opposite side at 4. Both sides should lift at the same number, so we need to correct this. We can either work on one link solely or work on both links at the same time. I prefer to work on both links to correct big tweaks. While it may sound more difficult, it keeps the roll bar around your desired horizontal position more than altering only one link length.

If it's a minor tweak, it's fine to only work on one. Since the left side is taking 2mm more to lift up the opposite side than the right side, we would consider this a major tweak, so we adjust both links. We need to increase the link length on the left side, so that at the same height, it is putting more pressure on the other side to lift up. Let's start by unscrewing ¼ of a turn on the left link. You must recheck both sides, because lengthening one will also affect how quickly the right side now lifts the left side up.

Let's say we check the right again, now it is 2.5 and the left is 3.5, this means we have half corrected the tweak and need to do the same again to make them equal at 3 each side. This is where the two-sided adjustment comes in; instead of lengthening the left link another ¼ of a turn, we will shorten the right link by ¼ of a turn. Effectively, it's the same thing; it's just keeping the roll bar from getting too high. Check that this change has translated, and you can tweak by less than ¼ of a turn if need be to get them perfect. The worst that can happen is that you get confused and need to reset them back to the same length left and right and start again.

Now you can reattach your shocks.

Interaction

Chassis stiffness can significantly impact the effectiveness of roll bars. A stiffer chassis makes the car more responsive to roll bar changes. Refer to Chassis Stiffness on page *122*.

Roll Centre

Level: Advanced

The roll centre of the car is the point around which the car will roll when cornering. By adjusting the roll centre, we can make the car roll more or less and therefore increase or decrease traction.

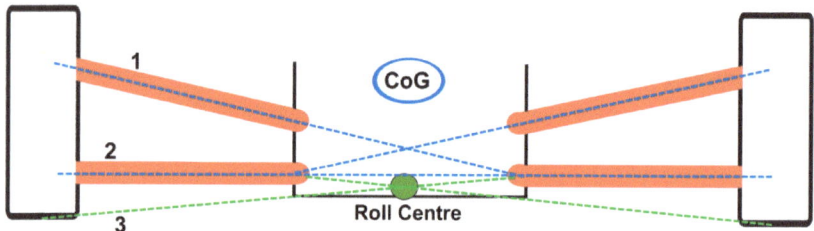

The illustration above shows the car from the front, including:

- The car's Centre of Gravity (CG) (refer to page *192*).
- The Roll Centre (green circle).

To calculate the front roll centre when the car is stationary:

1. Draw blue dotted line (1) through the camber link/upper arm.
2. Draw blue dotted line (2) through the lower suspension arm.
3. Where lines (1) and (2) meet is an imaginary point called the Instant Centre.
4. Draw green dotted line (3) from the Instant Centre to the middle of the tyre contact patch.
5. Repeat for the other side of the car.
6. Where the two green dotted lines meet is the Roll Centre.

When cornering, the car will roll as shown in the diagram on the right, with the Centre of Gravity (CG) rolling around the roll centre. By raising the height of the roll centre, the

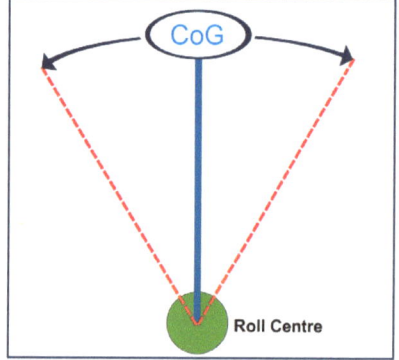

blue line becomes shorter. The car will therefore not roll as much, and traction will be reduced. It will take less time to roll, so the car will react to steering inputs more quickly.

By lowering the height of the roll centre, the blue line becomes longer. Therefore, the car will roll more and traction will be increased. It will take more time to roll, so the car will react slower to steering inputs and feels less responsive. Using a lower roll centre may assist to reduce traction rolling.

Note: We refer to camber links, but some cars (notably 1/8) may have an upper suspension arm at the front instead. Changes work the same way.

Changing the Roll Centre

The roll centre is determined by the relative angle between the camber links and suspension arms. To change this, some cars will use shims, and some will use blocks (option parts may be required). Refer to your car's manual. Always make the same change to the left and right sides of the car.

Adjusting the front or rear roll centre changes the balance of the car. Changing them both at the same time changes the overall handling and responsiveness.

Front Roll Centre	Change By	Effect
Lower	Lower the suspension arms towards the chassis or raise the **inside** camber links by adding shims	• Car rolls more at front. • Increases front traction. • More steering response. • More mid-corner and exit steering.
Higher	Raise the suspension arms away from the chassis or raise the **outside** camber links by adding shims	• Car rolls less at front. • Decreases front traction. • Less steering response. • Less mid-corner and exit steering.

Rear Roll Centre	Change By	Effect
Lower	Lower the suspension arms towards the chassis or raise the **inside** camber links by adding shims	• Car rolls more at rear. • Increases rear traction. • Increases forward traction (unless you go too low, then car will suddenly lose traction at rear on corner exit). • Less mid-corner and exit steering. • Best for low-grip tracks.
Higher	Raise the suspension arms away from the chassis or raise the **outside** camber links by adding shims	• Car rolls less at rear. • Decreases rear traction. • Decreases forward traction. • More steering response. • Easier to drive. • Better in chicanes. • Best for high-grip tracks.

The front suspension has a different roll centre to the rear suspension.

- Any changes made to the left front should also be made to the right front.
- Any changes made to the left rear should also be made to the right rear.

Roll centre is a complex area of vehicle mechanics and has been simplified here. If you are reading other texts on roll centre, you may find it helpful to know that it is the geometric roll centre described above (vehicle is stationary). When the suspension is compressed or lifted, the roll centre will move, and the roll centre at any point in time is called the instantaneous roll centre. How much the roll centre moves when the suspension compresses is determined by the relative angle between the top and bottom arms and the arm length.

Should I Change the Suspension Arm Angle or the Camber Link Angle?

Both have the same effect. However, you may need to shim the camber link by 1mm or more to equate to a 0.5mm change on the lower suspension arms. The suspension arms are therefore often changed first, while the camber link is often used for finetuning the roll centre.

Should I Change the Length of the Camber Link?

Many cars have alternative mounting points for the camber links in order to lengthen or shorten them. Shortening the camber link is similar to lowering the inside camber link. Lengthening is similar to raising the inside camber link. Always make the same change on the left and right. Front and rear may be set differently. In addition, longer camber links tend to improve grip, but the steering feels less precise. While shorter links make the car more responsive, it will roll less and may be harder to drive.

Interaction

Lowering the roll centre by increasing the angle of the front camber link will slightly increase the Camber Gain (refer to page *121*).

Rollout

Refer to *Gearing and Rollout* on page *160*.

Shock Absorber

Refer to Damping on page *126*.

Slipper Clutch

A slipper clutch is used to protect the drivetrain of:

- Most 2WD cars.
- 4WD cars that don't have a centre diff often use a centre slipper clutch.

It achieves this by slipping when:

1. Accelerating – this helps reduce wheelspin, which is very useful in low-traction to prevent spinning out when coming out of a corner or at any time you punch the throttle.

2. Landing a Jump – it protects your drivetrain when landing a jump by absorbing the impact that can cause your transmission gears to wear prematurely.

3. Driving over rough/choppy spots on the track – where one or more of the driven wheels may leave the ground.

Setting your Slipper Clutch

Set the slipper clutch as stated in your car's manual, then test that the slipper clutch is set correctly using the tests below.

Test 1 (2WD and 4WD)

Place your car at your feet, facing away from you, and pull full throttle. You should be able to hear a faint slipping sound for the first 1–2 feet (30–60cm). If the front wheels leave the ground or it immediately spins out, then the slipper is too tight (loosen the slipper 1/8th of a turn and retest). If the faint slipping sound lasts longer than 1–2 feet or if the car seems to lack acceleration, then tighten the slipper 1/8th of a turn and retest.

This faint slipping noise can be challenging to hear, so if you have a 2WD then try Test 2.

Test 2 (2WD only)

1. Car is race ready.
2. On your pit bench, push down on one rear wheel with the wrist of the hand holding your radio. Hold the other rear wheel with your free hand. Neither rear wheel should be able to turn.
3. Pull full throttle very briefly. The front tyres should come off the bench about 1/2 to 1 inch (1–3 cm).

   - If the slipper clutch is **too loose**, the wheels won't come off the ground and the slipper clutch will make a high pitched noise as it spins. Tighten 1/8th of a turn and retest.

   - If the slipper clutch is **too tight** the front tyres will come off the bench, but the slipper clutch will make a noise like a barking seal. Loosen 1/8th of a turn and retest. If no amount of loosening stops the barking noise, then the **ball diff** is too loose. Tighten the diff (page 144) and retest.

4. After testing, if your car's diff makes a barking noise on the track, then rebuild your ball diff.

Loose Slipper or Ball Diff?

A loose ball diff can act like a loose slipper clutch, so make sure the ball diff is not loose (page 144). During Test 2 above, you can observe the slipper clutch tensioning nut and/or spring. If the nut remains stationary whilst power is applied, the slipper is doing its job. If the nut rotates during the test, the diff is slipping!

Solid Axle (Spool)

Level: Basic

Although not common, a solid axle, also known as a spool, can be used at the front of the car (instead of a differential). A solid axle means that the left and right tyres rotate at the same speed at all times.

Solid axles reduce car weight. The drawback is less off-power steering.

A differential can be used instead of a solid axle (refer to page 141). A front diff will provide less steering response but more overall steering and cornering speed compared to a solid axle.

A one-way front axle was popular in the past but makes the car significantly harder to drive and has therefore fallen out of favour.

A spool can be used in 4WDs instead of a centre diff. If there is no centre diff then this has the same effect as a centre spool.

A detailed description of a spool is provided on page 147.

Steering Arm Ball Cup Location

Refer to Ackermann on page 107.

Steering Linkage Angle

Refer to Bump Steer on page 117.

Steering Throw/Lock

Level: Basic

The Steering Throw, also called Steering Lock, should be the same to the left as it is to the right. This makes the turning radius of the car the same in both directions. You can check this by putting the car on a flat piece of ground and driving slowly in a figure of eight. If the car doesn't turn the same to the left as it does to the right then you need to set the steering throw.

If you have a setup station, follow its instruction manual to set this. If not, you can set steering throw by:

1. Place your race ready car on a flat surface with the body off (wheels on).
2. Make sure the car is located safely (or remove the pinion gear) in case you touch the throttle trigger by mistake.
3. Turn on the radio and then turn on your car.
4. Check the Dual Rate on the radio is set to 100%.
5. Turn the steering all the way to the left and adjust your radio's steering servo End Point Adjustment (EPA) so that the steering arm turns until it starts to push against the c-hub, then back off one click. The steering arm mustn't turn past this point as it could damage the servo over time. Check that the wheels don't rub on the arms or chassis at full lock (if it does reduce the EPA until it doesn't).
6. Now check the right side using the same technique as step 5.
7. If your EPA % is the same left and right, and assuming the car is built correctly, then your wheels should turn the same amount to the left and right. However, it is not uncommon for small errors in the build or the car's manufacture to introduce a slight difference. Without a setup station you can only do your best "by eye" to reduce the EPA with the highest % to be closer to the side with the lowest % until both wheels turn equally in both directions. This provides balanced handling.

    If the left and right EPA % is not within 0–5%, it means your steering rack isn't quite centred, servo horn is not quite at 90-degrees, or your main steering links aren't equal lengths. Refer to How to Set Servo and Steering Alignment below.

Pro drivers sometimes reduce the Steering Throw to maximise corner speed.

How to Set Servo and Steering Alignment

Unscrew your servo horn from your servo, turn your radio and car on.

Check that your radio settings are: sub-trim 0, steering trim 0, End Points (EPA) 100% and Dual Rates (D/R) 100%.

The biggest mistake people make with this is making the servo horn at 90-degrees to the servo. The servo horn needs to be at a 90-degree angle to the steering link, not to the servo. This means it must create a right angle with the steering link as pictured. Get it as close as you can by locating the servo horn on the spline with the transmitter on and car powered up. You won't be able to get 90-degrees to the link exactly, but we can finetune it with sub-trim later.

Screw your servo horn on and tighten it heavily; I don't recommend using Loctite as you may not be able to get it off! Once you've done this, we can get the link and the servo horn at exactly 90-degrees using the sub-trim. Ignore what the steering rack is doing; we will get to that next.

You don't have to touch your steering trim or sub-trim from this point. Keep your transmitter on, as we need the steering powered up and centred. The **steering rack** now needs to be located perfectly in the centre; you can often do this by eyeballing the steering rack from above. Adjust the length of the servo linkage (the link between the servo and the steering rack) so that the steering rack is centred.

Once the steering rack is centred, we need to turn to the steering links and set toe-out. With your setup station attached, you can set the toe-out by adjusting these links. Shortening the links will increase toe-out, and lengthening the links will decrease toe-out. A typical toe-out setting is 1° (0.5° per side). Make sure you achieve this by ensuring both steering links are the same length. Different length steering links will give different steering angles on inner and outer wheels between left and right. For more information on toe-out refer to page *186*.

Once this is done, you can set the **steering throw** using the end points (EPA) on your radio (described above).

If you don't like to drive with full steering lock, you can turn it down with the Dual Rate setting on your radio (refer to page *167*).

Toe

Level: Basic

Toe-out is when the front of the wheel points away from the centreline of the car. Conversely, toe-in is when the front of the wheel points in towards the centreline of the car (although the diagram below only shows the front wheels, this actually works the same way for both front and rear wheels).

The greater the toe angle the greater the friction and therefore the lower the top speed. However, adding toe can stabilise the car. So you want to use the smallest toe angle possible while making the car easy to drive.

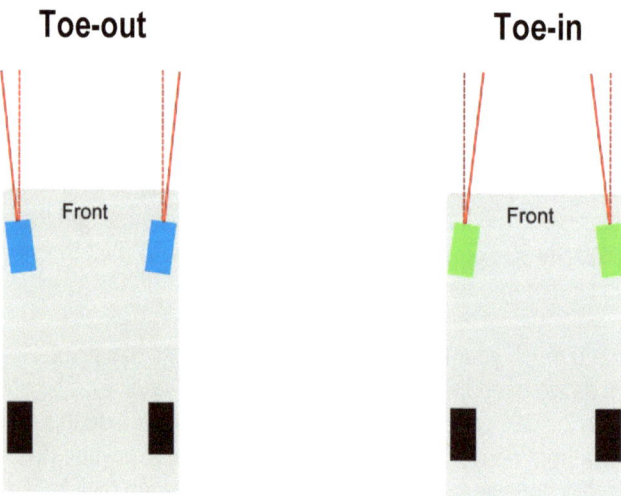

Measuring Toe

We recommend using a toe gauge. Toe is measured as an angle (in degrees) and therefore it is very difficult to measure front toe without one, although rear toe is often set using fixed blocks or shims.

However, if you must set front toe without a toe gauge, it can be done by measuring between the front of the wheels (red line, below) and the rear of the wheels (green line). Adjust the length of the Steering Linkages so that the red line is about 1mm longer than the green line. Make sure the left and right Steering Linkages are equal in length.

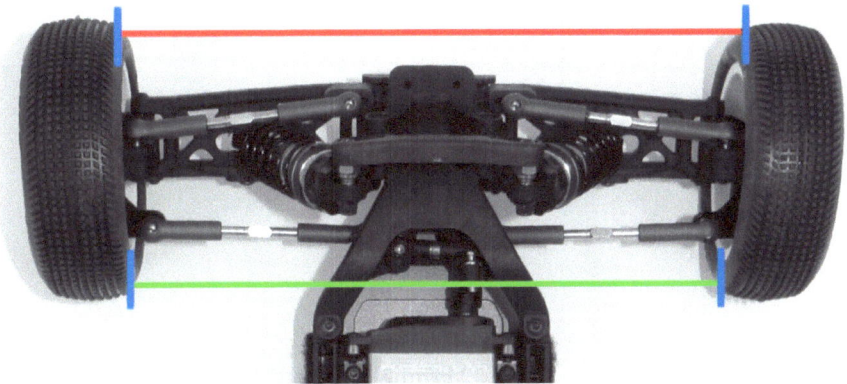

Front Toe Angle

A good starting point is front toe-out of 1°. Front toe-in is not recommended.

If you have just built your car, set the Steering Throw (refer to page 182) before setting the front Toe. Front toe must be the same on the left and right side of the car.

There is a great deal of confusion about front toe and its effects. To ensure this book contains the most accurate information, the following table was collated by interviewing several world and national champions:

Front Toe	Change	Effect
Toe-out	Increase (more toe-out)	• Car more stable on the straight. • Decreases steering (most noticeable at corner entry). • Less steering response. • Makes car easier to drive. • Car more prone to understeer.
	Decrease (less toe-out)	• Car less stable on the straight. • Increases steering. • More steering response. • Car is harder to drive. • Less prone to understeer.
Neutral Toe	Tyres straight	• Fastest straight-line speed. However, less than 0.5° of toe-out is not recommended.
Toe-in	Not recommended.	

Front toe can be a very important tool for finding the correct balance on the car. You should always use toe-out at the front.

Increasing front toe-out will smooth the car's steering response. This is especially good for high-traction, when the car is twitchy around neutral. It will also slightly decrease on-power steering and steering on sweepers.

Decreasing front toe-out will make the car more edgy and aggressive entering a corner. This can be good for low-traction in order to get aggression out of the car. It will also increase high-speed steering and on-power steering.

Rear Toe Angle

A good starting point is rear toe-in of 3°.

Rear Toe	Change	Effect
Toe-in	Increase (more toe-in)	• Increases traction. • More stable. • Greater understeer on-power. • Less cornering speed.
	Decrease (less toe-in)	• Reduces traction. • Less stable. • More cornering speed. • More on-power steering. • Better rotation.
Toe-out	Never used.	

In general, the more rear toe-in, the more stable your car will be. The rear wheels of your car should always be adjusted with some toe-in. Rear toe-out is never used.

Increasing the angle of rear toe-in will cause decreased straight line speed, but the car will be more stable. Rear toe-in must be the same on the left and right side of the car.

Increasing rear toe-in will give the car more rear traction overall. At low-speed, the extra toe can increase rotation and low-speed steering; particularly noticeable on hairpins. More rear toe is generally used on lower traction tracks where the car suffers from instability, especially on-power.

Decreasing rear toe-in will give the car less rear traction overall. If the traction is high, then this can give the car more corner speed and free it up through corners. If you use less rear toe-in low-traction, it can make the rear quite unstable, making it hard to get on the power.

Interaction

Changing the front Track Width will change the front toe setting.

If the front toe is adjusted, you should recheck your Steering Throw, refer to page *182*.

Transmission (2WD)
Level: Basic

Some cars have the option of different transmissions for use in various conditions (high or low-traction). Each type of gearbox may move the transmission weight forward or backwards and may change the number of gears in the transmission (refer to page *60* for the difference between three and four gear transmissions). Refer to the manufacturer's instructions.

Track Width
Level: Intermediate

Track width is the distance between the outside edges of the wheels. Most racing classes will have rules specifying the maximum track width.

The track width at the front may be different to the rear. It is important when making a change that it is made to both the left and the right, i.e. the left and right wheels must be the same distance from the centreline of the chassis.

Track Width can be adjusted via:

- the inner suspension mounts, or
- through the width of the wheel hexes.

It can also be changed if your wheels have an offset other than 0mm (page *90*).

The following table is accurate for cars that use c-hubs at the front (refer to page *105*). If your car uses a pillow ball instead of a c-hub on the front (some 1/8 cars), the front suspension angles are different, and the table below for the Front Track Width Effects may not apply.

Front Track Width	Effect
Wider	• Decreases front grip. • Slower steering response. • Increases understeer. • Easier to drive. • Reduces traction rolling. • Better for high-grip tracks.
Narrower	• Increases front grip. • Faster steering response. • Decreases understeer. • Better for low-medium grip tracks. • Better for bumpy tracks.

The following table is for the rear track width and applies regardless of which front-end the car has.

Rear Track Width	Effect
Wider	• Increases car stability. • Easier to drive. • Increases rear grip at corner entry and mid-corner. • More on-power understeer. • Decreases cornering speed. • Better for high-grip tracks.
Narrower	• Reduces car stability. • Increases car responsiveness. • Increases rear grip at corner exit. • Increases cornering speed. • Increases on-power steering. • Better for low-medium grip tracks. • Better for bumpy tracks.

Wheel Hexes

Narrower wheel hexes will decrease the car's track width and generate more traction. This will yield a more responsive and agile car. Narrow hexes, especially at the front, can increase high-speed steering and low-speed response. Narrow hexes at the rear can increase the rotation of the car, especially off-power in tight hairpins.

Wider wheel hexes will increase the car's track width and generate less traction. They will make the car easier to drive and more stable. Wider hexes, especially at the front, can be used to stop traction rolling in high-traction conditions. Wider hexes at the rear allow you to get more forward traction and stability.

Suspension Blocks

Altering the track width from the suspension blocks effectively alters three things; different length turnbuckle, different shock position on the arm, and changes front toe. This makes it a more substantial change than changing wheel hex width.

Widening the front via suspension blocks will give the car less steering overall, especially in the middle and exit of the corner. It can be used to decrease tyre wear or decrease tyre heat.

Widening the rear will make the car more stable off-power, with less rotation and less rear side bite on-power. However, it can increase the car's forward traction.

Narrowing the front will give the car more overall steering, especially mid-corner and corner exit. It will also give more steering at high-speed. It can cause the car to traction roll on high-traction tracks and cause higher front tyre wear.

Narrowing the rear will increase the car's rotation off-power and increase rear side bite on-power. It can cause the car to traction roll on high-traction tracks because it makes the rear of the car more active and aggressive.

Interaction

Changing the front Track Width via the inner hinge pins will change the front Toe setting (refer to page *185*).

Tyres and Additives
Level: Basic

Refer to page *76*.

Up Travel
Level: Intermediate

Up Travel is the amount the shocks can compress (travel up inside the shock body) from ride height before the shock is fully compressed.

Down Travel (also called Droop) is the amount the shocks will extend (travel down inside the shock body) from ride height before the tyres leave the ground. Down Travel/Droop is discussed on page *152*.

If changing to longer eyelets at the bottom of the shock, check that you are still getting enough up travel by pushing the car all the way down to the bench top. Does the chassis touch down (normal) or is there an air gap underneath?

External Limiters

If you wish to reduce Up Travel you can insert an external shock limiter (also called an up travel limiter). An external limiter is a bushing or washer that sits on the shock shaft just above the shock eyelet (outside the shock body) to limit the amount of compression.

Why limit Up Travel? 1. To prevent driveshafts from binding the diff outdrives during suspension compression or 2. If the front of the chassis is digging into the ground on a very bumpy track you can limit the front Up Travel to reduce this.

Weight

Level: Basic

Most racing classes have a minimum weight rule where the race ready car must be that weight or heavier. Depending on your car, battery, motor and electronics choices, this may mean it is necessary to add weight, or you may be looking for ways to reduce weight.

A heavy car will usually have more traction over bumps and be more stable than a lighter car. However, a lighter car will be faster than a heavy car. Because our goal is the fastest possible lap time, we normally run the car as close to the minimum weight as possible and change the setup of the car to provide the traction needed.

It can be risky to run too close to the weight limit, as cars found to be underweight after the race may be disqualified, and your scales may provide a different reading than the scrutineer's scales.

If you need to add weight, then do so as low on the chassis as possible and check that the car remains balanced left-to-right. Both of these are explained below.

Centre of Gravity

The Centre of Gravity (CG) of the car is the balance point of the mass of the car. The lower the CG, the better; this is achieved by placing all electronics as low as possible on the chassis and minimising any weight high up.

The higher the CG, the more the car will roll in a corner. It is better to keep the CG as low as possible and change the Roll Centre to increase chassis roll if required (refer to page 177).

Weight Balance (Side-to-Side)

Ideally:

1. The weight on your front left tyre should be the same as the weight on your front right tyre.
2. The weight on your rear left tyre should be the same as the weight on your rear right tyre.

You should always try to adjust the weight on your chassis so it is equal left-to-right. It doesn't have to be perfect but should be within 10g (0.02 pounds). This will assist with consistent handling and keep the ride height similar on both sides of the chassis. It is easiest to do this after building the kit, before securing your electronics in place.

Individual Scales

Make sure your pit board is perfectly flat by checking it with a spirit level (sometimes called a water level). Otherwise, the weight balance reading might not be accurate.

Individual scales show the weight supported by each tyre. The GForce X Weight Gauge shown above also shows calculates the total weight and the weight % left-to-right and front-to-rear

Weight Balancing

If your car is heavier on one side, then add weight or move the electronics/battery so that the car sits level. A 50%/50% left-to-right split is ideal as shown above (as shown it doesn't have to be exact and a few grams either way does not matter).

Many manufacturers will allow the servo and/or the battery to be shifted to the right or left side of the car to assist with weight balance. However, it is optimum to have these as close to the chassis centreline as possible.

Due to their construction, lipo batteries may be slightly lighter on the end with the plug.

A small amount of lead weight can be added to one side to balance the car if required. Modern cars are often underweight out of the box and require weight to be added.

Some classes may require a lot of weight to be added to meet the minimum weight rule. In this case, add the weight as low down and as centrally as possible. MR33 make a range of weights for this purpose, such as this one for placing under the battery:

Moving Weight (Front-to-Rear)

Redistributing existing weight can be a useful tuning tool. This is most easily done by moving the battery location (refer to page 112).

When it comes to moving weight, we can position it in order to finetune the handling of the car.

Weight at the rear will increase the car's on-power rear traction initially under acceleration, as well as increase steering into corners and at high-speed. It can make the car quite difficult to drive, causing traction rolling in high-grip and snap oversteer in low-grip.

Weight at the front will decrease steering into corners, decrease steering at high-speed, but add stability. It will make the car easier to drive in corners, especially in high-traction, where traction rolling is an issue. It will be more predictable in low-traction and reduce the car's aggression and steering capabilities. However, in 2WD in low-grip, if the weight is too far forward the car will lose forward drive and can spin out under power.

Adding Weight to Increase Steering or Rear Traction

Car handling is determined by weight transfer (refer to page 27). However, the car should be kept as close to the minimum weight for the class as possible.

Adding weight to the front for more steering or to the rear to increase rear grip ***does not work***. This is because it is the transfer of weight to one end of the car that changes car handling.

If you take any car and double its weight, then it will not be able to take the corner as quickly because it must change the direction of the additional weight. Adding physical weight to the rear of the car to correct oversteer could make the car oversteer even more because the car must now change the direction of this extra weight when cornering. As a general rule, the lighter your car, the better it will corner.

Although static weight certainly impacts handling, it should only be added in extremely slippery conditions such as a wet or extremely low-grip track. When adding static weight, make sure your car remains balanced left-to-right (as above), and add the weight as low down and as close to the centreline as possible.

To increase steering without adding weight, refer to the checklist on page *317*.

To increase rear traction without adding weight, refer to the checklist on page *314*.

If, after reading this, you still want to add weight at one end of the car, then I recommend no more than 10–15g (.02–.03 pounds).

Wheelbase

Level: Advanced

Wheelbase is the distance between the front and rear axle. The greater the distance, the longer the wheelbase; the shorter the distance, the shorter the wheelbase. Most cars have the option of changing the wheelbase. Refer to your car's manual.

By adjusting the wheelbase at one end of the car, you affect the traction at that end. For example, by shortening the wheelbase at the rear of the car, you place more weight over the rear wheels (resulting in more rear traction).

Wheelbase	Effect
Longer	<ul><li>More stability.</li><li>Easier to drive.</li><li>Less steering response.</li><li>Better for larger tracks.</li><li>Better for high-traction tracks.</li><li>Better for longer corners (sweepers).</li><li>Better in bumpy conditions and rhythm sections.</li></ul>
Shorter	<ul><li>Less stable.</li><li>More difficult to drive.</li><li>Better for tight technical tracks.</li><li>Better for tracks with many 180-degree corners.</li><li>The car rotates better in the centre of the corner.</li><li>Car carries more corner speed.</li></ul>

The front wheelbase usually has less adjustability than the rear wheelbase. It is a good tuning option to change the weight position over the tyres to finetune the car's balance.

Lengthening wheelbase

Lengthening the **front** wheelbase will increase the car's steering initially and corner speed in sweepers. However, it can make the car "wash out" mid-corner and understeer.

Lengthening the **rear** wheelbase will make the car more stable in general and decrease rotation or snap oversteer.

Shortening wheelbase

Shortening the **front** wheelbase will decrease the car's initial steering but will increase the overall steering and rotation of the car at low-speed.

Shortening the **rear** wheelbase will increase the car's rotation, especially on slower corners such as hairpins. It generates more forward traction as it allows more weight transfer over the rear end. It adds rear grip, which can be useful on loose tracks but will not handle bumps as well.

Wings

Ray Munday – Tech Talk

On an off-road buggy, the wing has a large effect on the car and is a valuable tuning tool that you should understand, test and be ready to change as track/weather conditions change.

What does the wing do?

In a nutshell, the wing provides downforce as it moves through the air due to aerodynamic effects. This pushes down on the chassis, giving more load on the tyres, and therefore more tyre grip, which means better acceleration, braking and cornering. The wing also has a large effect on jumping balance, especially for high-speed/large jumps.

Wing Theory

A wing works by creating a higher air pressure on one side of a large surface than the other. This high pressure, acting over the large area, creates a force that tries to push the wing down (downforce) or up (lift). A larger area (bigger wing) and/or larger pressure will provide more force.

It's important to understand with aerodynamic effects that the force is roughly proportional to speed squared – in other words, go twice as fast, and you will get four times the downforce. Wings don't work until you start moving, and they don't work well until you are going fast.

There are two basic styles of wing – the aerofoil and the spoiler.

- An **aerofoil** is the shape found on Formula 1 car wings and on aircraft. An aerofoil works on the Bernoulli Principle, which basically states that as air travels faster, it has lower pressure. The aerofoil has a very smooth curved shape, and the air must travel further around one side than the other, which means that the air on this side of the wing must move faster and therefore has less pressure. In the case of a race car, the longest surface is on the bottom, so the higher pressure on top of the wing pushes the wing down, creating downforce.

- A **spoiler** is a device that deflects air upwards. Air has a mass (even though it is relatively light), and the pressure of forcing this mass upwards creates a reaction pressure force that pushes the wing down. In the case of buggies, this is the main method of creating downforce with the wings we have.

A "**gurney**" or spoiler "lip" is a small vertical piece at the very back of the wing (known as the trailing edge). This lip helps to act as a spoiler but also helps to suck air under the wing, moving it faster and therefore creating lower pressure under the wing and making more downforce.

Drag is the resistance of the wing moving through the air. Drag pushes the wing backwards, slowing your car down and generally reducing top speed. The measure of a wing's efficiency is the lift to drag ratio. A more efficient wing creates lots of downforce with little drag. Top speed isn't affected too much by the wing drag, other than perhaps spec classes such as the 21.5 class.

The most efficient wing is a very long and slender wing, such as those seen on gliders; however, these aren't practical (or legal) on a race buggy. To help make the wings more efficient, we have **side plates** on the wings, which help to duct the air over the wing but also stop air from spilling from the top of the wing around the side and underneath the wing.

Off-road Wing Tuning

The main tuning points are:

1. **Wing style** – There are a number of manufacturers out there offering wings claiming to have better downforce and other benefits. It's best to choose one which has been designed for your vehicle and doesn't interfere with the tyres at full compression. I use the JConcepts wings all the time.

2. **Wing width** – A wider wing has more area and, therefore, will give more downforce. But you will also get more drag and the wing will be heavier.

3. **Gurney height** – A higher lip height gives much more downforce but also much more drag.

4. **Wing angle** – A steeper angle generally gives more downforce. This is usually adjusted using the wing mounts but can also be affected if you change the front/rear ride height of the car.

5. **Wing position (forwards/rearwards)** – Moving the wing rearwards will give the same total downforce but will have more effect on the rear tyres and less on the front. If the wing is mounted behind the rear tyres, any downforce will actually start to take weight off the front tyres but will add more to the rear. So move the wing backwards to get more stability, but be careful as it can cause the jumping performance to be too nose high.

6. **Wing height** – A higher wing moves the drag of the wing higher. The drag will lever the car backwards slightly – giving more load on the rear tyres but taking it off the front (it doesn't actually add grip but changes the balance of the car). Usually, we try to mount the wing as low as possible but still in "clean" air.

7. **Front wings** – These were often used in the rear-motor days and then became more common around 2015 as tracks started to become faster, and traction levels increased.

Balance

The key to tuning wings is to get the combination of total downforce and the front/rear balance correct. As described, wings become much more effective as they move faster. They are a kind of "free" grip, but if the balance is wrong (e.g. too much at the rear), you can have a car that has great steering at low-speed but has a lot of understeer at high-speed. If you have a car that changes its character totally from low-speed to high-speed corners, wings are the first thing to look at.

High-speed vs Low-speed Tracks

As you are travelling faster on a high-speed track, you don't need too much downforce. If the wing gurney is too big or mounted too far back, you will struggle with high-speed understeer. Conversely, for low-speed tracks, you may need a bigger wing to get enough downforce. Body design can also have a big influence, as this will control how much front downforce is available.

High-grip vs Low-grip Tracks

On a high-grip track, you don't always want too much downforce at the rear as it can lead to strong understeer. Generally, you use a smaller gurney to help with the jumps and a bit of high-speed stability. Sometimes I even shorten the wing to give less downforce.

On low-grip tracks, you usually need every bit of stability and grip you can get, so you should start with a higher downforce wing and even use a wider wing if necessary. A larger wing will help forward traction of a 2WD vehicle considerably.

Big Jumps

The rear wing on a buggy makes a surprisingly big difference to the jumping attitude of a car, especially on big/high-speed jumps. If you have no wing, the car will have a fast (often uncontrollable) nose down attitude. If the wing is too big, it will jump nose high no matter what you do. I recommend trying to jump with no wing (in practice of course) to see just how much difference it makes!

Wind

The speed of the air over the wing controls the downforce, so strong head/tailwinds can heavily influence the performance of the car. Usually, if the wind is very strong, I will reduce the size of the gurney and/or flatten out the wing angle. This is especially true if there is a headwind over a large jump.

– Ray Munday

Chapter 7

Tweak

What is Tweak?

Tweak is the adjustment of the suspension so that both rear tyres touch the ground with equal pressure, and both front tyres touch the ground with equal pressure. If the pressure is not equal, a car is said to be "tweaked".

A "tweaked" car displays inconsistent handling. For example, it may turn to one side when accelerating in a straight line, or it may oversteer on one corner and understeer at the next.

Off-road cars are less susceptible to suspension tweak than on-road cars because of the amount of suspension travel and the terrain that they run on. Both tend to make them more forgiving of tweak. However, you should still check for tweak before a race meeting or after a crash.

Tweak Causes

A "tweaked" car may be caused by:

1. Build Error/Setup Error

1. **Left and right settings unequal** – settings on the left of the car are different to settings on the right. Check:
    a. Roll bars not set the same left-to-right. Refer to page 174.
    b. Droop screws (if your car has them) may not be set the same left-to-right. Refer to page 152.
    c. Shock length may not be the same left-to-right. Refer to page 126.
    d. Shock spring preload may be different left-to-right. Refer to page 129.
    e. Other Damping settings may not be the same left-to-right. Refer to page 126.
    f. Shims or physical parts may not be the same on the left and right sides.
2. **Binding parts** – make sure that all suspension components move freely without binding, including suspension arms and hinge pins, pivotballs, ball cups, etc.

3. **Twisted chassis** – top deck/chassis stiffeners, transmission, bulkhead or motor mount screws have been tightened inconsistently or using an incorrect pattern. This is more likely to occur if you use an alloy chassis (a carbon fibre chassis is more likely to return to flat unless pushed well past its limit). See *Test for a Twisted Chassis* below.

4. **Springs are different** – Bezerk RC (bezerk.com.au) has tested hundreds of springs from various manufacturers and found that both length and rate can vary significantly when they should be identical. In new springs, this could be due to manufacturing tolerances. In used springs, they may fail to return to their full length over time. Only use springs of the same length (left-to-right). See *Test for Suspension Tweak* below.

2. Crash Damage

1. **Physical Damage** – cracked carbon fibre or plastic parts can cause unpredictable handling when the parts flex under load. Change any broken parts.

2. **Bent roll bars** – check that they are flat. Refer to Roll Bar Installation on page *174* for installation and setting roll bar tweak.

3. **Twisted or bent chassis** – a particularly hard crash may twist or bend your chassis. See *Test for a Twisted* Chassis below.

Chassis Tweak

Test for a Twisted Chassis

1. **Ruler Test** – a particularly hard crash might damage/bend the chassis. Place a straight edge such as a ruler against the chassis looking for gaps between the ruler and chassis that indicate the chassis has twisted. For minor twisting refer to *Untwisting the Chassis* below. If the chassis has been damaged it should probably be replaced.

2. **Rocking Test** – components that are screwed to the chassis might move in a crash and cause the chassis to twist, tweaking the car.

   For buggies, remove the rear wing. For all vehicles, remove the body and turn it upside down and place on a flat surface. The shock towers should sit flat. If pushing on the side of the chassis causes the car to rock from side-to-side then the chassis is twisted (tweaked).

Untwisting the Chassis

If the chassis is tweaked (twisted), then one or more of the components attached to the chassis may have moved:

1. Loosen all the screws under the chassis slightly (say half a turn) i.e. screws mounting the servo, motor, A–D Blocks, centre diff/slipper, transmission/bulkheads/uprights. This should remove the tension causing the tweak.

2. Gently tighten the screws using the following pattern:

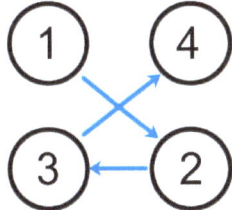

3. Before fully tightening the screws, recheck the chassis to see if it is still twisted.

   a. If the twist has been fixed, then proceed to Step c below.

   b. If the twist remains, then there may be components secured to the chassis from the top which are tweaked, therefore:

      i. Loosen screws holding the top deck/chassis braces, battery tray, transmission, etc.

      ii. With one hand, use a ruler to push down on both shock towers so that the chassis sits flat.

      iii. With the other hand, gently tighten the screws loosened in Step i. above using the pattern in Step 2 above.

      iv. Recheck the chassis to see if it sits flat. The twist should have been eliminated. If not, retry steps i–iii above. If this doesn't fix it, one or more components (such as the chassis) may be damaged/bent and need replacing.

   c. Fully tighten the screws using the pattern in Step 2 above. Recheck the chassis. If it is no longer twisted, then you have removed the tweak from your chassis. If the twist remains, then possibilities include: you have over-tightened screws or tightened them in the wrong order, or one or more components (such as the chassis or top deck/chassis braces) have been bent or damaged.

Note: If you can't identify the source of the tweak, don't have replacement parts, or don't have time to change them before the next race, then you can adjust shock preload to de-tweak the car. Refer to *Correct the Suspension Tweak* below.

Suspension Tweak

Test for Suspension Tweak

Remember that both rear tyres should touch the ground with equal pressure, and both front tyres should touch the ground with equal pressure. If this is not the case, we can identify it as follows:

1. Check that your camber, droop and ride height are set correctly. If you're uncertain whether your roll bars are set correctly, disconnect them.

2. Place your race ready car on a level surface (check it with a spirit level/water level; if the surface is not level then the test will provide false results).

3. Settle the car on its suspension by dropping it from 30cm (12") above the surface.

4. With your eyes level with this surface, use a hex driver under the centre of the chassis to lift up one end of the car (front or rear).

5. As the car lifts, the wheels should come off the ground at exactly the same time. If one wheel leaves the ground before the other, there is a problem (refer to *Tweak Causes* above). Minor tweaks can be corrected using *Correct the Suspension Tweak* below.

6. Repeat steps 3–4 on the other end of the car.

Correct the Suspension Tweak

1. Using the *Test for Suspension Tweak* above – as the car lifts up, the wheels should come off the ground at exactly the same time. If one wheel leaves the ground before the other, there is a problem. For example, if the rear right wheel leaves the ground slightly before the rear left. This means the front left needs more pressure on it. We need to correct this:

   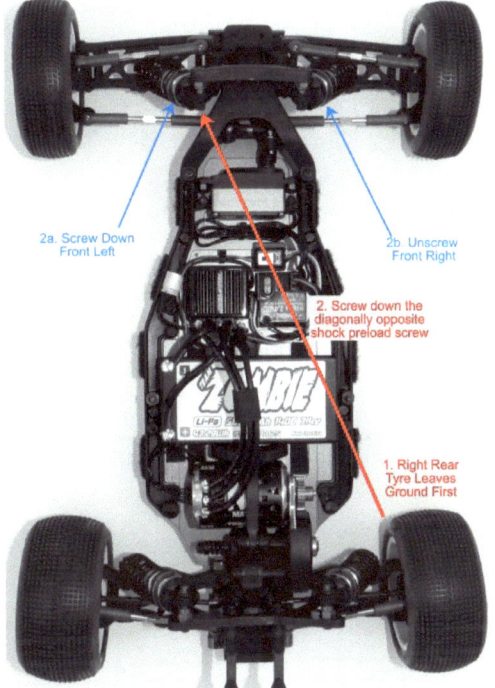

   a) Change the shock preload on the other end of the car by screwing down the collar diagonally opposite the wheel that leaves the ground early (as shown in the example photo on the right). Adjust the same on both sides, e.g. if you screw down the front left by 1/8th of a turn, then unscrew the front right by 1/8th of a turn (this helps to maintain ride height).

   b) Retest.

      NB: Excessive difference left-to-right – If the preload on the left and right sides of the car are different by more than a few mm (between front left and front right shocks, or between rear left and rear right shocks) then this is too much and could be because the shock tower has been tightened on an angle ("shock tower tweak"). Loosen the shock tower screws, twist the shock tower towards the side where the shock collar is screwed down more, and retighten. After doing this, you should now be able to back off that shock collar and tighten the opposite side, evening them up. Retest.

2. Once one end of the car is set, proceed to test the other end. For example, if you first tested the rear of the car, now test the front.

The up travel on the front and the rear should now be perfect, with both left and right tyres leaving the ground at exactly the same time. If not, then this could be because your weight distribution is slightly wrong, and you may need to add weight to balance your car side-to-side (refer to page *192*). However, unless the weight balance is significantly out, the procedure above should solve your tweak issues.

Assuming you changed the shock preload to correct the tweak, you will need to check your ride height again. Do this normally (refer to page *172*) by turning both left and right collars the same amount. Your ride height should now be the same on the left side of the car as on the right.

Equipment

The above procedures require no specialist equipment. However, some manufacturers provide setup wheels that make checking for tweak easier (using the *Test for Suspension Tweak* above). Bezerk's wheels (bezerk.com.au) are shown below.

Left: 1/10 DeTweak Wheels and right: 1/8 DeTweak Wheels

A set of four carbon fibre setup wheels replace the tyres. The setup wheel is heavier on one side, and when you lift the car with a driver, the wheel will rotate as it lifts from the ground. This provides obvious visual and noise cues as to which wheel lifted first.

Chapter 8

Trucks

Short Course Trucks

By Ray Munday

The 2WD Short Course Truck (SCT) class exploded onto the scene a few years ago with its mix of great scale looks, accessible performance and realistic handling that appealed to a far wider audience than any other class in recent history. 4WD SCTs are also available but are more commonly used for bashing.

What's Different About SCT?

SCTs are called 1/10 scale. However, they are quite different to 1/10 Buggy and Stadium Truck (ST) dimensions.

They are much longer and narrower than ST. The body is heavier and higher, which leads to a high Centre of Gravity (CG) and high roll inertia. This makes SCT roll a lot more, but they are quite stable under power.

The tyres are narrower and taller than ST, with higher profile sidewalls (refer to Tyres on page 87).

Driving SCTs Quickly

Low-speed

At low-speed, you can drive an SCT very aggressively. When properly set up they are very nimble at low-speed and the high CG doesn't have as much of an effect.

The longer travel and heavier weight makes them less sensitive to hitting curbs (something that is great for younger drivers).

Typically SCTs are rear-motor, or use a mid-motor setup with brass weights at the rear and the battery mounted further back. I recommend throwing the trucks into low-speed corners to get them lined up as early as possible for the following straight, and then you can punch out of the corner quickly.

High-speed

High-speed cornering is where SCT can be trickier.

The high roll angle and high roll inertia will quickly catch you out if you are too aggressive. If you "throw" the truck into a fast corner, the body starts to roll very quickly and can actually "throw" the vehicle into a rollover. This is not necessarily a traction roll – it is more of an inertia roll.

If the truck doesn't roll over, it will often lose the rear end if you are too aggressive, especially if you let off the power.

My suggestion for tackling high-speed corners is to be very smooth on the steering inputs on the way into the corner and also don't fully let off the power mid-corner.

SCT tends to be more stable on the power, so a slightly slower entry speed then applying power throughout a sweeper is usually the fastest method.

The suspension setup you use will have a huge effect on the driving style you need in fast corners.

If you have a very soft, underdamped setup, you will need to be very cautious and the truck will feel very nervous.

Run a firmer, more damped setup, and it will be much easier to push hard.

Jumping

With the large body, jumping becomes trickier, especially into a headwind.

The most important point is to get a level take-off. If you end up nose high, it's very hard to get the nose back down no matter how good your brakes are.

Should you get on the brakes too hard into a headwind, however, the large body will act like a wing and slam the car hard into the ground!

Jumps with flatter/more level take-offs are far more friendly to SCT, whereas jumps with steeper take-offs are always more difficult.

With a headwind, you will need to make a choice between going for the jump or not.

With a tailwind, you will pretty much be able to jump the same as a 2WD Buggy.

Crosswinds can also be tricky as the wind can easily get in the side of the wheel wells, firstly rolling the truck to one side, then making it turn in mid-air. The best way to counter this is to use the steering in the air to roll the truck into the wind. So if the wind is blowing from the right, turn to the left in the air (rolling the truck to the right). Just remember to straighten the wheel before landing.

It's always necessary with SCT to understand which direction the wind is coming from and whether it is a smooth wind or a blustery wind.

SCT Setup

Author's note: *The following setup tips were written for 2WD SCT. However, most also apply to 4WD SCT.*

Alignment

I find the following settings work in most conditions:

- 1° of negative camber front and rear.
- 1° of toe-out on the front.
- 3° of toe-in at the rear.
- 2° of anti-squat.
- Ride height is around 30mm for most tracks (other than carpet, which will be lower).

Weight Distribution

This depends on the brand of SCT you are running. For my Team Associated 2WD SCT, I typically run the weight more rearward than in my 2WD buggy. With my SCT, I usually run a standup transmission, battery rearwards, brass C block weight and rear shocks behind the arms to give more forward traction.

Tyres

I usually run the same tyre front and rear where possible.

Within the JConcepts range, I use similar tyre patterns to my 2WD buggy.

SCT tyres are larger than buggy tyres and therefore overheat less, so you can usually get away with a slightly softer compound than the Buggy.

Front tyre choice is very important to balance the high-speed steering feel. Sometimes we will use front tyres which are more worn than the rears – this will make it much easier to drive. Simply move the tyres from the rear to the front when they are worn – it keeps the cost of racing down as well!

As with all tyres using Closed Cell inserts, make sure you punch 2 x 3mm holes in the tyre and rim before gluing up (refer to page 77).

If the track is super high-traction, you can get a little more stability by using double sided tape between the insert and the rim to minimise tyre flex.

Springs and Shocks

These are critical to the performance of an SCT which seem to like a heavy damping feel, may benefit from extra weight, and needs more pack than a Buggy (refer to page 133).

Don't be afraid to go harder with the springs and heavier with the oil – the suspension will feel a bit slow to react on the bench, but it will make the truck much easier to drive. Generally, a very stiff front spring will help make the truck easier to drive and heavier oil will smooth out the transitions.

Lay down the rear shocks on the shock tower. This tends to smooth out the steering and it will ride the bumps a little better.

Roll bars

These have a huge effect on SCTs.

I've found in testing that using both front and rear roll bars helps to keep a good balance in the truck but makes it sit much flatter through high-speed sections and can be driven more like a Buggy than a truck.

This is probably the single biggest change I have made to my SCT, and on tracks with good grip and/or sweeping corners, I can't rate roll bars highly enough.

Differential

An SCT is much heavier than a buggy and has more weight transfer, so you will need to run the differential tighter. This helps reduce the inner rear wheel spinning when coming out of corners and also helps extend diff life.

Body Tuning

Most bodies now come with multiple cut-out options to allow the air to vent out and reduce the parachute effect. I recommend cutting them out as much as you can, especially at the front of the truck, to minimise the effect of headwinds.

I always use the JConcepts Hi-Flow body as it looks great, is super durable and has many cut-outs from the front grill/fender area.

One of the most effective tuning tools I've found is the pitch of the body. If you have trouble jumping into headwinds, try lifting the rear of the body up as far as possible (with the front as low as possible). I have found this to really help, and it also gives a little more downforce into higher speed corners.

I also highly recommend using an over-tray for your chassis. If you run on a wet track, this is critical for keeping mud out of your chassis, which adds weight, makes maintenance a pain, and is a risk for electronics. You can buy an over-tray made for your chassis, or you can make one using a 2WD buggy body cut to fit over the chassis side pods.

– Ray Munday

Stadium Trucks

Stadium Truck (also called Racing Truck) is a historical racing class whose popularity has fallen in recent years.

Stadium Trucks often have a longer chassis (wheelbase) than a similar buggy and are wider, with larger tyres (refer to page 87). Most setup recommendations in this book can successfully be applied to Stadium Trucks.

Racing Stadium Trucks are typically 2WD, while 4WD versions are often used for bashing.

Trucks 8

Monster Trucks

Although not normally raced, their large tyres make these vehicles very stable for bashing. While some of this book is relevant to Monster Trucks, they are not referred to specifically within these pages.

Monster Trucks come in both 2WD and 4WD versions. Refer to the glossary on page 296 for a brief comparison between 2WD and 4WD drivetrains.

Redcat Racing Blackout XTE (www.redcatracing.com)

Chapter 9

1/8 Scale

1/8 Buggy

Electric 1/8th scale buggies are often referred to as eBuggies (Eco Buggies) or just EP (Electric Powered) to differentiate them from Internal Combustion (IC) Nitro powered buggies. The setup advice in this book for 1/8 buggies applies to both eBuggies and Nitro buggies.

Throughout this book, setup options and case studies for 1/10 4WD buggies also apply to 1/8 buggies. Where 1/8 buggies setup varies, it is specified in the text of the relevant section.

On average, 1/8 buggies are approximately 25% longer and 25% wider than their 1/10 counterparts and are more than twice as heavy. They typically use 4S lipo batteries to provide the 14.8V required (rather than the 2S 7.4V lipos used in 1/10 vehicles) to propel that extra mass around the track at Modified speeds. They typically run on much larger tracks than 1/10 vehicles. These tracks are usually shared with 1/8 nitro vehicles.

Motor power is measured in Kv rather than a number of turns. Motors around 1,900 Kv work well. Lower powered motors (say 1,700 Kv) may work well on smaller tracks while higher powered motors (say 2,100 Kv) may work well on larger tracks. Higher Kv motors will reduce battery run time and this may be a consideration when longer race lengths are required.

Refer to Final Drive Ratios on page *161* for gearing recommendations and page *90* for 1/8 wheel sizes.

1/8 Scale

Serpent Cobra SRX8

Some vehicles offer alternative battery placement options (above and below).

1/8 Scale

1/8 Truggy

Truggy is a contraction of Truck and Buggy. Electric 4WD 1/8 Truggies are often referred to as eTruggies (or Eco Truggies) or just EP (Electric Powered) to differentiate them from Internal Combustion (IC) nitro powered truggies. Most setup advice in this book for 1/8 Buggies applies to 1/8 Truggies.

Truggies usually have a longer chassis (wheelbase) than a similar buggy, with larger tyres (refer to page 90). They are therefore heavier and use different gearing ratios than 1/8 buggies (refer to page 290 for gearing ideas).

eTruggies may use larger motors than eBuggies (check your local rules).

Essential Off-road RC Racer's Guide

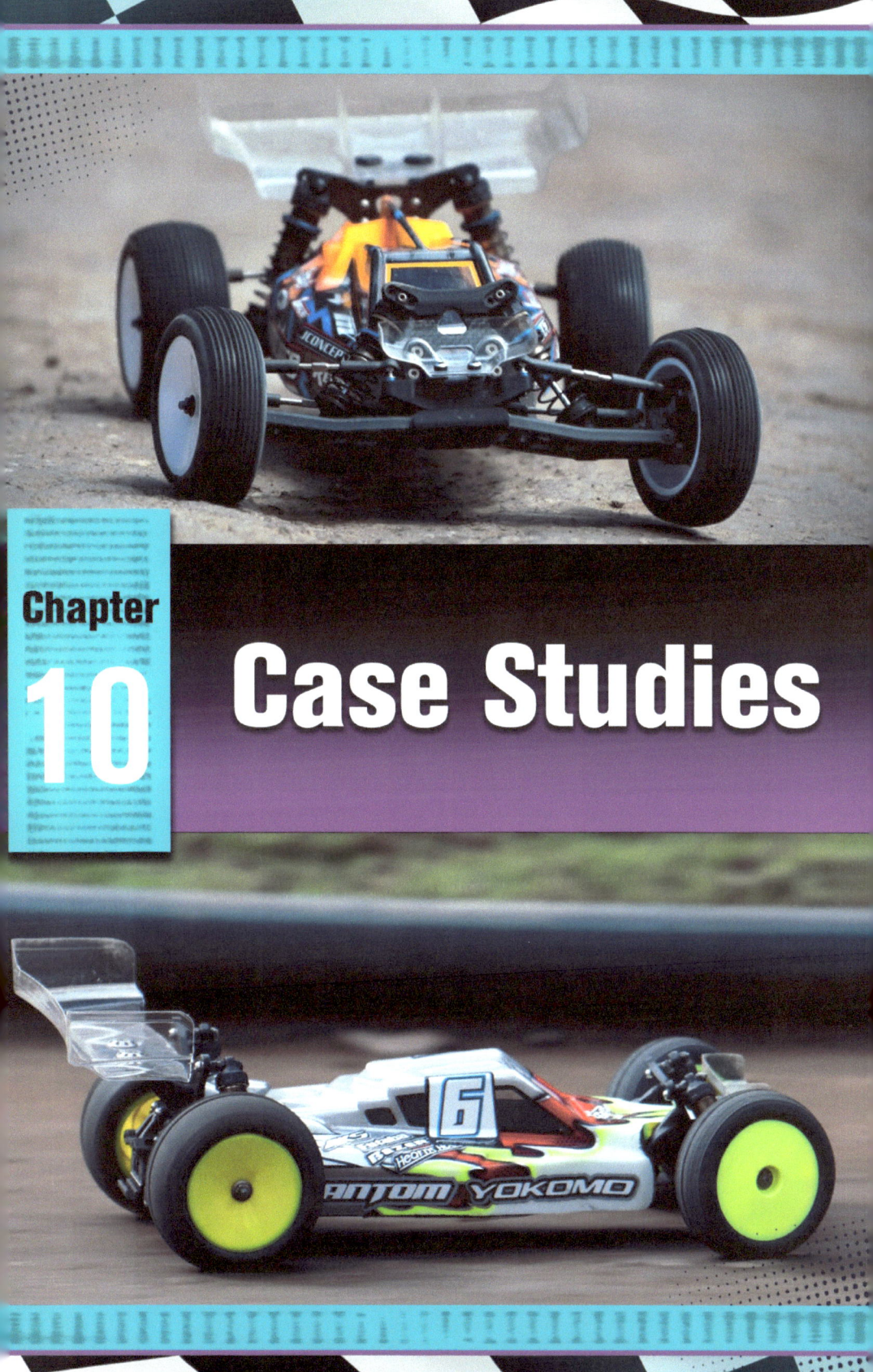

Chapter 10: Case Studies

This chapter describes actual race meetings and how skilled drivers approached their setup, what changes they made, why, and how car performance improved.

Different cars have unique handling characteristics. Even with the same chassis, driver style varies. That is why it's not recommended that you copy a world champion's car setup without understanding the settings. Instead, identify the differences between the world champion's setup and your car's setup and make one change at a time. Determine whether your car handles better or worse, based on your skill level and driving style, and finetune from there.

Stock vs Modified

The Clay case study provides setups for Stock and Modified. However, space limitations prevent providing this for all case studies. Modified setup windows tend to be narrower than Stock setup windows, i.e. a Modified setup should work for a Stock car but the reverse is not necessarily true. Therefore, the Modified case studies provided are relevant to Stock classes except for motor, gearing and ESC settings.

COVID-19

Very little racing took place in 2020 and early 2021 due to the COVID-19 (coronavirus) pandemic. The 2019 world championship featured was the most recent world championship at the time of writing.

Dirt Case Studies

Starting Setup

If you have not raced at a particular track before, then we recommend starting with your chassis manufacturer's base setup. You may also wish to search your chassis manufacturer's website for another driver's setup at that track so you can note the changes they made. We do not recommend using another driver's setup without knowing why they made the changes they did. However, it can be very useful to note the differences to the manufacturer's kit setup and then try each change, one at a time, and note whether it feels better or worse.

Clay Case Study

Race

2021 ROAR 1/10 Electric Off-Road Nationals, The Track, Gaithersburg, Maryland, USA.

Foreground: Dakotah Phend's winning 4WD and 2WD Buggies

Track Conditions

Indoor, small-medium, clay sealed with glue, grooved, very high-traction, damp. Tight track.

Control Tyre

Modified Classes – any tyres. Stock Classes:
- Rear Tyres 2WD/4WD – Raw Speed Stage Twos.
- Front Tyres 2WD/4WD – Raw Speed Radars.

Control Additive

Modified Classes – any additive. Stock Classes – SXT Baja Max (SXT00043). Manufacturer recommends applying for 15–30 minutes as needed and wipe off tyres 10 minutes before the run.

Modified 4WD Buggy

1st Dakotah Phend, 2nd Spencer Rivkin, 3rd Ryan Maifield, 4th Cole Tollard, 5th Tom Rinderknecht, 6th Charlie Maiorana, 7th Ryan Cavalieri, 8th Aydin Horne, 9th Dreighton Stoub, 10th Broc Champlin

TQ and 1st – Dakotah Phend – TLR 22 X4

Dakotah is the current World Vice-Champion (4WD) and multiple ROAR National Champion.

I stayed with the kit clay setup for:
- Rear toe-in 3°.
- Front toe-out 1°.
- Caster block 9°.
- The kit roll bars were used.
- Front and rear camber –2°.
- Wheel hexes left as kit.

Changes from the kit setup:
- A JConcepts F2 body with front wing was used. Rear wing was JConcepts Aero Type S with angle increased from 2° to 4° and cut below gurney.
- Ride height was set to 16mm front and rear.
- Changed chassis from aluminium to carbon fibre. This was the biggest change I made and allowed me to run softer springs.
- Used Lunsford titanium screws to give total weight of 1,605g.
- Changed carbon front steering brace from kit to optional TLR331049.
- Rear axle hole (CV pin position) changed from 2 to 1.
- Diffs:
  - Front diff fluid remained at kit setting (7K).
  - Centre slipper replaced with diff in rearward position using 500K fluid.
  - Rear diff fluid remained at kit setting (5K).
  - All diff metal gears replaced with composite ones to save weight.
- Anti-squat changed from 2° to 1.5°.

- Kick-up was reduced.
- Arm sweep increased.
- Front suspension arms changed from Standard to Stiffezel.
- Roll centre:
  - Rear camber link inner position changed from high (2) to low (1).
  - Rear outer camber link ball stud hole moved rearwards from A to B (longer link).
- Shocks:
  - Position – Rear shock position stood up on tower from middle to outside position. Front as kit.
  - Oil:
    - Front reduced from 42.5 WT to 40 WT.
    - Rear reduced from 37.5 WT to 35 WT.
  - Springs were changed to Associated v2 blue front and Associated v2 grey rear. These are softer and more progressive than kit.
  - Pistons, Shock Limiters and Eyelets were left as kit.
  - Spring cups – Front changed from High to Mid. Rear changed Mid to Low.
  - Stroke:
    - Front decreased from 23.5mm to 22.3mm.
    - Rear increased from 30.5mm to 31.2mm.
- Tyres – I ran JConcepts Ellipse Silver with Dirt Tech insert front and rear. I sanded the tyres down to slicks and applied FDJ additive. No tyre warmers.

Photo taken before some changes were made

- Motor:
  - Trinity Phenom 6.0T motor with 30-degrees of end bell timing.
  - FDR 11.25:1.
- Pro Performance ESC with 11% initial brake, no drag brake, 6° Turbo, no Boost.

6th – Charlie Maiorana – TLR 22 X4

I stayed with the kit clay setup for:
- Rear toe-in 3°.
- The kit roll bars were used.
- Caster block 9°.

Changes from the kit setup:
- A Pro-Line Axis body with front and rear wings was used. Rear wing angle increased from 2° to 4°.
- Ride height was set to 18mm front and rear.
- Front and rear camber reduced from –2° to –1°.
- Front toe-out reduced from 1° to 0°.
- Rear wheel hex changed from 5mm to 4.5mm.
- Diffs:
  - Front diff fluid increased from 7K to 10K.
  - Centre slipper replaced with diff using 500K fluid.
  - Rear diff fluid increased 5K to 7K.
  - All diff metal gears replaced with composite ones.
- Roll centre:
  - Rear camber link inner position changed from high (2) to low (1).
- Shocks:
  - Position – Front and rear shock position stood up on tower from middle to outside position.
  - Oil – Front reduced from 42.5 to 40 WT. Rear reduced from 37.5 to 35 WT.
  - Springs were changed to Associated v2 Yellow front and rear.
  - Pistons were left as kit.
  - Shock Limiter – Front removed internal from 1mm to 0mm.
  - Stroke – Front decreased from 23.5mm to 23mm. Rear unchanged (30.5mm).
- Tyres:
  - I ran Pro-Line S3 Shadows front and rear with included inserts.
  - Treatment – I sanded the tyres down to slicks. Applied yellow liquid wrench penetrating oil before each run.

8th – Aydin Horne – Associated RC10B74.1D

I did not make any track specific changes. This setup is the baseline that I use everywhere I race. However, I would only recommend this setup for very high-traction clay surfaces (typical in America), where we run long wear, slick tyres with tread removed. I would not recommend trying this setup on carpet, astroturf or loose dirt.

I was satisfied with vehicle performance in the main events. Unfortunately I didn't qualify well, but the car was capable of competing for the podium.

I stayed with the kit dirt setup for:
- Rear toe-in 3°.
- Front and rear camber –1°.
- Battery position.

Changes from the kit setup:
- A Pro-Line Axis body was used as it seems to drive a bit smoother than the kit body.
- Ride height was set to 17mm front and rear. When the traction is very high, the lower ride height makes the car less likely to traction roll, while also driving flatter.
- Kick-up 8°(instead of the kit 9°) + Caster block 9° = total Caster 17°. Made the car easier to drive.
- Front toe-out from 1° to 0° to give the car a little more corner speed.
- Front roll bar from 1.2mm to 1.3mm which is a bit more stable and easier to drive on high-traction. Rear roll bar 1.3mm (kit).
- Diff – I increased the oil viscosity in all three diffs to make the car a little more "numb", less reactive and ultimately easier to drive:
  - Front diff fluid increased from 10K to 20K.
  - Centre diff fluid increased 200K to 350K.
  - Rear diff fluid increased 10K to 15K.
  - All diff metal gears replaced with plastic ones to save weight, making the car more agile.
- Diff heights from +1mm to 0mm front and rear as this seems to have a bit more grip, and stays more planted on the track.
- Front wing removed – Provides a little more high-speed steering.
- Anti-squat increased from 0° to 0.5° for a little more corner entry steering.
- Total weight: 1,655g.
- Steering spindles shaved/ground down slightly to provide more steering throw.
- Front suspension arm hinge Pin Width from 0mm to –1.4mm to make it easier to drive.

- Roll centre – front outer camber link ball stud shim decreased from 2mm to 1mm to provide more steering.
- Chassis stiffness – Moved one front chassis brace screw from 3rd from right to 2nd from right position. Added one screw (2nd from left) to rear chassis brace. This provided the best combination of flex and stability.
- Rear camber link spacing shim reduced from 2mm to 1mm. The longer rear camber link helps stop traction rolling and makes it easier to drive with a less reactive rear end.
- Shocks:
  - Front shocks stood up one position from 2 to 3 on shock tower for more initial steering.
  - Rear shocks laid down one position from A to B on suspension arm to help with stability.
  - Oil – front increased from 40 WT to 42.5 WT as easier to drive. Rear left as 35 WT (kit).
  - Springs – Rear spring stiffness changed from kit Blue (2.2 lbs) to Kyosho Gold which are a little softer, making the car easier to drive with a less reactive rear end. Front as kit.
  - Shock Limiters:
    - Front added 1mm external limiter. Removing front up travel made the car easier to drive, with less front roll.
    - Rear removed 1mm external limiter. Adding up travel in the rear helped to handle the bumpy terrain.

- o Stroke:
  - Front reduced from 22mm to 20.6mm. Removing front droop helps the front end to stay flatter on the track, making it easier to drive.
  - Rear increased from 27.5mm to 28.8mm and rear eyelet length increased from short to long. Adding rear droop helped the car to land better.
- Tyres:
  - o I run Pro-Line S3 Shadows front and rear with included inserts.
  - o Treatment – I sanded the tyres down to slicks and used tyre warmers to burn in yellow liquid wrench penetrating oil (similar to WD40) for more grip each run.
- Motor:
  - o Reedy Sonic M4 5.5T with 15-degrees end bell timing (timing reduced to make the car easier to drive).
  - o FDR 10.83:1.
- ESC Reedy Blackbox 510R
  - o All changes were to smooth out the feel of the throttle and the brakes. This makes it easier for me to repeat the same lines every lap.
  - o Throttle: Punch Level 3, Init Throttle 0%, Drive Freq 8KHz, Dead Band 6%, Current Limit 100%.
  - o Brake: Drag Brake 4%, Brake Strength 75%, Init Brake 0%, Drag Freq 1.5KHz, Brake Freq 3KHz, Brake Punch Level 1, No Dynamic Drag Brake.
  - o Dynamic Timing: no Boost, no Turbo.
- Radio – EPA: Throttle 100%, Brake 96%. Expo: Throttle –6%, Brake 0%.

13.5 4WD Buggy

1st Matthew Gonzales, 2nd David Batta, 3rd Brennan Schimmel, 4th Sammy Moran, 5th Doug Lariviere, 6th AJ Marasco, 7th Sam Isaacs, 8th Nate Sutherland, 9th Allen Horne, 10th Kyle Gough

TQ and 1st – Matthew Gonzales – Associated RC10B74.1D

I stayed with the kit dirt setup for:
- Rear toe-in 3°.
- Front toe-out 1°.
- Anti-squat 2°.

Changes from the kit setup:
- A JConcepts S1 Yokomo body was used with a JConcepts High Clearance rear wing. Front wing removed.
- Ride height was set to 16mm front and rear.
- Front and rear camber increased from –1° to –2°.
- Flex:
  o Front and rear suspension arms changed from kit to carbon.
  o Chassis brace support from 2mm kit to 2.5mm carbon front and rear.
  o Front and rear chassis brace screws – all used.
- Battery position moved full forward from position 3 to position 4.
- Wheelbase – front and rear changed from arms forward to arms back.
- Kick-up 8°(instead of the kit 9°) + Caster block 8° = total Caster 16°.
- Front roll bar from 1.2mm to 1.3mm. Rear roll bar from 1.3mm to 1.4mm.
- Diff:
  o Front diff fluid increased from 10K to 20K.
  o Centre diff fluid unchanged at 200K (kit setting).
  o Rear diff fluid increased 10K to 20K.
  o All diff metal gears replaced with plastic ones.
- Diff heights from +1mm to 0mm front and rear.
- Total weight 1,590g.
- Front suspension arm hinge Pin Width from 0mm to –1.4mm.
- Axle height rear changed from +1mm to +2mm.
- Roll centre – rear outer camber link ball stud shim decreased from 2 to 1mm.
- Shocks:
  o Tall shock towers and tall shocks were used with 24mm shock bodies and 21mm shafts.
  o Rear shocks stood up one position from B to A on suspension arm.
  o Oil – front changed: 40 WT to 600 cSt. Rear changed: 35 WT to 450 cSt.
  o Springs – Rear spring stiffness changed from kit Blue (2.2 lbs) to X-Gear Gold to provide more support. Front were kit Yellow.
  o Pistons:
    ▪ Front – 2 hole piston changed from 2x1.6mm to 2x1.7mm with one hole drilled out to 1.8mm.
    ▪ Rear – 2 hole piston changed from 2x1.7mm to 2x1.8mm with one hole drilled out to 1.9mm.
  o Shock Limiters – Rear removed 1mm external limiter.

- o Stroke:
    - Front reduced from 22mm to 21.5mm and rear eyelet length changed from Long to Yokomo Line.
    - Rear increased from 27.5mm to 28.8mm and rear eyelet length increased from Short to Long.
- Tyres – Spec tyres on RM2 inserts. I sanded the tyres down to slicks.
- Motor – Fantom ICON V2 13.5T with 45° of end bell timing. FDR 7.2:1.
- ESC Muchmore Fleta Euro – Non-timing (Blinky) mode.
- Radio Settings – Throttle EPA 100%, Brake EPA 100%.

3rd – Brennan Schimmel – TLR 22 X4

I stayed with the kit clay setup for:
- Rear toe-in 3°.
- Front toe-out 1°.
- The kit roll bars were used.
- Caster block 9°.
- Front and rear camber –2°.
- Wheel hexes left as kit.

The most significant changes I made were:
1. Lowering the rear inside camber link from the upper position to the lower position for a quicker transition in the corner.
2. Changing the front shock piston holes which allowed me to long jump the front second double into the face of the table top. The change added a little more pack, providing a less harsh landing.

Changes from the kit setup:
- A TLR body was used with rear wing angle increased from 2° to 4°.
- Ride height was set to 16mm front and 17mm rear.
- Battery pushed all the way forward.
- Total weight of 1,675g.
- Rear axle hole (CV pin position) changed from 2 to 1.
- Diffs:
  - Front diff fluid increased from 7K to 10K.
  - Centre slipper replaced with diff in forward position using 1 million cSt fluid.
  - Rear diff fluid increased from 5K to 10K.
  - All diff metal gears replaced with composite ones to save weight.
- Roll centre:
  - Front camber link inner position changed from high (2) to low (1).
  - Rear camber link inner position changed from high (2) to low (1).
- Shocks:
  - Position – Rear shock position laid down on tower from middle to inside position. Front as kit.
  - Oil – as kit.
  - Springs – Front as kit. Rear changed from Pink to Red.
  - Pistons – Front piston holes from 2x1.6 to 2x1.5mm.
  - Eyelets and Stroke as kit.
  - Shock Limiters:
    - Internal front limiter removed (1mm to 0mm).
    - External limiters removed front and rear (1mm to 0mm).
  - Spring cups – front changed from High to Mid. Rear as kit.
- Tyres – Spec tyres sanded down to slicks. I applied FDJ Green additive before each run with tyre warmers set to 57°C (135°F) for 5 minutes.
- Motor – Fantom 13.5T motor with about 45-degrees end bell timing. FDR 7.5:1.
- Fantom ESC – Non-timing (Blinky) mode. 100% Throttle and Brake.

7th – Sam Isaacs – Xray XB4 '21

I stayed with the kit setup for:
- Front toe-out 1°.
- Standard chassis.
- Kit wheel hexes.

At this track, the key was making the car easy to drive in the high-grip conditions. Gluing the front sidewalls and lowering the front roll centre were key changes.

Changes from the kit setup:
- An Xray Gamma D light body was used with optional 323510 rear wing cut lower than kit (line 3 to line 2). Wing position lowered from Up to Middle.
- Ride height was set to 16mm front and 17mm rear.
- Camber front was changed from –2° to –1°. Rear remained at –2° (kit).
- Rear toe-in changed from 3.5° to 2°.
- Anti-squat from 2° to 1.5°.
- Kick-up changed from 10° to 9° + C-hub Caster from 9° to 6° = total Caster 15°.
- Track width front changed from –1.5mm to +1.5mm.
- C-hub longer bushings changed from Up to Down.
- Roll bars – Front reduced from 1.2mm to 1.0mm. Rear 1.3mm (kit).
- Diffs:
  - Front oil changed from 10K to 30K.
  - Rear oil changed from 10K to 15K. Rear diff height raised from 3-dots-down to 1-dot-up.
  - Centre oil changed from 100K to 500K.
- Bump steer:
  - Shims under steering link decreased from 2mm to 1mm.
  - Shims on steering plate reduced from 5mm to 1mm.
- Wheelbase – The car felt more stable and easier to drive after changing:
  - Rear upright wheelbase shim in front of arm changed from 1mm to 2mm.
  - Front and rear shims in front of arms removed (2mm to 0mm).
- Shocks:
  - Springs – Rear changed from 60mm 2 dot to 57mm 2 dot. Front 45mm 2 dot (kit).
  - Oil:
    - Front changed from 600 cSt to AE 47.5 WT.
    - Rear changed from 500 cSt to AE 42.5 WT.
  - Position – lower shock position moved inwards on suspension arm front and rear.
  - Shock Pistons as kit.
  - Stroke changed from 22mm to 23mm front and from 27mm to 29mm rear.
  - Travel – No limiters were used. Front upstop removed (1mm to 0mm) and rear downstop removed (2mm to 0mm).
- Rear upright shims changed from 2mm to 0mm.
- Rear driveshaft length increased from 75mm to 77mm.
- Rear brace changed from Medium to Hard.
- Roll centre:
  - Raised front inner camber link from position 1 (down) to 2 (up).
  - Lowered front outer camber link by removing shim (2mm to 0mm).
  - Lowered rear outer camber from 4mm to 3mm.

- Motor:
    - Fantom 13.5T with 30-degrees of end bell timing.
    - FDR 8.1:1.
- ESC – Hobbywing XR10 Pro G2 in non-timing (Blinky) mode.
- Tyres:
    - Spec tyres. I sanded the tyres to slicks, and glued the front sidewalls to make the car easier to drive in the high-traction. I used tyre warmers for about 5–8 minutes which helped the tyres have grip from the moment the car was put down.
    - The race used a "spec" additive. However, this rule was not enforced and almost all drivers in Stock used a different sauce.

Modified 2WD Buggy

1st Dakotah Phend, 2nd Ty Tessmann, 3rd Cole Tollard, 4th Spencer Rivkin, 5th Ryan Cavalieri, 6th Aydin Horne, 7th Charlie Maiorana, 8th Tom Rinderknecht, 9th Lee Setser, 10th Dreighton Stoub

TQ and 1st – Dakotah Phend – TLR 22 DC 5.0 Elite

Dakotah is the current World Vice-Champion (4WD) and multiple ROAR National Champion.

I stayed with the kit setup for:
- Front toe-out 0°.
- No roll bars were used.
- Ball diff (1/4 turn tighter than kit).
- Slipper clutch with kit pads.
- Kick-up shims 3mm.

The biggest changes were shock positions, increasing rear toe-in and anti-squat.

Case Studies **10**

Changes from the kit setup:
- A JConcepts P2 body with high small front wing was used. Rear wing was JConcepts Astro 7" with kit angle (4°) and cut at 2nd line.
- Ride height was set to 21mm front and rear.
- Camber changed from –1° to –2° front and rear.
- Rear toe-in increased from 3° to 3.5°.
- Anti-squat increased from 2° to 3°.
- Caster block changed from 5° to 0°.
- Bump steer shims changed from 1mm to 0mm.
- Front axle spacing increased from 0mm to 1mm.
- Steering Trail setting reduced from 4mm to 3mm.
- Battery position moved forward from position 3 to 4.
- Rear driveshaft changed from 67mm to X68mm.
- Used Lunsford titanium screws and 63g under the LCG battery to give total weight of 1,545g.
- Roll centre:
  - Front camber link inner shim changed from 1mm to 0mm.
  - Rear outer camber link ball stud hole moved rearwards from C to B (shorter link).
- Shocks:
  - Front and rear shock towers changed from Carbon +2mm to Carbon Std.
  - Position – as kit.
  - Oil – as kit (32.5 WT front and 27.5 WT rear).
  - Springs – front was changed to Associated v1 grey. Rear was left as kit.
  - Pistons:
    - Front – kit 2x1.6mm but drilled a 3rd hole (1mm).

- Rear – kit 1x1.7mm/1x1.8mm but drilled a 3rd hole (1mm).
  - Shock Limiters:
    - Front internal limiter removed (1mm to 0mm). No external limiter (kit).
    - No rear internal or external limiters (as kit).
  - Eyelets were left as kit.
  - Spring cups:
    - Front Mid.
    - Rear Low.
  - Stroke:
    - Front increased from 22mm to 22.7mm.
    - Rear increased from 28.5mm to 31mm.
- Tyres – I ran JConcepts Smoothie 2 Silver with Dirt Tech insert front and rear. I sanded the tyres down to slicks and applied FDJ additive before each run. I didn't use tyre warmers.
- Motor:
  - Trinity Phenom 7.0T motor with 22-degrees of end bell timing.
  - FDR 9.03:1.
- Pro Performance ESC with 11% initial brake, 11% drag brake, no turbo or boost.

6th – Aydin Horne – Associated RC10B6.3D

I did not make any track specific changes, this setup is my baseline for very high-traction clay surfaces.

I stayed with the kit dirt setup for:
- Front toe-out 0°.
- Rear toe-in 3°.
- Front and rear camber –1°.
- Ball diff.
- No roll bars.
- Laydown transmission.

Changes from the kit setup:
- Ride height was set to 18.5mm front and rear.
- A Pro-Line Axis body was used.
- Changed from standard chassis #91892 to long chassis #92893 (+3mm). The long chassis doesn't transfer weight as fast, making the car much smoother and easier to drive on high bite surfaces.
- Front wing removed. Provides a little more high-speed steering.
- Kick-up 25°(kit) + Caster bushing 0° = total Caster 25°. I run the 0° caster inserts to smooth out the steering on high bite.
- Front suspension arm from standard to hard. Rear arm was not changed. The hard front suspension arm seems to make the front end/steering smoother and

more predictable. The rear carbon arms take away too much grip for my liking on that surface and so were not used.
- Anti-squat reduced from 2° to 1°. I took out some Anti-squat to settle the rear end a bit. It makes the car easier to drive and less likely to flip.
- Weight:
  - 22g weight added under the battery and 13g added under the ESC/receiver. This makes the car feel more planted into the track, and adds stability.
  - 14g added behind the servo to get some more weight on the front tyres. This adds steering.
  - Total 49g added.
- Battery placement moved forward one position from 4F to 5F to get a little more steering. It also rounds off the corners better than having the battery back.
- 2 pad slipper clutch optional parts #91802 and #91806 with #92289 pads. The slipper clutch parts are just vented plates so it doesn't overheat. The LCF pads seem to engage smoother than the kit pads.
- Shocks:
  - Oil reduced – front from 35 WT to 32.5 WT and rear from 35 WT to 30 WT. This makes the car absorb the bumps better and generates more traction.
  - Front piston changed from 2x1.6mm to 1x1.6mm + 1x1.7mm. I drilled one hole in my front piston to 1.7mm to get extra steering.
  - Front spring stiffness increased from Gray (3.61 lbs) to Blue (3.91 lbs). The blue front spring is a little smoother to drive, making the front end slightly more numb feeling.
  - Rear spring stiffness reduced from Gray (2.00 lbs) to White (1.91 lbs). Generates more rear traction.
  - Added rear shock external limiter (from 0 to 1mm). Reduces up travel which results in better landing and more stable cornering.
  - Stroke – front increased from 21mm to 23.4mm and eyelet length increased by 2mm, rear increased from 27.5mm to 29mm. I added droop all the way around the vehicle to get it to land better.
- Tyres:
  - I ran Pro-Line S3 Shadows front and rear with included inserts.
  - I also tried Pro-Line S3 Positron rear and Electron front, but they were not any better.
  - Treatment – I sanded the tyres down to slicks and used tyre warmers to burn in yellow liquid wrench penetrating oil for more grip each run.
- Motor:
  - Reedy Sonic M4 7.5T with 20-degrees end bell timing (the default setting).
  - FDR 9.66:1.

- ESC Reedy Blackbox 510R
  - All changes were to smooth out the feel of the throttle and the brakes. This makes it easier for me to repeat the same lines every lap.
  - Throttle: Punch Level 6, Init Throttle 0%, Drive Freq 8KHz, Dead Band 6%, Current Limit 100%.
  - Brake: Drag Brake 16%, Brake Strength 75%, Init Brake 0%, Drag Freq 1.5KHz, Brake Freq 4KHz, Brake Punch Level 1, No Dynamic Drag Brake.
  - Dynamic Timing: Boost Timing 3°, Boost RPM 5,000–15,000, Throttle Limit Off, no Turbo.
- Radio Settings:
  - Throttle EPA 100%, Brake EPA 96%, Throttle Expo –6%, Brake Expo 0%.

Compared to Aydin's 4WD motor and ESC setup earlier, the 4WD is overall more aggressive as the 5.5T motor has more punch, whereas the 7.5T in 2WD needs some boost. The 4WD can handle harder acceleration and braking.

10th – Dreighton Stoub – Associated RC10B6.3D

I stayed with the kit dirt setup for:
- Front toe-out 0°.
- Rear toe-in 3°.
- Front and rear camber –1°.
- Ball diff.
- No roll bars.
- Laydown transmission.
- Front and rear wing.
- Kick-up 25°(kit) + Caster block 5° = total Caster 30°.

The changes that made the largest difference were:

1. Moving my rear arms back. Given I was running the short chassis (kit), my car was already on the shorter side. On top of that I was running the short (73mm) rear arms which also made the car more aggressive. To compensate for those two things, I moved my rear arms back. This allowed me to gain the comfort and stability I needed, but still allowed the car to be quick in and out of the corners.

2. Changing the axle height. Raising my rear axles from +2 to +3 at the hub took rear grip out of the car. Obviously, on a glued surface the grip is already high enough, so raising that hub "freed up the car," ultimately making it more comfortable to drive.

Changes from the kit setup:
- Ride height was set to 18mm front and rear.
- A JConcepts F2 body was used.
- Ackermann changed by reducing ball stud shim from 1mm to 0mm.
- Axle height changed from +2mm to +3mm.
- Rear arm spacing from forward to rearward 2mm.
- Roll Centre – Rear camber link length increased (position 3 outer to 1 inner) and ball stud shim reduced from 3mm to 2mm.
- Shocks:
  - Oil reduced – Front from 35 WT to 32.5 WT. Rear from 35 WT to 30 WT.
  - Spring stiffness changed – Front from V2 Gray to V1 Gray, and rear from V2 Gray to V1 White.
  - No internal or external limiters (as kit).
  - Stroke – Front increased from 21mm to 23.5mm. Rear increased from 27.5mm to 28.5mm.
  - Eyelets – Reduced front and rear from Long (+2) to Short.
- Tyres – I ran AKA Chainlink Clay fronts and AKA X-link rears. Both with Red inserts and sanded down to slicks. I used FDJ "green/yellow" dot sauce before each run with no tyre warmers.
- Motor:
  - Fantom Super D 7.0T with 30-degrees end bell timing.
  - FDR 9.22:1.
- ESC Fantom FR10 with 3° boost and 3° turbo. With hindsight, I would have removed both. It would've calmed the car down enough to make a noticeable difference while driving on a track as high bite and tight as the track we were running on that specific weekend.

17.5 2WD Buggy

1st Matthew Gonzales, 2nd Sammy Moran, 3rd David Batta, 4th Doug Lariviere, 5th Kyle Gough, 6th AJ Marasco, 7th Justin Green, 8th Allen Horne, 9th Matt Wilbert, 10th Brennan Schimmel

TQ and 1st – Matthew Gonzales – Associated RC10B6.3D

I stayed with the kit dirt setup for:
- Rear toe-in 3°.
- Anti-squat 2°.
- Ball diff.
- No roll bars.
- Laydown transmission.
- Kick-up 25°(kit) + Caster bushing 5° = total Caster 30°.
- Battery placement 4F.

Changes from the kit setup:
- Ride height was set to 19mm front and rear.
- A JConcepts S2 lightweight body was used with front wing and the JConcepts Astroturf rear wing.
- Front and rear camber changed from –1° to –2°.
- Front toe-out from 0° to 1°.
- Ackermann – inner steering link ball stud shim from 1mm to 0mm. Steering plate changed from +1 to +0.
- Rear arm spacing changed from forward position to 2mm in front of arm.
- I ran the ball diff tighter than kit.
- Slipper clutch – changed from 11mm to 19mm pads.
- Track Width decreased:
   - Rear hex changed from 5mm to 4mm.
   - Rear hinge pin width decreased from +1.4mm to –1.4mm.
- Changed from standard chassis #91892 to long chassis #92893 (+3mm).
- Weight total: 1,545g.

- Roll Centre – rear:
  - Inner camber link shim reduced from 3mm to 0mm.
  - Outer camber link shim reduced from 2mm to 1.5mm.
  - Camber link spacing reduced from 1mm to 0mm.
- Shocks:
  - Position – Rear shocks laid down on tower from position 3 to position 2.
  - Pistons – Front piston changed from 2x1.6mm to 1x1.7mm + 1x1.8mm. Rear piston changed from 2x1.7mm to 1x1.8mm + 1x1.9mm.
  - Oil – Front from 35 WT to 500 cSt and rear from 35 WT to 450 cSt.
  - Springs – Front and rear changed from V2 Gray to V1 Gray.
  - Limiters – Added rear external limiter (from 0 to 3mm).
  - Stroke – Front increased from 21mm to 22.5mm. Rear increased from 27.5mm to 28.5mm.
- Tyres:
  - Control tyres sanded to slicks. Control additive applied before each run.
- Motor:
  - Fantom Icon Torque V2 17.5T.
  - FDR 6.93:1.
- ESC Muchmore Fleta Pro in non-timing (Blinky) mode.

10th – Brennan Schimmel – TLR 22 5.0 Elite

I stayed with the kit setup for:
- No roll bars were used.
- Laydown transmission.
- Ball diff.
- Slipper clutch with kit pads.
- The kit body was used.

Changes from the kit setup:
- Ride height was set to 19mm front and 20mm rear.
- Camber changed from –1° to –2° front and from –1° to –3° rear. This change made the biggest difference and allowed me to drive the car harder into the corners.
- Front toe-out increased from 0° to 1°.
- Kick-up shims changed from 3mm to 2mm.
- Rear toe-in increased from 3° to 4°.
- Anti-squat increased from 2° to 2.5°.
- Bump steer shims changed from 1mm to 0mm.
- Front axle spacing increased from 0mm to 1mm.
- Steering Trail setting reduced from 4mm to 3mm.
- Total weight of 1,550g.
- Roll centre – Front camber link outer shim changed from 2mm to 1mm.

- Shocks:
    - Front and rear shock towers changed from Carbon +2mm to Carbon Std.
    - Position – Front stood up from position 2 to position 3. Rear as kit.
    - Oil – Front changed from 32.5 WT to 40 WT and rear from 27.5 WT to 35 WT.
    - Springs – Front was changed from TLR Green to Associated v1 Gray. Rear from TLR White to TLR Yellow.
    - Pistons:
        - Front – Changed from 2x1.6mm to 2x1.5mm.
        - Rear – Changed from 1x1.6mm + 1x1.7mm to 2x1.7mm.
    - Shock Limiters:
        - Front internal limiter removed (1mm to 0mm). No external limiter (kit).
        - No rear internal or external limiters (as kit).
    - Eyelets were left as kit.
    - Spring cups:
        - Front Mid.
        - Rear Low.
    - Stroke:
        - Front from 22mm to 24.5mm.
        - Rear from 28.5mm to 30.5mm.
- Tyres – Control tyres sanded to slicks. Control additive applied before each run.
- Motor – Fantom 17.5T motor with 43-degrees of end bell timing. FDR 6.17:1.
- Fantom ESC in non-timing (Blinky) mode.

Modified 2WD Stadium Truck

1st Cole Tollard, 2nd Dakotah Phend, 3rd Ty Tessmann, 4th Chase Lemieux, 5th Ryan Cavalieri, 6th Aydin Horne, 7th Charlie Maiorana, 8th Ron Devoll, 9th Tater Sontag, 10th Chase Chandler

6th – Aydin Horne – Associated RC10T6.2

I did not make any track specific changes, this setup is my baseline for very high-traction clay surfaces.

I stayed with the kit dirt setup for:
- Front toe-out 0°.
- Rear toe-in 3°.
- Ball diff.
- Front and rear camber –1°.
- Kick-up 25° + Caster block 5° = total Caster 30°.
- Laydown transmission.

Changes from the kit setup:
- Associated T6.2 Kit Body and spoiler (#71126) was used.
- Ride height was set to 24mm front and rear.
- Front roll bar from 1.3mm to 1.4mm which is a bit more stable and easier to drive on high-traction. Rear roll bar none (kit).
- Bump steer shim reduced from 1mm to 0.5mm.
- Rear hub spacing from Forward to Mid-position.
- Roll Centre – Front inner camber link ball stud increased from 1mm to 2mm.
- Diff height changed from 2mm to 3mm.
- 2 pad slipper clutch optional parts #91802 and #91806 with #92289 pads. The slipper clutch parts are just vented plates so it doesn't overheat. The LCF pads seem to engage smoother than the kit pads.
- Anti-squat increased from 2° to 2.5°.
- Weight:
  - 13g added under the ESC/receiver. This makes the car feel more planted into the track, and adds stability.
  - 7g added behind the servo to get some more weight on the front tyres. This adds steering.
- Battery placement moved forward one position from 4F to 5F. This provides a little more steering. It also rounds off the corners better than having the battery back.
- Shocks:
  - Rear mounting position changed from rear of arm to front of arm.

- o Rear shock position changed from B to A (innermost hole) on suspension arm, and from 2 to 1 (innermost hole) on shock tower.
- o Oil increased – Front from 30 WT to 37.5 WT. Rear 30 WT (kit).
- o Front piston changed from 2x1.6mm to 1x1.6mm + 1x1.7mm. I drilled one hole in my front piston to 1.7mm to get extra steering.
- o Rear spring stiffness reduced from White (2.4 lbs) to Green (2.2 lbs). Front spring unchanged from Gray (4.45 lbs).
- o Added front shock internal limiter (from 0 to 2mm).
- o Stroke – Front increased from 27.5mm to 27.9mm, rear reduced from 35mm to 33.6mm.
- Tyres:
  - o I run Pro-Line S3 Positrons front and rear with included inserts.
  - o Treatment – I sanded the tyres down to slicks and used tyre warmers to burn in yellow liquid wrench penetrating oil for more grip each run.
- Motor:
  - o Reedy Sonic M4 7T with 28-degrees end bell timing.
  - o FDR 10.67:1.
- ESC Reedy Blackbox 510R – Non-timing (Blinky) mode.
- Radio Settings – Throttle EPA 100%, Brake EPA 96%.

9th – Tater Sontag – TLR 22 4.0

I stayed with the kit dirt setup for:
- Front toe-out 0°.
- Rear toe-in 3°.
- Front and rear camber –1°.
- Ball diff.
- Kick-up 25° + Caster block 5° = total Caster 30°.
- Anti-squat 2°.
- Laydown 3-gear transmission.
- The kit body was used.

Changes from the kit setup:
- Ride height was set to 27mm front and rear.
- Weight:
  - o 10g added behind the servo.
  - o Total truck weight: 1,753g.
- Rear Hub spacing changed from middle to 2mm. This made the truck less likely to tip in the high-speed sections.

- Battery placement – Removed battery strap to provide more flex and taped full forward to provide more rotation.
- Camber link length shortened at front inner from position 1 to position 2 which frees up the car in the corner and less likely to hook.
- Camber link rear spacer from –1mm to +1mm. Allows the truck to generate more side bite through the corner while taking away some forward bite.
- Changed slipper from HDS to SHDS which has better pads and springs.
- Shocks:
    - Rear shock mounting changed from front-to-rear.
    - Position:
        - Front shock position laid down on tower from middle (2) to inner position (1).
        - Rear shock position laid down on suspension arm from inside to middle position.
    - Oil:
        - Front increased from 32.5 WT to 42.5 WT.
        - Rear increased from 32.5 WT to 37.5 WT.
    - Springs and pistons were left as kit.
    - Shock Limiter:
        - Front removed from 1mm to 0mm.
        - Rear removed from 2mm to 0mm.
    - Stroke – Rear decreased from 33mm to 32mm. Front unchanged (28mm).
- Tyres:
    - I ran Pro-Line S3 Positrons front and rear with included inserts.
    - Treatment – I sanded the tyres down to slicks. Applied green FDJ additive using tyre warmers before each run.
- Motor:
    - Trinity Xfactor 7.0T with about 30° end bell timing (kit setting).
    - FDR 12.45:1.
- ESC Muchmore Fleta Pro V2 – Drag Brake 2%, Initial Brake=Drag Brake. No Dynamic Timing (Boost/Turbo) was used.
- Radio Settings:
    - Throttle EPA 90%, brake EPA 85%.

Packed Dirt Case Study

Race

2019 World Championship, Hudy Arena, Trencin, Slovakia.

4WD layout above. A different layout was used in 2WD

Track Conditions

Indoor, medium size, low-traction, bumpy, hardpacked dirt, dry. Mixed track with both fast and technical sections.

Control Tyre

- 2WD Rear/4WD Front and Rear – Pro-Line Worlds Hole Shot 2.0 2.2" M3 compound with stock inserts.
- 2WD Front tyres are Pro-Line 4-Rib M3 with stock inserts.

Control Additive

Additive and tyre warmers were not allowed.

Special thanks to JConcepts for the World Championship photos.

4WD Modified

1st Bruno Coelho (Xray), 2nd Dakotah Phend (Losi), 3rd Michal Orlowski (Schumacher), 4th Daniel Kobbevik Jr (Xray), 5th Ty Tessmann (Xray), 6th Marco Baruffolo (Xray), 7th David Ronnefalk (Hot Bodies), 8th Yusuke Sugiura (Yokomo), 9th Ryan Maifield (Yokomo), 10th Spencer Rivkin (Associated)

Bruno Coelho top qualified, but a mistake in A1 allowed Dakotah Phend to take the win after an extremely close race. Bruno 2nd and Michal Orlowski 3rd. Bruno led strongly in A2 until going slightly wide before the quadruple gave Dakotah an opening. They launched over the quad side by side, touched in mid-air and Bruno got the worst of it dropping to second. A couple of laps later Dakotah rolled over and Bruno re-took the lead and the win in A2, Dakotah 2nd and Michal 3rd. So the winner of A3 would determine the world championship. A3 started with Dakotah pushing Bruno hard for the first few laps until Dakotah rolled over and dropped to 4th. He fought his way back to 2nd and charged after Bruno, but another mistake gave David Ronnefalk 2nd place, Dakotah taking 3rd. With well-deserved wins in A2 and A3, Bruno became the 4WD world champion for the second time.

TQ and 1st – Bruno Coelho – Xray XB4 '20

I stayed with the kit setup for:
- Front toe-out 1°.
- Rear toe-in 3°.
- Front and rear camber –2°.
- Diffs – Front and rear diff oil both 10K.
- Kick-up 7° + C-hub Caster 9° = total Caster 16°.

These changes from the kit setup made the largest difference on track:
- Changed from standard chassis to 2.5mm chassis.
- Roll bars changed to increase traction:
  - Front reduced from 1.8mm to 1.2mm.
  - Rear reduced from 1.8mm to 1.3mm.

- Centre slipper clutch replaced with centre diff (200K oil) to generate traction.
- Motor settings were tuned to make the car easy to drive:
  - Hobbywing 7.5 with 30-degrees of end bell timing.
  - FDR 8.44:1.
  - ESC Hobbywing XR10 Pro. I used very low boost with very high drive frequency to make it smooth and also pretty high turbo as the straight was long.

Other changes from the kit setup:
- A lightweight Xray body was used.
- Ride height was set to 19mm (front and rear) for this track.
- Track Width reduced with wheel hexes changed from 0 to –0.75mm.
- Bump steer shims – increased from 0mm to 2mm.
- Anti-squat from 2° to 3°.
- Rear shock position to inner hole on the suspension arm.
- Rear shock up-stop shim reduced from 3mm to 2mm.
- Front and rear suspension arms changed from Short to Long.
- Rear Axle Height eccentric bushing inner top 1°.
- Front driveshaft length increased from 81mm to 83mm.
- Steering block from Hard to Graphite.
- Caster block from Hard to Graphite.
- Front and rear suspension arms from Hard to Graphite.
- Roll centre:
  - Front lowered inner camber link.
  - Rear camber link length increased from position 3 to position 4.
- Rear upright from 0mm to 2mm shims.
- Rear insert changed from centre to top left.

You can see detailed photos of Bruno's winning buggy on page *20*.

Case Studies 10

3rd – Michal Orlowski – Schumacher CAT L1

Michal is a multiple European champion and multiple EOS series champion.

Michal stayed with the kit dirt setup for:
- Diff oil 10K front and rear.
- Shock oil front 550cSt and rear 400cSt.

Changes from the kit setup:
- A Penguin CAT L1 body was used.
- Ride height was set to 22mm front and rear.
- Front camber –2°. Rear camber –2.5°
- Rear toe-in increased from 3° to 3.5°.
- Front toe-out increased from 0° to 0.5°.

- Diff height rear changed from high to low. Front diff height was low (kit).
- Battery moved from middle to front position.
- Slipper clutch changed from 2-plate to 3-plate.
- Roll Bars – Front from 1.4mm to 1.2mm. Rear from 1.4mm to 1.8mm. This gave more rotation and more steering. The very thick rear roll bar gave me forward drive and stability exiting corners.
- Yoke changed from 10° to 8° Caster. This provided more initial steering and added some grip to the front axle.
- Front Pin Angle changed from 10° to 8° Kick-up. So Total Caster is 8+8=16°.
- Front Pin Width changed from mid to narrow.
- Front hub spacer changed from high to low.
- Front hub height changed from low to high. This gives more exit steering and slightly less initial, compared to the hub low position.
- Driveshafts changed from kit universals to Roche CVDs.
- Wheelbase reduced in the front, which added some steering.
- Ackermann from mid to forward setting.
- Roll centre:
  - Front outer camber link washers from 4mm to 3.5mm.
  - Rear inner camber link washers from 2mm to 5mm.
  - Rear camber link lengthened by moving ball stud to outermost hole on hub.
- Anti-squat reduced from 2° to 1°.

- Rear strap changed from low pin to high pin.
- C/F shock towers.
- Front topdeck from 2.5mm to 1.6mm S2.
- Centre top deck was fitted.
- Track width reduced by changing front and rear hex from 0mm to −0.75mm.
- Suspension arms changed from kit to flexible, front and rear. Rear arms dremeled and moved 1.0mm forward.
- Shocks:
  - Position
    - Front shocks stood up one position on shock tower from hole 4 to hole 3 (middle). (Number 1 being the outermost hole.)
    - Rear shocks laid down one position on shock tower from hole 4 to hole 5.
  - Springs – Front Blue (3.7 lbs/in), rear Green (2.2 lbs/in). This is my standard spring setup for low-traction in 4WD.
  - Pistons – Front holes drilled out from 1.6mm to 1.7mm. Rear changed from 3 hole at 1.6mm to 2 hole at 2.1mm.
  - Shock Limiters – Front internal limiter added from 0mm to 1mm.
  - Stroke:
    - Front increased from 22mm to 22.2mm.
    - Rear increased from 27.3mm to 28.5mm.
- Total weight: 1,730g.
- Tyres – control tyres with included inserts.
- Motor:
  - LRP X22 7.0T with 12.5mm rotor and 19-degrees end bell timing.
  - FDR 9.24:1.
  - Battery only charged to 8.2V rather than 8.4V.
- ESC LRP Flow-X:
  - Brakes – Auto-brake 15%, Brake Type X, Brake Ramp SP, Initial Brake 3%.
  - Throttle – Initial Drive 1%, Torque Feel 4 (out of 5), Turbo Timing 18°, Ramp 5°/10K RPM, Delay 5K RPM.
- Radio Settings:
  - Throttle EPA 95%, Throttle Expo -10%, Brake EPA 85%.

2WD Modified

1st Spencer Rivkin (Associated), 2nd Davide Ongaro (Associated), 3rd Yusuke Sugiura (Yokomo), 4th Bruno Coelho (Xray), 5th Ryan Maifield (Yokomo), 6th Joona Haatanen (Associated), 7th Martin Bayer (Xray), 8th Ty Tessmann (Xray), 9th Ryan Cavalieri (Yokomo), 10th Neil Cragg (Associated)

After five rounds of qualifying, Spencer Rivkin put his Associated buggy on pole. The current 1/8 nitro world champion Davide Ongaro won A1, with Spencer 2nd and Bruno Coelho 3rd. In A2, it was extremely tight, with Spencer taking the win by only half a second from Davide with Ryan Maifield 3rd. It was all on the line in A3, and Spencer drove a superb race to win and take the world championship. Davide 2nd to secure 2nd overall and 3rd in A3 was Yusuke Sugiura. Yusuke's 4th place in A1 was enough to achieve 3rd place overall. With wins in A2 and A3, Spencer locked in his second 2WD world championship.

3rd – Yusuke Sugiura - Yokomo YZ-2 DTM3

Multiple Japanese National champion, Yusuke Sugiura, shares his setup:

The track was very large and the surface was hard and slippery, making it difficult to secure traction. Also, the control tyres had open cell inserts, not the closed cell of today, so we had to find a setting that would work for this situation. We introduced several prototype parts to secure traction as much as possible. In particular, new front tyres were edgy and did not work well, so we used only one set of front tyres all weekend.

Due to the very large and slippery track, we needed to soften the suspension and apply traction more aggressively than we normally would on this type of surface. We determined the ride height by considering the balance between the jump landings and the roll feeling in the corners. Normally, I use the same ride height for both front and rear, but with the track surface being low-grip with undulations, we set the front ride height higher than the rear.

My setup was as follows:
- A JConcepts body with front wing, high clearance rear wing and JConcepts centre divider wing.
- Ride height was set to 24mm front and 22mm rear for this track.
- Standard DTM3 chassis.
- Front and rear camber –2°.
- Front toe 0°.
- Rear toe-in 3.5°.
- Anti-squat 2°.
- Standard Kick-up and 5° caster block.
- Ball diff. Diff height lowered from 2mm to 0mm.
- No roll bars.
- Lay up gear box 2mm.
- Ackermann – Inner steering link ball stud shims reduced from 2mm to 1mm.
- Shocks:
    - Oil – Front 35 WT, rear 32.5 WT.
    - Springs – Front Orange (YS-A750), rear KY White.
    - Pistons – Front 1x1.6mm, rear 2x1.7mm.
    - Limiters – Front internal 1mm and external 2mm. Rear internal 1mm and external 0mm.
    - Stroke – Front 20mm, rear 27.5mm. Long eyelets on both.
- Roll centre – Rear camber link outer shim from 3mm to 2mm.
- Motor – Muchmore 7.5T with FDR 9.45:1.
- ESC Muchmore Fleta Pro V2.

4th – Bruno Coelho and 7th – Martin Bayer – Xray XB2 '20

Bruno and Martin worked together and ran the same setup. Martin has won multiple national off-road championships (2WD, 4WD and 1/8).

We stayed with the kit dirt setup for:
- Front toe-out 1°.
- Rear toe-in 3°.
- Front and rear camber −2°.
- Kick-up 26° + Caster bushing 5° = total Caster 31°.
- Ball diff.
- 2 pad slipper clutch.
- No roll bars.

Changes from the kit setup:
- A lightweight Xray Alpha2 body was used.
- Front wing installed.
- Rear wing – Xray Rank with center fin added to improve stability.
- Ride height was set to 22mm front and 23mm rear for this track.
- Changed from standard chassis to long chassis (Aluminium 2.5mm).
- Front and rear suspension arms from hard to graphite to increase stiffness.
- C-hub from hard to graphite.
- 60g weight added under the battery because we used the LCG battery and therefore needed to add weight to maintain the same balance.
- Battery placement to the rear.
- Shocks:
  - Oil increased from 500cSt to 550cSt front and rear.
  - Front eccentric shock ball changed from rear to front orientation.
- Wheelbase:
  - Front – Changed from 2mm to 1mm shim to reduce wheelbase to make the car turn in to tight corners more easily.
  - Rear – As far forward as possible.
- Servo linkage ball stud shims from 1mm to 3mm.
- Roll centre – Rear camber link inner shim from 4mm to 3mm.
- Tyres:
  - Front – Pro-Line 4-Rib M3 with stock inserts.
  - Rear – Control tyre.
- Motor:
  - Hobbywing G3 8.5T with 30-degrees end bell timing.
  - FDR 9.4:1.
  - Dynamic timing – boost 0°/turbo 20°.

We were very happy with the setup.

Carpet Case Study

Carpet Setup

By Ray Munday

Tyres

With the high-traction available, carpet front tyres and rims are normally narrower than for dirt. They are designed to give smooth steering without flexing under. You also don't need to run inserts in the front. The most common type is a staggered rib but some use pins.

Rear tyres are often a sharp pin and use closed cell inserts.

Both front and rear are a hard compound and the tread is designed to dig into the track. They can be used with or without traction compound.

Starting Setup

Due to the high-grip and smooth nature of the tracks, carpet setups tend to have much stiffer front springs, heavier oils front and rear, more weight in the front and a much lower ride height.

Driving Style

It is very different to racing on dirt! Your first impression of driving on carpet is the traction. It is much higher than the traction you will experience on dirt tracks, even highly sugared tracks.

You can still feel the car slide around a little and the limit feel is quite smooth, unlike heavily sugared tracks which tend to be very unforgiving at the limit.

You will need to use a smoother style than for dirt and you will also need to use the brakes a lot more. Rather than driving "point and shoot", it is critical to take a racing line through each section. You will also need to use less steering lock in the fast corners, or you will risk getting the car sideways and traction rolling.

Going fast on carpet is a balance between being smooth and aggressive. Too smooth and your lap times will be too slow, too aggressive and you risk traction rolling.

In the low-speed sections you can be a little more aggressive and feel your way up to the traction roll limit but in the higher speed sections you will lose a lot of time if you are too aggressive.

One trick on high-traction surfaces like carpet is to apply the steering a little slower than on dirt. On dirt, the tires have some delay before they grip and the grip level is lower, so you generally need to flick the steering to get the car to turn in. On carpet, the tyre response is much faster and the grip is higher, so if you turn the steering too fast you risk traction rolling as you are turning faster than the chassis can react.

Try working your way up to the limit over a few laps. When the car starts to lift a wheel and feel like it is going to traction roll, you have pretty much found it!

Generally, jumps on carpet tracks are made of wood, with either a carpet or wood face. If you have a track with wooden jump faces you will need to be careful as the level of traction is very low with the hard carpet tires!

Forward traction is very high so you can be aggressive with the throttle, to a point. It is very easy to wheel stand if you are too aggressive and if your slipper clutch is set too tight. In fact slipper clutch setting is critical on these sorts of surfaces. You should set it so that you can accelerate hard with the front tires just coming off the ground. If you have enough weight over the front, you will be able to steer on-power, but with too much throttle it can be easy to get the front very light out of the corner and have strong on-power understeer. So you will need to tailor your driving style to the car setup. It's important to smoothly apply the power until you have completed the corner; after that, full power!

Something you have to be careful of is "diffing out" as the car comes into the corner under brakes. You can brake very hard in a straight line and the car will turn in very strongly, but it is possible to lift a rear inside tyre under brakes and therefore lose some of your braking from the inside tyre. If your diff is too free, this will feel like a sudden loss of braking and the car may feel very unpredictable.

Carpet rewards a smooth transition from braking to cornering.

One of the fun parts of carpet driving is that it's very consistent from lap to lap and day to day. On a dirt track, the traction level can change wildly with sun coverage, ambient temperature, wind, moisture and tyre condition. With carpet I have found it very consistent, allowing you to focus on your lines, your technique, your setup and your consistency.

Wheel Standing

To prevent wheel standing, it is important to have the weight biased towards the front of the car and why you see the mid-motor laydown transmission designs used in conjunction with lots of additional weight at the front bulkhead.

Traction Rolling

To prevent traction rolling, you need to make the car as wide as possible and lower the Centre of Gravity (CG) as much as possible. The easiest way to lower the CG is to run a low ride height. This does help reduce traction rolling but has the downside of poor landing from jumps.

Jumps

Jumps are what separate this from a pure handling exercise and turn setup into a compromise. If there were no jumps, you could run very low ride heights with minimal droop. However, the reality is that carpet tracks often have large jumps and if you can't land off the jump well, you can't get on the power quickly and/or your car will crash on landing.

The car still needs good down travel so that the shock can start absorbing the jump early and needs enough ride height to stop it from bottoming too easily, especially as the carpet tends to "spring" the car up a little if you flat land.

Where a jump is immediately followed by a corner, it is very tempting to turn as soon as the car lands, but if it hasn't settled, then it will often flip over.

When landing a jump on carpet you have to land straight! On dirt, you can get away with landing the car at an angle; in fact if there is a corner directly afterward, you often need to get the car angled towards the apex for the fastest lap. On carpet, if you land at an angle the tyre generates so much grip it will make you roll almost immediately. Don't try "whipping" the car on carpet!

Settings

Ride Height – Around 18mm for 2WD, 16–18 mm for 4WD.

Droop – Similar to a dirt setup. Any less and jump landing suffers.

Weight Bias – With the 2WD, you need a lot of weight up front. Changing components to aluminium and/or adding weight, helps. 60–70g added to the front of the car is not unusual. Of course, if you can remove a similar weight from the rest of the car by using lighter components then this can also help and allows you to place the weight lower down.

Run a shorty battery all the way forward and the ESC right up against the servo. Install a "laydown" transmission to move the motor further forward.

Total Weight – Run it heavy! Adding weight down low helps lower the CG but it also seems to calm the cars down and make them easier to drive. Adding weight under the battery can really help.

Diffs – You can run a ball diff but you will need to tighten it a long way to prevent slippage and then it becomes a little too tight. Gear diffs are therefore the way to go without question. The 4WDs can be sensitive to front oil changes. A centre diff can make the car feel unpredictable on carpet unless very heavy oil is used (e.g. 1 million cSt). I replace the centre diff with a locked/slipper clutch assembly.

Alignment – More camber helps take away grip and reduce traction rolling. 2°–2.5° negative camber is a good starting point. No front toe-in or toe-out. At the rear, less toe-in (start with 1° instead of 3°) helps to smooth out the steering.

Shocks – Run them 5–10 WT heavier than a dirt setup (or reduce the piston hole size) to control the speed of body roll and stop traction rolling.

Springs – Front springs in particular need to be much stiffer than on dirt to minimise body roll and make the car more driveable. I run 4–5 spring rates heavier at the front and 1–2 rates heavier at the rear.

Shock Position – Moving the shocks out on the tower can improve stability and make the car more linear to drive.

Roll Centres – Lower roll centres smooth out the car and make it feel easier to drive with less traction rolling.

Flex – Harder suspension arms make a huge difference to the feel of the car in high-traction. Be careful though, they can be much more brittle than the standard arms, especially in cold weather.

Slipper Clutch – The slipper clutch setting makes a big difference. In the 2WD, set it to just allow wheel stands but soft enough that the front tyres don't get higher than 1–2 inches from a standing start. The more weight you have at the front, the tighter you can run the clutch and the more forward acceleration you will have (up to a point, eventually you will start to wheelspin). In the 4WD, it can help stop the car flipping end over end under brakes.

Power – There is no substitute for power on these surfaces! I use a Reedy 6.5T motor in my 2WD (8.5T on dirt) and a 5.5T in my 4WD (instead of 6.5T). Everything gets hot on carpet due to the high load, so make sure you have plenty of cooling for the ESC and motor.

Wing – With the higher speeds and traction, a lower downforce rear wing helps reduce high-speed understeer.

Roll bars – Run much thicker roll bars.

Starting Setup

If you have not raced at a particular track before, then we recommend starting with your chassis manufacturer's base setup. You may also wish to search your chassis manufacturer's website for another driver's setup at that track so you can note the changes they made. We do not recommend using another driver's setup without knowing why they made the changes they did. However, it can be very useful to note the differences to the manufacturer's base carpet setup and then try each change, one at a time, and note whether it feels better or worse.

Case Studies

Carpet Case Study Race

European Off-road Series (EOS) Round 1 2020, Daun, Germany.

Over 450 entries filled the sports hall in Daun Germany with entries from 13 countries. They were treated to an exciting and challenging layout that rewarded consistency in driving.

Photo courtesy of Red RC (eos.redrc.net/2018/01/track-focus-daun)

Track Conditions

Indoor, carpet, large size, smooth, high-traction. Mixed track with both fast (38m straight) and highly technical sections.

Air Temperature

18°C (64°F)

Special thanks to EOS for the photos. www.eurorcseries.com

Control Tyre

- 4WD – Schumacher Fusion fronts and Schumacher Cactus Yellow rears. Both with medium inserts.
- 2WD – Schumacher Cut Stagger Yellow fronts (no insert) and Schumacher Cactus Yellow rears with Medium insert.

Control Additive

No additive or tyre warmers allowed.

4WD Modified

1st Michal Orlowski (Schumacher), 2nd Bruno Coelho (Xray), 3rd Jorn Neumann (Schumacher), 4th Joona Haatanen (Associated), 5th David Ronnefalk (Hot Bodies), 6th Martin Bayer (Xray), 7th Lee Martin (Yokomo), 8th Daniel Kobbevik (Xray), 9th Micha Widmaier (SWORKz), 10th Bartosz Zalewski (Xray)

Round 1 of the EOS season opener saw 135 entries in 4WD Modified.

TQ and 1st – Michal Orlowski – Schumacher CAT L1 Evo

Michal is a multiple European champion and multiple EOS series champion.

I stayed with the kit dirt setup for:
- Front and rear camber –1°.

The most important changes for carpet were:
- Rear toe-in reduced from 3° to 0.5° to reduce rear grip.
- Ride height was set to 12mm front and rear.
- Tyre Treatment – Rear tyres cut off both the inside and outside row of pins from the surface tread to free the rear of the car. Glued front tyre sidewalls.
- Shocks:
  - Shock oil as kit (front 550cSt and rear 400cSt).
  - Springs – Front changed from Blue to Black. Rear changed from Green to Black.
  - Pistons – Rear changed from black 3 hole to red 2 hole. Front as kit (black 2 hole).
  - Shock Limiters – Front and rear internal limiters as kit (0mm).
  - Rear shock stand-off spacing increased from 0mm to 3mm.
  - Stroke:
    - Front reduced from 22mm to 21.8mm.
    - Rear increased from 27.3mm to 28mm.

- Position – Front shocks stood up one position on shock tower. Rear shocks as kit.

Other changes from the kit setup:
- A Penguin PCB003 body was used with low rear wing and no front wing.
- Roll Bars – Front from 1.4mm to 1.9mm. Rear from 1.4mm to 2.1mm.
- Flex:
  - The Flex chassis was used.
  - Front top deck thickness reduced from 2.5mm to 2mm.
  - Front and rear suspension arms changed from Medium to Carbon.
  - Bumper from Stiff to Carbon.
- Track Width – Rear hex increased from 0mm to 1.5mm.
- Wheelbase – Front changed from Long to Short. Rear changed from Medium to Long.
- Front toe-out decreased from 1° to 0.5°.
- Diff:
  - Oil changed from 12K to 10K front and rear.
  - Diff height rear changed from low to high. Front diff height changed from high to low.
- Battery moved from middle to front position.
- Slipper clutch changed from 2-plate to 3-plate.
- Yoke changed from 10° to 8° Caster. This provided more initial steering and added some grip to the front axle.
- Front Pin Angle changed from 10° to 8° Kick-up. So Total Caster is 8 + 8 = 16°.
- Front Pin Width changed from mid to narrow.
- Front hub spacer changed from high to low.
- Driveshafts changed from kit universals to Roche CVDs.
- Ackermann from mid to forward setting.
- Roll centre:
  - Front outer camber link washers from 2mm to 4mm.
  - Rear inner camber link washers from 2mm to –0.5mm. It is negative because we can raise the rear camber plate. So, positive 2mm lowers the inner ball stud, but when it's negative it's higher because the whole plate is raised (onto which the ball stud is screwed). We do this to achieve more rotation and free the rear of the car.
  - Rear camber link shortened by one hole on the hub.
- Anti-squat reduced from 2° to 1°.
- Rear strap changed from low pin to high pin.
- Gearbox riser fitted.
- Total weight: 1,630g.

- Motor:
  - LRP X22 5.0T with 12.3mm rotor and 24-degrees end bell timing.
  - FDR 11.29:1.
- ESC LRP Flow-X:
  - Brakes – Auto-brake 15%, Brake Type BDX-0, Brake Ramp 70, Initial Brake 5%.
  - Throttle – Initial Drive 5%, Torque Feel 2 (out of 5), Turbo Timing 24°, Ramp 10°/10K RPM, Delay 5K RPM.
- Radio Settings – Throttle EPA 100%, Brake EPA 95%

2nd – Bruno Coelho and 6th – Martin Bayer – Xray XB4 '20

Bruno and Martin worked together and ran the same setup. Martin has won multiple national off-road championships (2WD, 4WD and 1/8).

Xray do not publish a carpet setup for the XB4 '20 or '19, so the comparison has been made with the XB4 '18 carpet setup.

We stayed with the kit setup for:
- Front toe-out 2°.
- Front camber –2° and rear camber –3°.
- Kick-up 8° + C-hub Caster 9° = total Caster 17°.
- Centre slipper clutch.
- Battery position front.
- Rear wing cut to the lowest line.
- All chassis flex screws used in order to minimise flex.

Changes from the kit setup were:
- A lightweight Xray body was used.
- Ride height was set to 13mm front and rear for this track.
- Changed from standard chassis to 2.5mm chassis.
- Rear toe-in from 3° to 2°.
- Diffs – Front oil increased from 10K to 40K, rear increased from 10K to 30K.
- Roll bars – Front increased from 1.3mm to 2mm. Rear increased from 1.2mm to 2mm.
- Bump Steer – Inner shims increased from 2mm to 5mm. Outside shims left at 2mm.
- Anti-squat from 2° to 3°.
- Servo saver changed from Medium to Tight.
- Ackermann – Inner steering link position moved from 1 (rear) to 2 (front).
- Flex:
    - Front steering blocks changed from Medium to Graphite.
    - Front caster block from Hard to Graphite.
    - Rear brace (graphite) added.
    - Front upper plate changed from Standard to Steering Brace.
    - Front and rear suspension arms from Hard to Graphite.
- Track Width – Front and rear offset both changed from 0 slots to 4 slots.
- Roll centre:
    - Rear camber link inner position from 1 (low) to 2 (high). Outer camber link has 4mm of shims.
    - Rear hinge pin height changed from +0.75mm to –0.75mm.
- Shocks:
    - Short shocks used in the front with 5 dot 42mm springs cut to fit and 750 cSt oil. Rear shocks 3 dot 57mm with 650 cSt oil.
    - Rear collar –2mm (this option became publicly available on the XB4 '21).
    - Position – Front suspension arm position changed from inner to outer, laying shocks down.
    - Stroke – Front from 23mm to 22mm, rear from 28mm to 29mm.
    - Limiters – 1mm internal limiter added front and rear. External limiters changed from rear 3mm to 1mm and front from 3mm to 2mm.
    - Shock pistons were not changed – Front 2x1.6mm, rear 2x1.7mm.
- Motor:
    - Hobbywing 5.5 with 30-degrees of end bell timing.
    - FDR 10.65:1.
- ESC:
    - Hobbywing XR10 Pro.

You can see photos of Bruno's World Champion winning dirt XB4 '20 on page 20.

2WD Modified

1st Michal Orlowski (Schumacher), 2nd Lee Martin (Yokomo), 3rd Bruno Coelho (Xray), 4th Micha Widmaier (SWORKz), 5th Martin Bayer (Xray), 6th David Ronnefalk (Hot Bodies), 7th Joona Haatanen (Associated), 8th Jorn Neumann (Schumacher), 9th Marcel Schneider (Schumacher), 10th Elias Johansson (Hot Bodies)

There were 164 entries in 2WD Modified.

Michal Orlowski fought back from a mistake in A1 to take the win from Lee Martin. In A2 Michal was unchallenged and took the overall win. In A3 Lee fought a long battle with Bruno Coelho and won to secure second spot on the podium; Bruno coming home in third for Xray.

TQ and 1st – Michal Orlowski – Schumacher Cougar LD

Michal is a multiple European champion and multiple EOS series champion.

I stayed with my kit carpet setup (as shown on petitrc.com) for:

- Ride height 14mm.
- Front toe-out 0°.
- Rear toe-in 1.5°.
- Anti-squat 2°.
- Caster 5° Yoke.
- Low rear wing.
- Kit side pods.
- 3 plate slipper clutch.
- Roll bar – Front none, rear 1.2mm.
- Diff with 7K oil and 2 gears (but changed height from mid to high).
- Battery posts forward, battery in front position.
- Shocks – Front 550 cSt, Black springs, 3x1.5mm pistons. Rear 400 cSt, black springs, 3x1.6mm, but some changes made to the rear shock setup as listed below.

Case Studies 10

The most important changes I make on carpet are the rear toe-in to reduce rear grip, the shock package, ride height and modifying the rear tyres by removing the inside and outside stagger pins from the tread.

Changes from the kit setup:
- Shocks – Kit setup as listed above, but changed rear stroke from 28.5mm to 28mm, removed 0.5mm rear internal limiter and changed rear shock position on tower from fully laid down (position 5) to position 4.
- An Aerox body was used with no front wing.
- Changed to a –5mm chassis (U7679).
- Camber – Front reduced from –1.5° to –1°. Rear left at –1°.
- Total weight of 1,520g:
    - 18g under the servo.
    - Trishbits nose weight.
    - Brass electric plate.
    - Brass weights moved from chassis front to under radio tray.
    - Motor plate from alloy to carbon fibre.
- Flex – X-Brace with centre post.
- Track Width – Rear hex reduced from 1.5mm to 0mm. Front hex –0.75mm.
- Ackermann – Internal steering link shims from 2mm to 1mm.
- Roll centre:
    - Front inner camber link washers from 0mm to –2mm. It's negative 2 because we used a modified front camber plate to lower the front inner ball

stud to achieve more steering. It says –2 because it's 2mm lower than you could go with the standard camber plate.
    - Rear inner camber link washers from 6mm to 4mm.
    - Rear camber link lengthened by one hole on hub.
    - Rear pin height from high to low.
- Motor:
    - LRP X22 5.5T with 12.7mm rotor and 24.5-degrees end bell timing.
    - FDR 10.12:1.
- ESC LRP Flow-X:
    - Brakes – Auto-brake 15%, Brake Type BDX-0, Brake Ramp 70, Initial Brake 3%.
    - Throttle – Initial Drive 3%, Torque Feel 2 (out of 5), Turbo Timing 24°, Ramp 10°/10K RPM, Delay 10K RPM.

2nd – Lee Martin – Yokomo YZ-2 CAL3

Lee is a six times European Champion, thirteen times National Champion and three times EOS Champion.

- JConcepts P2K body with an LMR27 rear wing and LMR front wing.
- Gear diff (2 gear) with 100K oil at height 3. LC Transmission. This made the biggest difference to the car's handling.
- Ride height was set to 17mm front and rear.
- Front toe-out 1°.
- Caster block 5°.
- Rear toe-in 3°.
- Anti-squat 2°.
- Camber –2° front and rear.
- Roll Bars – Front 1mm and rear 1.4mm.
- Battery position forward (kit position).
- Total weight of 1,573g including 50g under the battery.
- Track Width – Front hex 4.3mm, rear hex 5mm.
- Axle Height – Rear 0.5mm up.
- Roll centre:
    - Rear outer camber link ball stud shim reduced from 3mm to 2mm.
    - Rear suspension arm hinge pin height lowered.
- Shocks:
    - Position – Middle (kit) position on the towers front and rear. Rear shocks stood up on suspension arm from outside position to next position towards chassis.
    - Springs – Front was changed to Racing Performance RP-103PU Purple (a medium spring) and rear to RP-089PU Purple (a hard spring).

- Case Studies

        - Oil – Front 42.5 WT and rear 37.5 WT.
        - Pistons – Front 2x1.6mm and rear 2x1.8mm.
        - Shock Limiters – internal 1mm front and rear. No external limiters.
        - Eyelets – Front short, rear long.
        - Stroke – Front 22mm, rear 28mm.
- Motor:
        - Scorpion 5.5T motor with 12.3mm rotor and 30-degrees of end bell timing.
        - FDR 10.4:1.
- ESC Scorpion Vanguard with 15° boost and 25° turbo.

3rd – Bruno Coelho and 5th – Martin Bayer – Xray XB2 '20

Bruno and Martin worked together and ran the same setup. Martin has won multiple national off-road championships (2WD, 4WD and 1/8).

We stayed with the kit carpet setup for:
- Front toe-out 1°.
- Front and rear camber –2°.
- Anti-squat 2°.
- 3 pad slipper clutch.
- Front LCG Gearbox.
- A lightweight Xray Beta2 body was used.

Changes from the kit setup:
- Ride height was set to 14mm front and rear for this track.
- Changed from standard chassis to short chassis (Aluminium 2.5mm).
- Wings – Front wing added to the upper deck. Rear wing Xray Tec cut to the lowest rear and side lines.
- Kick-up reduced to 23° + Caster bushing 5° = total Caster 28°.
- Rear toe-in reduced from 3° to 2°.
- Track Width – Front reduced from 0mm to –0.75mm.
- Roll Bars – Added front 0.8mm and rear 1mm.

- Gear diff oil from 5K to 8K and changed from 4 gears to 2. Height high (kit).
- Weight:
    - Front arm mount and bell crank arms changed from Composite to Aluminium.
    - Front roll center holder from Hard to Aluminium.
    - 45g weight added under the battery because we used the LCG battery and therefore needed to add weight to maintain the same balance.
    - 17g added under the ESC.
    - Servo moved forward one position from position 4 (rear) to 3.
- Battery holder to the front (position 1, long side front) with battery at position 5 (slightly rear of middle).
- Ackermann – Steering arm reduced from 2 slots to 1 slot. Inner steering link shims from 0mm to 2mm.
- Servo linkage ball stud shims from 1mm to 5mm.
- Flex:
    - Caster block from Hard to Graphite.
    - Rear upright from Hard to Aluminium.
    - Front and rear suspension arms from Hard to Graphite.
- Shocks:
    - Oil – Front decreased from 500 cSt to 550 cSt. Rear increased from 450 cSt to 500 cSt.
    - Springs – Front from 3 dots to 2 dots (42mm). Rear 2 dots (kit).
    - Pistons, Shock Body, Eyelets and Internal Limiters as kit.
    - External Limiters – Front from 2mm to 5mm. Rear from 4mm to 2mm.
    - Stroke – Front from 22mm to 24mm. Rear from 29mm to 31mm.
    - Position – Front laid down on shock tower from position 3 (outside) to 2 (middle).
- Wheelbase – Front changed from 0mm to 2mm shims. Rear from 0mm to 1mm.
- Roll centre – Rear camber link inner shim from 2mm to 4mm and rear outer link from 4mm to 2mm. Changed Rear Roll Centre Holder to #323043 and used hole 2 (forward and shorter camber link length). Rear hinge pin height from –0.75mm to +0.75mm.
- Motor:
    - Hobbywing G3 6T with 30-degrees end bell timing.
    - FDR 8.99:1.

Astroturf Case Study

Starting Setup

If you have not raced at a particular track before, then we recommend starting with your chassis manufacturer's base setup. Most manufacturers will not publish a base astroturf setup so start with their carpet setup. You may also wish to search your chassis manufacturer's website for another driver's setup at that track so you can note the changes they made. We do not recommend using another driver's setup without knowing why they made the changes they did. However, it can be very useful to note the differences to the manufacturer's base carpet setup and then try each change, one at a time, and note whether it feels better or worse.

Race

European Off-road Series (EOS) Round 2 2020, Arena 33, Andernach, Germany.

Track Conditions

Outdoor, medium size, high-traction, bumpy, astroturf, dry. Mixed track with both fast and technical sections. Air temperature 20°C (68°F).

Control Tyre

- 4WD – Schumacher Mini Dart front and rear.
- 2WD – Schumacher Mini Dart rear and Schumacher Cut Stagger front.

Control Additive

No additive allowed.

Special thanks to EOS for the photos.
www.eurorcseries.com

4WD Modified

1st Jorn Neumann (Schumacher), 2nd Bruno Coelho (Xray), 3rd Michal Orlowski (Schumacher), 4th Hupo Honigl (Xray), 5th Martin Bayer (Xray), 6th Micha Widmaier (SWORKz), 7th Wesley Van Helmond (Schumacher), 8th Max Götzl (Xray), 9th Jesper Rasmussen (Associated), 10th Aaron Munster (Xray)

Race summary courtesy of EuroRCSeries.com:

A1 saw a great battle between Coelho and Neumann, with Coelho leading the first half of the race before a small slide gave Neumann the small chance he needed to move through and take the lead. Although Coelho didn't let him get away, the Portuguese driver couldn't find a way through and ended up less than half a second behind at the line.

In A2, it was time for the mistake to come from Neumann, an error on lap four pushed him back a few places. Out front, Coelho was then being chased by Orlowski and just before half distance, the Xray driver made a small error and allowed the Schumacher pilot into the lead. But the race wasn't over, and a few laps later Orlowski returned the favour and Coelho was back to the lead and took the victory by just one tenth of a second. Behind, Neumann had recovered to third.

This meant any of the top three drivers could take the overall win in A3, but Coelho's chances faded quickly as he dropped to the back of the pack on lap one. Out front, the Schumacher duo circulated comfortably clear of the field and, although Orlowski kept Neumann honest, it was clear that the German driver was in control and ran out to take the overall victory and complete the "double" win of 4WD and 2WD at this event.

2nd – Bruno Coelho and 5th – Martin Bayer – Xray XB4 '21

Bruno and Martin worked together and ran the same setup. Martin has won multiple national off-road championships (2WD, 4WD and 1/8).

We stayed with the kit carpet setup for:
- Front toe-out 1°.
- Front and rear camber –2°.
- Centre slipper clutch.
- Anti-squat 2°.
- Roll bars 1.8mm front and rear.
- Bump Steer – Inner shims 5mm. Outside shims 2mm.
- An Xray Gamma 4C body was used (lightweight).

Changes from the kit setup were:
- Rear wing cutting line from 2 to 1 (lowest).
- Ride height was set to 15mm front and 16mm rear for this track.
- Changed from standard chassis to 2.5mm chassis.
- Rear toe-in from 2° to 3°.
- Kick-up 7° + C-hub Caster 12° = total Caster 19°.
- Diffs – Front and rear oil decreased from 10K to 8K. Rear diff height changed from 2 dots high to 3 dots high (highest).
- Driveshaft – front from CVD to ECS.
- Flex:
    - Front steering blocks changed from Hard to Graphite.
    - Front caster block from Hard to Aluminium.
    - Front T-brace screws added in outer position.
    - Front and rear suspension arms from Hard to Graphite.
    - Steering plate changed from Hard to Graphite.
    - Rear upright from Hard to Aluminium.
- Suspension Arms – Front and rear changed from Short to Long.
- Track Width – Front hex offset changed from 0 slots to 2. Rear from 0 to 3.
- Roll centre – Rear outer camber link from 4mm to 2mm of shims.
- Shocks:
    - Springs – Front 2 dot changed to 3 dot. Rear 3 dot changed to 2 dot.
    - Oil – Front reduced from 700 cSt to 600 cSt. Rear from 550 cSt to 400 cSt.
    - Rear collar changed from Standard to –2mm.
    - Position – Front and rear suspension arm positions changed from inner to outer, laying front and rear shocks down.
    - Stroke – Unchanged (Front 22mm, rear 27mm).
    - Limiters – 2mm external limiter removed from front.
    - Shock pistons were not changed – Front 2x1.6mm, rear 2x1.7mm.

- Motor:
  - Hobbywing G3 5.5T with 30-degrees of end bell timing.
  - FDR 11.25:1.
- ESC – Hobbywing XR10 Pro.
- Tyre treatment:
  - Front – Glue on sidewall, cut 3 out of tyre, cut 1 in on insert.
  - Rear – Cut 1 out of tyre, cut 1 in on insert.

Bruno chases the leader Jorn Neumann over a jump

8th – Max Götzl – Xray XB4 '21

Max is the 2021 Czech National Champion in 1/8 scale (electric and nitro).

I started with the kit carpet setup for:
- Front toe-out 1°.
- Standard chassis.
- Anti-squat 2°.
- Bump steer.
- Centre slipper clutch with kit settings.
- Wheelbase.
- Ackermann.

Changes that made the biggest difference were:
- Short Suspension Arms front and rear. This makes the car easier to drive, especially in bumpy conditions. Track width settings changed to maintain the cars width: front offset changed from 0 to 3 and rear offset changed from 0 to 4. Front hinge pin width changed from +1.5mm to –1.5mm.
- Increased Caster: Kick-up 7° + C-hub Caster 12° = total Caster 19°.
- Adding the T brace outer screws (noted under Flex below).
- Diffs – Front and rear oil increased from 10K to 15K. Rear diff height changed from 1 dot high to 3 dots high (highest). Front diff height high (highest).

Other changes from the kit carpet setup were:
- A lightweight Xray Gamma 4CL body was used.
- Rear wing settings as kit except rear line cut at lowest line (1 rather than 2).
- Ride height was set to 16mm (front and rear) for this track.
- Front camber changed from −2° to −1.5°. Rear camber −2°.
- Rear toe-in from 2° to 3°.
- Roll bars – Front and rear decreased from 1.8mm to 1.6mm.
- Servo saver changed from Medium to Tight.
- Flex:
    - Added outer T brace screws.
    - Front steering blocks changed from Hard to Graphite.
    - Front caster block from Hard to Aluminium.
    - Rear upright changed from Hard to Aluminium.
    - All chassis flex screws used in order to minimise flex.
    - Front and rear arms from Hard to Graphite (and from Short to Long).
- Roll centre – Outer camber link shims reduced from 4mm to 2mm.
- Shocks:
    - Springs – Front 4 dots changed to 2 dots. Rear 3 dots to 2 dots.
    - Oil – Front 700 cSt changed to 600 cSt. Rear from 550 cSt to 400 cSt.
    - Position – Front suspension arm position changed from inner (1) to outer (2), laying shocks down. Rear suspension arm position changed from outer (2) to inner (1), standing shocks up.
    - Stroke – Front from 22mm to 24mm, rear from 27mm to 29mm.
    - Limiters – Rear changed internal from 2mm to 0mm and external from 0mm to 2mm. Front 0mm internal and 2mm external.
    - Shock pistons were not changed – Front 2x1.6mm, rear 2x1.7mm.
- Driveshafts – Front changed from CVD to ECS.
- Motor:
    - Hobbywing 5.5T with 35-degrees of end bell timing.
    - FDR 10.65:1.
- ESC Hobbywing G2 with 7° boost and 20° turbo.
- Tyre treatment – Front Tyres: Cut some pins from tyre to lower traction and reduce the steering and roll of the front of the car, making it easier to drive.

9th – Jesper Rasmussen – Associated RC10B74

Jesper is the 2021 Danish National Champion (4WD and 2WD).

I stayed with the kit carpet setup of:
- Front and rear diff oil 10K.
- Front and rear chassis brace screws.
- Diff heights front and rear at 0mm.
- Anti-squat 2°.

Changes from the kit carpet setup:
- A JConcepts kit lightweight body was used. Front wing removed. JConcepts Aero rear wing cut low with 0° wing angle. Rear wing mount lowered using a Dremel.
- Ride height was set to 15mm front and rear.
- Camber – Front from –1° to –1.5°. Rear from –1° to –2°.
- Front toe-out from 0° to 1°.
- Rear toe-in reduced from 3° to 2°.
- Centre diff with 500K oil. This made a big difference at this track. The car was very nervous under braking when I used the slipper clutch.
- Kick-up 8° + Caster block 10° = total Caster 18°. Changing the Caster block from 9° to 10° is a good option to help with corner entry and at mid-corner. It gives a little more on-power steering. I like that on bumpy high-grip tracks where it's important to have an easy car to drive.
- Roll bar – Front from 1.7mm to 1.8mm. Rear from 1.6mm to 1.8mm.
- Arm Sweep – Front arms set to maximum arm sweep.
- Flex:
    - Front and rear arms changed to Hard.
    - Top Plate Brace not used.
- MSP Battery mount, fully forward. The MSP battery system provides more equal flex in the car due to its o-ring system.
- Track Width – Rear increased from 5mm hex to 6mm.
- Front Axles changed from CVA to DCV.
- Rear CVA bone length increased from 62mm to 66mm with shims 1mm in.
- Rear hub spacing from Mid to Back.
- Axle Height – Front from +3mm to +2mm. Rear from 0mm to +1mm. This made the car easier to drive.
- Bump Steer – This setting is sensitive to the size of tyres. So is it is important to work with bump steering shims inner and outer to tune for the tyres at each track:
    - Steering link outer ball stud spacing shim changed from 1mm to 0mm.

- o Steering link inner ball stud spacing reduced from 3mm to 0mm. This provides a lot more direct steering going into the corner which suits my driving style. Other drivers might prefer a setting nearer to 1mm.
- Roll centre:
  - o Front outer camber link ball stud shim decreased from 2mm to 1mm.
  - o Rear inner camber link ball stud hole from position 2 (mid) to 1 (low).
  - o Rear axle pin height from 0mm to –0.7mm.
  - o Rear camber link length increased by changing camber link spacing shim from 2mm to 1mm.
- Shocks:
  - o Ruddog low shock towers used and AE 2WD shocks used front and rear.
  - o Front shocks laid down one position from 2 (mid) to 1 (inner) on shock tower.
  - o Oil – Front reduced from 50 WT to 40 WT. Rear from 35 WT to 30 WT. I prefer a soft car compared to many other drivers so others may wish to go 2.5–5 WT harder oil than I use.
  - o Springs – As kit.
  - o Pistons – Front 2x1.6mm. Rear increased from 2x1.7mm to 2x1.75mm. This small change made a big difference in the bumpy part of track, allowing the rear to remain in contact with the surface more of the time.
  - o Shock Limiters – internal 1mm limiters removed front and rear.
  - o Stroke – Front reduced from 24mm to 22mm. Rear from 29mm to 28mm.
  - o Eyelets long (kit).
  - o Cup Offset – Rear changed from 5mm to 0mm. Front 5mm.
- Motor:
  - o Reedy Sonic M4 6T with 30° end bell timing.
  - o FDR 9.75:1. I started with a 19T pinion but changed to a 20T to provide a little more top speed.
- ESC Reedy Blackbox 510R with 3° boost and 15° turbo.

2WD Modified

1st Jorn Neumann (Schumacher), 2nd Max Götzl (Xray), 3rd Bruno Coelho (Xray), 4th Martin Bayer (Xray), 5th Michal Orlowski (Schumacher), 6th Hupo Honigl (Xray), 7th Marcel Schneider (Associated), 8th Wesley Van Helmond (Schumacher), 9th Micha Widmaier (SWORKz), 10th Aaron Munster (Xray)

Race summary courtesy of EuroRCSeries.com:

The A Finals were a battle between Coelho and Neumann, as the two fastest qualifiers circulated up to half a second per lap quicker than the rest of the closely matched field. In A1, Bruno made full use of his pole position to lead every lap of the race, with Jorn keeping him honest but ultimately having to settle for second place.

In A2, Coelho immediately had to drive at 100% to keep the German behind him. This led to an early mistake from the two-time 4WD World Champion, leaving Neumann out front and Gotzl up to second. There was no change up front, as Neumann built a lead of around three seconds and took a controlled win. Coelho fought back through the pack, but was only able to reach fifth place by the buzzer.

The showdown in A3 never materialised, as a mistake from Coelho on lap one again dropped him down the order, leaving Neumann to control the race and build a comfortable lead. Gotzl made the most of the error from his teammate to take over second place, which he would hold until the finish and thus secure the overall runner up spot.

Above: Max's entries in 2WD, Stadium Truck and 4WD

2nd – Max Götzl – Xray XB2 '20

Max is the 2021 Czech National Champion in 1/8 scale (electric and nitro).

I started with the kit carpet setup of:
- Front toe-out 1°.
- Rear toe-in 3°.
- Anti-squat 2°.
- No roll bars.
- 3 pad slipper clutch.
- Chassis Aluminium 2.5mm standard length.
- Front LCG Gearbox.
- Kick-up 26° + Caster bushing 5° = total Caster 31°.

Changes that made the biggest difference were:
- Weight:
  - Front roll center holder from Hard to Aluminium.
  - Front arm mount from Composite to Aluminium.
  - 70g weight added under the battery.
  - 17g added under the ESC.
  - Servo moved forward one position from position 4 (rear) to 3 and 20g added.
- Front wing added to the upper deck.
- Diff changed from gear diff to ball diff and diff height from Highest (3 dots) to next highest position (2 dots).

Other changes from the kit carpet setup:
- A lightweight Xray XB2 '21 D body was used. Rear wing cut to the lowest rear and side lines.
- Ride height was set to 16mm front and rear for this track.
- Battery holder position 1 (front), long side rear, with battery at position 5 (slightly rear of middle).

- Front and rear camber changed from –2° to –1°.
- Flex:
  - Caster block from Hard to Graphite.
  - Rear upright from Hard to Aluminium (with camber ball stud hole facing the hex).
  - Front and rear suspension arms from Hard to Graphite.
- Shocks:
  - Oil – Rear decreased from 450 cSt to 350 cSt. Front 550 cSt (kit).
  - Springs – Front from 3 dots to 2 dots.
  - Pistons – Front 2x1.6mm, rear 2x1.7mm (both as kit). Tried making piston holes conical (homemade change) but no noticeable difference.
  - Shock body and shaft changed from short to long.
  - Eyelets as kit.
  - Limiters – Front and rear, internal and external limiters as kit.
  - Stroke – Front from 22mm to 24mm. Rear from 29mm to 31.5mm.
  - Position – Front laid down on shock tower from position 3 (outside) to 2 (middle).
  - Rear eccentric shock ball changed from front-to-rear orientation.
- Wheelbase – Reduced: Front changed from 0mm to 2mm shims. Rear from 0mm to 2mm.
- Roll centre:
  - Rear camber link inner shim from 2mm to 1mm.
  - Front camber link length increased by changing outer ball stud location from 1 (inner) to 2 (outer).
  - Changed Rear Roll Centre Holder to #323043 and used hole 2 (forward and shorter camber link length).
- Motor:
  - Hobbywing G3 6.5T with 30-degrees end bell timing.
  - FDR 8.99:1.
- ESC Hobbywing G2 with no boost and 18°turbo.
- Tyre treatment – Rear Tyres: Cut one row of pins from the inside and outside to gain more rotation in 180 turns.

5th – Michal Orlowski – Schumacher Cougar LD

Michal is a multiple European champion and multiple EOS series champion.

I stayed with my kit carpet setup (as shown on petitrc.com) for:
- Front toe-out 0°.
- Caster 5° Yoke (changed to alloy).
- 3 plate slipper clutch.
- Rear wing gurney cut to lower line.
- Kit side pods.

You can see Michal's carpet setup for this car (EOS Round 1) on page 267.

The changes which made the biggest difference were rear toe-in, ride height and shock setup.

Changes from the kit setup:
- A Penguin Laydown body was used with no front wing.
- Changed to a –5mm chassis (U7679).
- Ride height 16mm.
- Rear toe-in from 1.5° to 2.5°.
- Camber – Front reduced from –1.5° to –1°. Rear left at –1°.
- Anti-squat from 2° to 1°.
- Roll bars – Not used.
- Diff with 10K oil and 2 gears (changed height from mid to low).
- Flex – No X-Brace used. Rear Link mount from Alloy to Kit.
- Track Width – Rear hex increased from 1.5mm to 3mm. Front hex –0.75mm.
- Ackermann – Internal steering link shims from 2mm to 1mm.
- Total weight of 1,530g:
  - 18g under the servo.
  - No nose weight.
  - Brass electric plate.
  - Brass weights moved from chassis front to under radio tray and added 60g under Lipo.
  - Motor plate from alloy to carbon fibre.
- Battery posts from forward to rearwards and battery position from front-to-rear with Klinik battery cradle.
- Roll centre:
  - Front inner camber link washers from 0mm to 1mm.
  - Rear inner camber link washers from 6mm to 2mm.
  - Rear camber link lengthened by one hole on hub.
- Shocks:
  - Oil – Front from 550 cSt to 500 cSt, rear from 400 cSt to 350 cSt.
  - Springs – Rear from Black springs to Red progressive. Front Black.
  - Pistons – Rear from 3x1.6mm to 3x1.8mm, front 3x1.5mm.

- o Stroke – Front from 20.5mm to 22.2mm. Rear 28.5mm.
- o Limiters – Removed all internal limiters. No external limiters (o-rings).
- o Position – Changed rear shock position on tower from fully laid down (position 5) to position 4.
- o Other – Shock Cap Aeration front and rear. Shock Top Stand-off Spacing rear 3mm.
- Hubs – Front hub height from Low to Middle. Rear from outer pin position to inner (on the arm).
- Wheelbase – Front from 3mm to 4.5mm. Rear from Long to Medium.
- Motor:
  - o LRP X22 6.0T with 12.7mm rotor and 19.5-degrees end bell timing.
  - o FDR 8.8:1.
- ESC LRP Flow-X:
  - o Brakes – Auto-brake 15%, Brake Type BDX-0, Brake Ramp SP, Initial Brake 3%.
  - o Throttle – Initial Drive 1%, Torque Feel 4 (out of 5), Turbo Timing 18°, Ramp 3°/10K RPM, Delay 15K RPM.
- Battery – Only charged to 8.2V.
- Tyres – I cut the outside and inside row of pins from the rear tyres. No insert used in the front.

Above: Michal pressures teammate Jorn Neumann

1/8 Case Study

Race

2021 Mugen Challenge, LCRC Raceway, Pennsylvania, USA. 383 entries.

Track Conditions

Outdoor, large, low-medium traction, smooth, low dust on the racing line (dusty off the racing line), hardpacked, dry.

There was loam outside of the race line but as long as you stayed on the line it was fairly dust-free. All the dirt on the track was pretty well tamped down. For the majority of qualifying it was dry, with a little moisture at night. The organisers watered the track from time to time to help the surface hold together and to keep dust down. They would blow off the track before applying water, but as it dried out there would be more dust.

Unfortunately, the A-mains were rained out and the meeting was called on qualifying.

Temperature

Air 29°C (85°F).

Control Tyre

Tyres were open.

Case Studies 10

1/8 eBuggy

1st Adam Drake (Mugen Seiki), 2nd Jason Schreffler (Hot Bodies), 3rd Paul Ciccarello (Xray), 4th Gaven Gibler (Xray), 5th Gavin Vucina (Xray), 6th Bryan Kata, 7th Niko Pribojan, 8th Jared Bardin, 9th Kyra Bach, 10th Colin Morse III (Associated)

There were 51 entries in eBuggy.

1st – Adam Drake – Mugen Seiki MBX8 Eco

Adam is a 3xROAR National 1/8 Buggy Champion.

I stayed with the kit dirt setup for:
- Front Suspension:
  - Upper Arm Spacer 2mm.
  - Upper Plate E2148D.
  - Kingpin ball spacer top and bottom 1mm.
  - Kick-up.
- Front toe-out 1°.
- Rear toe-in 7° (kit).
- Tension Rod.

Changes from the kit setup:
- A JConcepts Silencer body with JConcepts F21 wing on E2428 +15mm wing mount (using kit positioning/holes). The JConcepts body has additional steering over the stock Mugen body. The F21 wing has slightly less downforce and is much better for jumping in windy conditions.
- Ride height was set to 25mm front and 26mm rear for this track. This is my standard setting for ride height for the MBX8 Eco.
- Roll bars – Front reduced from 2.3mm to 2.2mm. Rear reduced from 2.7mm to 2.4mm. The thinner roll bars allowed the car to roll more and help generate more grip.
- Camber:
  - Rear camber reduced from –3° to –2°.

- o Front −2.75° using a 1mm washer for the upper and lower arm. This is our standard setting for most tracks.
- Wheelbase:
  - o Front and rear lower arm spacers increased from 0mm to 1mm.
  - o Rear upright spacer reduced from 2.5mm to 1mm.
- Track Width – Front increased from E0240 (1mm) to E0241 (2mm).
- Flex:
  - o Lower Arm Plate Front changed from E2144A,B (kit) to E2155 1.2mm. Lower Arm Plate Rear changed from E2144A,B (kit) to E2157 1.2mm.
- Front Suspension:
  - o E2168 −3mm front upright arms improves the initial steering response and makes the car more stable through the middle and exit of the corner.
  - o Upper arm position from mid to low.
- Ackermann – Inner steering link hole moved rearwards from position 3 to position 4 (out of 5).
- Anti-squat – 2° (lower arm position from mid to low).
- Servo saver arm changed from E2301A to E2310 (aluminium).
- Shocks:
  - o Oil – Rear reduced from 550 cSt to 400 cSt. Front 550 cSt (kit).
  - o Pistons – Front and rear from E2525 (8 hole x 1.3mm) to MIP 6 hole.
  - o Springs – Front slightly heavier from 9 lb (E2517) to 9.25 lb (Clear Valve). Rear 10.5 lb E0554 (kit).
  - o Position – Front laid down one hole from position 3 to position 4 (out of 5). Rear kept at position 3 (kit).
  - o Pivot ball position and damper stays as kit, front and rear.
  - o Emulsion caps front and rear.
- Rebound Stop (Droop) – Rear reduced from 117mm to 114.5mm. Front 104mm (as kit). Measurements are from the centre of the ball studs at the top and bottom of the shock.
- Roll centre – rear camber link length increased by changing ball stud hole from mid to outer.
- Axle Height – rear hinge pin location changed from bottom to top on the hub.
- Center driveshafts changed from E2261, E2262 to E2228, E2229.
- Weight – Added 20g ballast at the rear centre.
- Diff oil:
  - o Front from 5K to 10K.
  - o Centre from 5K to 10K.
  - o Rear from 2K to 7K.
- Tyres – JConcepts Stalker (Blue and A2) front and rear with standard inserts. Blue compound was used when there was still some moisture in the track (darker colour). When the track dried out (lighter colour) I made the switch to the A2 compound. I didn't used additive or tyre warmers.

- Motor:
    - Tekin 1900KV Gen 3 with factory motor timing.
    - Gearing – Front and rear diff gears both 44/13T (kit) with a 16T pinion (kit). Changed centre diff gear from 46T to 44T which provides smoother power delivery and more top-end.
- ESC Tekin RX8 Gen 3 with 5° of dynamic timing.

10th – Colin Morse III – Associated RC8B3.2e

The biggest changes I made were roll bar, shock pistons, and diff fluid. Thinner roll bars let the car roll more on lower grip and carry more speed through the corners. The shock pistons and oil gave me better handling in the bumps, high-speed corners, and high temperatures because they gave the car more support overall. The pistons also helped over the bigger jumps. The thicker diff fluid helped the car to not diff out when the grip and heat came up. Thicker fluid in the front made the car turn less on-throttle. Thicker in the centre gave the car more acceleration out of the corners. Thicker rear fluid gave the car more stability in the rear and kept the car from randomly breaking traction in the corners. It also gave the rear less grip when the heat and grip came up.

- A Bittydesign Vision body with AE high wing was used.
- Ride height was set to 24mm front and 26mm rear for this track.
- Front toe-out 3°.
- Rear toe-in 3.2° (kit).
- Roll bars – Front 2mm. Rear 2.4mm.
- Wheelbase – Front wheelbase shim 1mm. Rear 0mm.
- Track Width – Front reduced from +1mm to 0mm. Rear hex +1mm (kit)
- Anti-squat – increased from 2° to 3°.

- Front Suspension:
    - Upper Arm Mount pills higher front and rear reducing initial steering but providing more through the middle to exit of the corner. If you reduce the upper arm height you'll get more initial steering and less mid to exit.
    - Lower Arm Mount pills – B pill moved from centre to top position. A pill centre position (kit) reducing kick-up by 1°.
- Camber:
    - Rear camber –2°.
    - Front camber – upper ball shim 1.4mm, lower ball shim 1mm.
- Ackermann – Inner steering link hole forwards (closest to front). Steering arm plate +2. Both as kit.
- Flex:
    - Suspension arm inserts graphite, front and rear.
    - Chassis braces – short, front and rear.
    - Suspension arms – all changed from kit to heavy duty arms.
    - Gearboxes changed to heavy duty.
- Driveshafts – CVAs front and rear.
- Shocks:
    - Oil – Front increased from 35 WT to 42.5 WT. Rear increased from 30 WT to 40 WT.
    - Pistons – Changed from kit 8 hole x 1.2mm front and rear to: front 2x1.4mm and 3x1.5mm (5 holes total) and rear 3x1.5mm, 2x1.6mm. Schelle pistons used.
    - Springs – Front from AE V2 Blue to AE Grey. Rear from V2 Blue to Hot Bodies Yellow.
    - Bladders – hard, front and rear.
    - Shock Length (Droop) – Rear increased from 124mm to 127mm. Front 105mm (as kit). Measurements are from the centre of the ball studs at the top and bottom of the shock.
- Battery position rearwards 15mm.
- Diff oil:
    - Front from 5K to 10K.
    - Centre from 5K to 10K.
    - Rear from 5K to 7K.
- Tyres – Front and rear AKA Doubledown SSLW compound with red inserts. I didn't use tyre warmers or additive.
- Motor:
    - Tekin 1900KV.
    - Gearing: 46T Spur and 17T Pinion. 44/13 Diff Gears used front and rear to provide more top-end speed.
- ESC Hobbywing SCT. Dynamic timing: 10° of turbo with 0.15s delay.
- Radio Settings – EPA: Throttle 100%, Brake 90%. No throttle or brake Expo.

1/8 eTruggy

1st Paul Ciccarello, 2nd Ian Cameron, 3rd Matt Williard, 4th Ty Payne, 5th Brett Butter, 6th Kevin Siller, 7th Cody Saner, 8th Binh Quan, 9th Cam Romberger, 10th Scott Hartman

There were 58 entries in eTruggy.

3rd – Matt Williard – Xray XT8E '22

I stayed with the kit dirt setup for:
- Ride height was set to 37mm front and 39mm rear.
- Front toe-out 1°.
- Rear toe-in 3°.
- Diff oil – Front 10K, Centre 15K, Rear 5K.
- Ackermann at the inner steering link ball stud was forward (position 3).
- I used the Xray kit body.

Changes from the kit setup:
- Rear wing changed from composite to lexan mounted to the front.
- Roll bars – Front reduced from 2.6mm to 2.2mm. Rear reduced from 3.0mm to 2.6mm.
- Caster – Caster Block 16° (kit) and Caster Bushing from 0° to +1°.
- Track Width – Front narrowed from +2mm to 0mm.
- Kick-up – Reduced by 1°.
- Battery – saddle pack front layout.
- Servo saver from Medium to Tight.
- Shocks – as kit except:
  - Oil – Front increased from 550 cSt to 600 cSt.

- Springs – Changed from Xray 3 dot (front and rear) to front Tekno TKR 8769 and rear Agama 9114.
- Shock Length (Droop) – Front 110mm. Rear 132mm. Measurements are from the centre of the ball studs at the top and bottom of the shock.
- Position:
  - Front moved outwards on suspension arm from inner position 1 to mid-position 2. Moved in on shock tower from outer hole (4) to hole 3. Overall the shocks were laid down slightly.
  - Rear suspension arm position moved from inner (1) to mid (2) laying down the shocks slightly.
- Camber – Front and rear camber reduced from –2° to –1°.
- Wheelbase – shortened by:
  - Front shim in front of arm added from 0mm to 2mm.
  - Rear shim in front of arm removed from 2mm to 0mm.
- Flex:
  - Steering block and C-hub both changed from Composite to Aluminium.
  - Rear upright changed from Medium to Hard.
  - Rear graphite brace added (2-pieces).
  - Rear suspension arms from Medium to Hard.
  - Side guard from Soft to Medium.
- Roll centre:
  - Front camber link outer 2mm shim added on top of caster block and front inner link location lowered/moved away from centreline (position 3 to 5).
  - Rear camber link lengthened: outer hole changed from 1 (inner) to 2 (mid).
- Tyres – Pro-Line M4 Buckshot tyres front and rear with no additive or warmers.
- Motor:
  - Hobbywing Gen3 2250Kv.
  - I ran a 48T spur with a 16T pinion but a 15T might have been better.
- ESC Tekin RX8 Gen3 with no dynamic timing (boost/turbo).

Case Studies 10

5th – Brett Butter – Associated RC8T3.2e

- AE kit body with VP Pro high wing (19mm gap to tower).
- Ride height was set to 22mm front and 24mm rear for this track.
- Front toe-out 3°.
- Rear toe-in 3°.
- Roll bars – Front 2.4mm. Rear 2.8mm.
- Kick-up and Anti-squat as kit.
- Pillow ball adjustment set very loose. Loose pillow balls make the car easier to drive. It keeps the suspension very "accommodating" and it doesn't fight you. This change made the largest impact on handling.
- Camber:
  - Rear camber –2°.
  - Front upper ball shim 0.7mm, lower ball shim 0.35m.
- Wheelbase – Front wheelbase shim 1mm in front of arm, rear 1mm in rear of arm.
- Ackermann – Inner steering link moved from front to middle hole.
- Flex:
  - Suspension arm inserts plastic, front and rear.
  - Chassis Braces – long, front and rear.
- Driveshafts – CVAs front and rear.
- Roll Centre – increased rear camber link length by moving outer ball stud hole outwards on hub from A to B.
- Shocks:
  - Oil as kit: front 40 WT, rear 35 WT.
  - Springs as kit: AE V2 Blue front and rear.
  - Shock Length (Droop) – Rear increased from 128mm to 130mm. Front increased from 107.5mm to 110mm. Measurements are from the centre of the ball studs at the top and bottom of the shock.
- Diff oil – Front 10K, Centre 10K, Rear 5K. All as kit.
- Tyres – VP Pro Frontier SSLW compound front and rear. No tyre additive or tyre warmers used.
- Motor:
  - Tekin 2000KV Truggy.
  - Gearing: 46T Spur and 16T Pinion.
- ESC Tekin RX8 Gen3. 15° of timing boost from 8,000–15,000 RPM.
- Radio Settings – EPA: Throttle 100%, Brake 55%. No Expo on-throttle or brake.

6th – Kevin Siller – Mugen Seiki MBX8T Eco

I stayed with the kit dirt setup for:
- Front toe-out 1°.
- Front Suspension:
  o Upper Arm Spacer 2mm.
  o Kingpin ball spacer top 0mm and bottom 1mm.
  o Upper arm position.
  o Kick-up.
- Rear toe-in.
- Anti-squat.
- Tension Rods front and rear.

The biggest difference in handling is choosing the correct tyre tread pattern and compound based on the track condition. Then I made a number of adjustments to make the car handle the way I like.

Changes from the kit setup:
- I used a Pro-Line body with JConcepts F21 wing on E2428 +15mm wing mount (using 3rd position from top).
- Ride height was set to 35mm front and 36mm rear for this track.
- Roll bars – Front reduced from 2.4mm to 2.0mm. Rear increased from 2.7mm to 2.8mm.
- Camber – Rear –3°. Front approximately –2° to –3°.
- Track Width – Rear increased from E0239 to E0241 (2mm).
- Flex:
  o Lower Arm Plates: Front changed from E2161A,B (kit) to E2166. Rear changed from E2162A,B (kit) to E2167.
  o Carbon shock towers.
- Rear Suspension:
  o Lower arm spacer increased from 0mm to 1mm.
  o Rear hub changed to E2131.
  o Axle Height – rear hinge pin location changed from bottom to top on the hub.
- Front upright arm E2168 –3mm replaced with E2153.
- Ackermann – Inner steering link hole moved rearwards from position 3 to position 4 (out of 5).
- Servo saver arm changed from E2301A to E2310 (aluminium).
- Shocks:
  o Oil – Rear reduced from 600 cSt to 550 cSt. Front 600 cSt (kit).
  o Pistons – Front and rear from E2525 (8 hole x 1.3mm) to MIP 6 hole x 1.3mm with clear front, and blue rear, valves.

- o Springs, Shock Position and Pivot Ball Position – As kit, front and rear.
- o Emulsion caps front and rear.
- Rebound Stop (Droop) – Front increased from 105mm to 106mm. Rear 127mm (as kit). Measurements are from the centre of the ball studs at the top and bottom of the shock.
- Center driveshafts changed to E2268, E2269.
- Diff oil – Centre changed from 10K to 15K. Front 10K and rear 7K (as kit).
- Tyres – Pro-Line Holeshot S3 with included inserts, front and rear.
- Motor:
  - o Tekin 2000KV.
  - o Gearing – Kit spur gear 46T with a 16T pinion.
- ESC Hobbywing with no boost or turbo needed.

Appendix A – eBook

This book is available as an eBook at a discount to those that have already purchased the physical book.

The eBook is available for any device with a web browser: Windows and Mac, iOS and Android, etc.

Additional eBook features include:

- Full-text search.
- Annotate content, including:
    - Highlight text.
    - Add your own notes to any text.
- Annotations are available across all of your devices, i.e. make notes on your phone and they are available on your tablet and computer.
- Cross-referencing is hyperlinked.

Visit www.DaveBStevens.com for details and to purchase.

Appendix B – Glossary

This section explains common terms used in this book (if they are not otherwise explained as part of the relevant chapter).

For a diagram of car parts refer to page 105.

2S/4S	Lipo batteries are made from a number of cells, each with a 4.2V maximum charge. A 2S battery has two cells and a total of 8.4V (used in 1/10 scale). A 4S battery has four cells and a total of 16.8V when fully charged (used in 1/8 scale).
2WD	Two-wheel drive cars typically only drive the rear wheels. Front-wheel drive cars are not common in off-road.
4WD	Four-wheel drive cars drive all four wheels. A driveshaft from the motor to a front differential is required to provide drive to the front wheels. A centre differential or slipper clutch is also used. This adds weight and complexity to the drivetrain in return for significantly better grip.
A, B, C, D Block	The A block (sometimes referred to as FF for Front-Front) holds the front of the front suspension arm hinge pins. The B block (RF) holds the rear of the front suspension arm hinge pins. The C block (FR) holds the front of the rear suspension arm hinge pins and the D block (RR) holds the rear of the rear suspension arm hinge pins. Changing the hinge pin inserts (also called pills) can change settings, including roll centre, track width, anti-dive, rear toe, arm sweep and kick-up.
A-arm	Another term for suspension arm.
Aggressive	An aggressive car has a greater steering response initially.
Bashing	Bashing is racing without rules or regulations, or simply driving and testing the limits of your RC vehicle. Any time you are driving on a surface that is not an RC track, you are bashing.
Bite	Also called grip and traction.

Brushed/ Brushless Motors	Ready-To-Run (RTR) vehicles often come with brushed motors and ESCs to reduce cost. Brushless motors replaced brushed motors in competition from about 2007–2009. Brushless motors are more consistent out of the box, require less maintenance and can have their timing set dynamically (refer to *ESC Settings* on page *158*). NB: A brushed ESC will not necessarily drive a brushless motor (check the manual).
Corner Entry	Corner entry is when you first turn-in to a corner until you stop turning the steering wheel on your radio. The car begins to roll, and this sets up the line to be taken through the corner. It is often defined as the segment of the turn from the turn-in point to the apex.
Corner Exit	Corner exit is where you are reducing the steering input and commence accelerating. The car starts to roll back level. It is often defined as the segment of the turn from the apex until the corner has been completed.
cSt	Centistokes (cSt) is a measurement of oil viscosity (typically shock oil and diff oil). It is a standard unit of measurement which can be compared between manufacturers. Another common measurement is Weight (WT or just W). However, Weight is not a standard unit of measure and therefore cannot be compared between manufacturers.
CVA	A type of driveshaft with Constant Velocity where the cup is on the axle (as opposed to a CVD where the cup is on the shaft/bone). CVAs have become more popular than CVDs.
CVD	A type of driveshaft with Constant Velocity where the cup is on the shaft/bone (as opposed to a CVA where the cup is on the axle). CVAs have become more popular than CVDs.
DNF	Did Not Finish a race that the car started.
DNS	Did Not Start in a race that the car entered.
Dog Bones	Entry-level kits sometimes use driveshafts called dog bones. They are not as effective as CVAs or CVDs and are not attached to the drivetrain, so might come out in a crash.
ESC	The Electronic Speed Controller (ESC) controls the speed and direction of the motor.

Glossary – Appendix **B**

Forward Traction	Forward traction is how much grip you have when accelerating in a forward direction.
Hook	Hooking means sudden oversteer.
Loctite	Loctite is a brand of thread locker which has become a generic term for any brand of thread locking liquid. It is used on screws where they are screwed into aluminium. The Loctite cures into a plastic that locks the threads together, preventing the screw from working loose from vibration. The screw can still be unscrewed using a driver or screwdriver. Do not use Loctite when screwing into plastic as you may not be able to unscrew it again.
Loose	Loose is another word for Oversteer.
Mid-corner	Mid-corner is the part of the corner where steering input is constant (the steering wheel is turned at a constant angle and is neither increasing nor decreasing). The car is at maximum roll. The apex is normally taken during the mid-corner (refer to page *29*).
Off-power Steering	This is when trying to change the direction of the car while the throttle is neutral or under braking. Letting off the power causes the car to dive at the front and rise at the rear. Braking causes this effect to increase, i.e. the car dives more at the front under braking.
On-power Steering	This is when trying to change the direction of the car while holding or increasing the throttle. For example, coming out of a slow corner and then accelerating through a sweeper, the driver is accelerating while changing the steering angle. Under power, the car will rise at the front and squat at the rear.

298

Oversteer (Loose)	Oversteer is a cornering situation where the rear wheels do not track behind the front wheels but instead slide out toward the outside of the turn. Oversteer can cause the car to spin. Put simply, when you turn into a corner, oversteer is when the car turns more than you expected. It is often referred to as the car being "loose" or where the driver "loses" the back-end. Rear-wheel drive cars are generally more prone to oversteer than 4WD, in particular when applying power in a tight corner. This occurs because the rear tyres must handle both the lateral cornering force and engine torque. Sudden weight transfer, such as swerving, can cause oversteer. For solutions to oversteer refer to the checklist for *Too Much Steering (Oversteer)* on page *315*.
Push	Push is another word for Understeer.
Slip Angle	Slip angle is the angle between a rolling tyre's actual direction of travel and the direction which it is pointing. In other words, it's the difference between where the tyre is pointing and where it's actually going.
Stock	The "Stock" class designation for motors is a standard across all manufacturers separate from the "Modified" class which has no restrictions. The purpose is to maintain a slower and less expensive class. For example, 17.5T 2WD Buggy is a Stock class.
Traction Roll	A traction roll occurs in a corner when the suspension has compressed as far as it can, but the car wants to roll further. The car will then roll or flip over.

Turns (Motors)	The number of turns in a motor is the number of times the copper wire has been wound around the armature. The higher the number of turns the greater the torque but the lower the RPM. The lower the RPM the slower the top speed. For example, a 21.5 motor is normally slower than a 17.5 motor. Motors can also be rated by kV. When comparing two motors from the same manufacturer, a motor with a higher kV will have higher RPM but less torque.
Understeer (Push)	Understeer is a cornering situation where the car turns less sharply than the driver intends. This typically occurs when the front tyres have insufficient traction for the car to follow the intended line. Put simply, when you turn into a corner, understeer is when the car turns less than you expected. It is also often referred to as "pushing", or refusing to turn-in. Too much speed when entering a corner can also cause understeer. It is common for a manufacturer's base setup to have a slight tendency to understeer by default. If a car understeers slightly, it tends to be more stable (for drivers of average ability). For solutions to understeer refer to the checklist for *Not Enough Steering (Understeer)* on page 317.
Universal	A type of driveshaft common in 1/8 scale (while 1/10 tends to use CVAs).
Viscosity	Viscosity is the thickness of the oil. It is measured in cSt (a standard unit of measurement which can be compared between manufacturers) or Weight (which cannot be compared between manufacturers).
Wishbone	Another term for suspension arm.
WT	Refer to cSt above.

Appendix C – Beginner's Guide

If you are a complete beginner and have just bought your first car (or are about to), then the content of this book may seem overwhelming at first.

To assist, this appendix assumes you know nothing about RC cars or racing and provides knowledge which is assumed elsewhere in this book. It also highlights some common rookie mistakes to avoid.

Buying Considerations

Key considerations when buying an off-road car include:

1. **Who else runs it at your local track?** – If another racer has a car that handles well, and is prepared to share their ideas, then buying the same model of chassis may be a smart move. So an early step is to visit your local track and talk to other racers.

2. **Parts availability** – If parts are on the shelf at your local hobby shop, then that's a big advantage when you break something. Next would be an online store with fast shipping. If you can't find a store that stocks parts, either locally or online, then don't buy the kit.

3. **Online Community** – Is there a strong online community where you can ask questions, share setups, and see what issues other drivers are experiencing? This may also be a great place to look for reviews.

4. **Second-Hand** – Buying second-hand means no manufacturer's warranty and parts might be bent or missing. The price needs to reflect this risk. However, buying from a respected local racer can be a great way to get a bargain. If they race at your club, they are more likely to sell you a reasonable car.

5. **Minimum Specification**

	Cheaper Cars	Recommended
Chassis and Shock Towers	Plastic or FRP	Carbon Fibre
Shock Absorbers	Foam-filled, with spacer collars for adjustment	Oil-filled with screw thread collars for adjustment
Screws	Various	Metric hex screws
Bearings/Bushings	Bushings	Ball Bearings
Motor	Brushed	Brushless

Learning to Drive on a Track

Complete each step without crashing before moving on to the next one:

1. First, drive slowly, sticking to the middle of the track, until you can do it without crashing. Drive over the jumps slowly so that the wheels never leave the ground.
2. Then, without increasing speed, drive the track on the racing line (refer to page 28). Once you can do this without crashing, you can start going faster.
3. Gradually increase speed until you start crashing and then slow down and practice taking each section of the track as quickly as you can without crashing.

What's the big deal about crashing? That's what marshals are for, isn't it? No. Crashing costs you time. A lot of time. If you crash several times in a race then you'll lose any time you gain by driving faster. Learn to drive without crashing, and you'll start to beat other racers.

Beginner Advice

When I started, just trying to complete one circuit of the track without crashing seemed incredibly difficult. With perseverance, I gradually got better. I was no longer coming last, but I was nowhere near the race leaders. What to do? I did a lot of reading and decided to invest in a new ESC. This did seem to make the car a little quicker, but in hindsight wasn't the best use of my money. I tried a lot of things to make the car quicker and handle better, most of which were not time or money well spent. If I were starting again, these would be my top tips to myself, as a beginner:

1. If your car uses bushings instead of ball bearings, then changing these is your first priority. Bearings will enhance performance, reliability and run time.
2. Buy two reasonable quality Lipo batteries. You should go noticeably faster compared to the NiMH batteries that come with most Ready-to-Run (RTR) kits. You can get away with one battery, but having two makes life much easier. It also ensures you should be able to start every race with a full battery. This is important because batteries lose voltage as they discharge and lower voltage means less speed. Note: you will need a charger capable of handling Lipo batteries. Charging a Lipo battery with a non-Lipo charger is extremely dangerous.
3. Tamiya RTR cars are still popular today, but they come with Tamiya plugs between the ESC and battery. These tend to come loose, fault or melt, and don't conduct electricity as well as other connectors. I use Deans Ultra Plugs or bullet connectors. There is nothing more frustrating than your car stopping in

the middle of the race with a problem that could have been prevented. Changing plugs between the battery and ESC can save a great deal of frustration.

If you use bullet plugs then make sure you can't plug them in the wrong way around. Connecting the positive side of the ESC to the negative side of the battery is the fastest way to destroy your ESC. Decide on the battery location and then make sure only the correct polarity cable will reach the furthest bullet terminal on the battery.

4. Make sure the on/off switch is easy to get at with the body on. However, don't mount it on the chassis with the switch protruding because the car might get turned off in a crash. Very frustrating!

5. Having difficulty turning the wheel on the radio the correct amount to get around corners? Then turn down the dual rate setting on your radio. Some RTR radios don't have dual rate, in which case an upgrade is recommended. Even a mid-level radio makes driving much easier when compared to an RTR radio. If you buy a new radio, remember to set the servo End Point Adjustment (EPA), refer to page *183*. Not setting the servo EPA will overdrive the servo (making a whining noise) and possibly cause damage.

6. Tightening screws – Don't over-tighten screws into plastic as this will strip the plastic. If screwing into metal, then use a dab of Loctite on the screw to prevent it coming undone accidentally (you'll still be able to unscrew it later as long as you don't use too much Loctite).

7. Not setting the slipper clutch correctly (page *181*) and/or not setting the ball diff correctly (page *145*).

8. RTR wheel nuts don't always have nylon in the centre, or a good locking mechanism, to prevent them coming off in a race. Buy some and save yourself a lot of frustration.

9. Practice! To finish first, first you must finish. In the beginner class it's not necessarily the fastest car that wins but the car that gets around the track with the least number of crashes!

Practice – ask advice from people at your local club – and have fun!

Common Build Errors

1. Shocks are not the same left-to-right

The length of the shock absorbers from tip-to-tip must be the same on the front left as on the front right. Similarly, the length of the rear left must be the same as the rear right. Differences in length will cause unusual handling. Then when you set the ride height make sure the preload collars are wound down the same amount on the left and the right (front and back). Refer to page 129.

2. Shims, Inserts and Lengths are not the same left-to-right

If you draw an imaginary line down the centre of the chassis from the front axle to the rear axle then everything you do to the left half of the car should also be done to the right side. We've already covered this for the shocks above but it also applies to all other settings. For example:

- The length of linkages must be the same left-to-right (front and rear camber links, steering links).

- All shims installed on the left must also be installed on the right (same thickness).

- All inserts, sometimes called pills, that hold the inner suspension arm hinge pins must be the same left-to-right. Note that in this case, "the same" actually means that they are mirrored in the imaginary line down the centre of the chassis. These are typically installed in the A Block, B Block, C Block and D Block (defined in the Glossary on page 296):

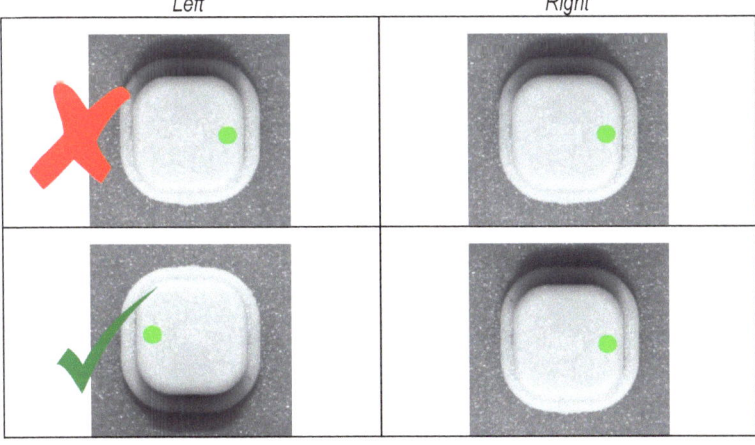

3. Gear mesh too tight or too loose

The pinion gear is the gear attached to the motor. The gap between the pinion gear and the spur gear is the gear mesh. If the gear mesh is too tight, then your car will not be fast and you will burn out motors more easily. The slower the motor, the larger the gear mesh gap is able to be without causing problems. However, if the gear mesh is too loose, the plastic spur gear could strip and leave your car stranded. Refer to page *162* for more gear mesh information.

Way Too Loose   *Too Loose*   *Good in Stock*

Good in Modified   *Too Tight*

In the photos, the spur gear is on the left and the pinion is on the right. Do not under-tighten or over-tighten (and strip) the pinion grub screw. To achieve this, the right tool can save you hours of frustration (refer to Tools on page *308*).

4. Binding in the steering or suspension

a. Linkages – steering links, camber links and the servo link should move freely. Ensure that the ball cups are perfectly free on the balls. If there is binding, sometimes squeezing the ball cup with pliers or heating it up quickly with a heat gun or cigarette lighter is all it takes to free it up.

b. Suspension Arms – Disconnect the shocks. Each suspension arm should move completely freely and fall under its own weight, i.e. lift the suspension arm and let it go and it should fall smoothly to the end of its travel and not bind up anywhere. If it doesn't then it may be rubbing on the inner hinge pin. File a small amount from the suspension arm hinge pin hole and try again. Otherwise it could be binding on the camber links (see a. above).

c. Steering – Disconnect the steering servo from the front wheels, the wheels should turn completely freely (and I mean you can move the wheel backwards and forwards with the slightest pressure from your little finger). If you can't, then something is binding. It could be the c-hub (you may need to back off screws slightly, or file excess material that is causing rubbing). It could be the steering links (refer to a. above).

It can be difficult to identify where binding is occurring until you gain experience. Simply ask someone at your club for assistance.

5. **Level surface**

Use a reasonably level surface when checking ride height, camber and droop. If the surface is not level, then it may skew the settings (depending how far out of level it is). Note: flat and level are two different things. You are looking for both. A kitchen bench is usually flat and level. A pit table might be flat but may not be level (of course it may not be flat either, and that's why you'll see most racers using a setup board or piece of glass).

6. **Car keeps rolling over (traction rolling or flipping)**

Ride height is probably too high. Refer to page *168* for recommended ride height. If your ride height is correct, then refer to the Traction Rolling Checklist on page *325* and Flipping Checklist on page *323*.

7. **Blowing motors**

A common way of trying to go faster is to turn the motor end bell timing up as far as it will go and drop the gearing to maximise speed on the straight, right? This is a great way to blow your motor. Refer to page *160* for detailed instructions on maximising your speed without burning out motors.

8. **Battery not charged**

Most beginner's start with one battery and quickly buy a second one. A common error is to forget to charge the battery you are using for the next race. To prevent this from happening, develop a system that works for you.

You might:

    a. Check the voltage of your battery before each race.

    b. Always store uncharged batteries in a lipo bag marked "Not charged" or conversely, store charged batteries in a lipo bag marked "Charged".

    c. Designate a place on your pit table for uncharged batteries and when you remove the battery from the car, put it in this area.

9. **Wiring the ESC backwards or plugging the battery wires in backwards – boom!**

Unlike most battery chargers, your ESC does not contain protection circuitry from connecting the + cable to the – terminal (or vice versa). Running power through your ESC the wrong way, even for a millisecond, is the top reason that racers buy a new ESC (and the most frustrating).

So when soldering wires on your ESC, check twice and solder once.

If you use bullet connectors, then make sure that one of the leads is only long enough to connect to the correct terminal on the battery. That way you can't connect them backwards (at least when the battery is installed in the car). For example, in the photo below the negative lead from the ESC is just long enough to reach the negative terminal of the battery. It is impossible to plug it into the positive terminal by mistake.

When buying a new battery that uses bullet connectors, double-check that the new battery has the + and – terminals on the same sides as your old battery. Not all manufacturers use the same layout!

10. **Car veers to one side under power**

There are two main possibilities:

a. The car has not been built the same way on the left side as on the right (refer to points 1 and 2 above).

b. The car may be "tweaked". When I started out, I tended to crash a lot. Every crash has the potential to bend or break parts or to move components slightly out of alignment. If you can't see anything obvious, ask someone at your club for assistance, or refer to page *201* for instructions on how to diagnose this.

Tyres Unglued

Checking that your tyres have not come unglued should be part of your routine after every run. If a tyre needs regluing, there are many different techniques you might use. I recommend using very thin (runny) glue with an applicator that has a small hole and only allows a small amount of glue to flow.

Lay the tyre on a flat surface and run the glue around the circumference of the rim where it meets the tyre. The glue will find its way in between the rubber tyre and the wheel rim. With this technique you shouldn't get glue on your fingers, glue your finger to the tyre, or glue the tyre in the wrong position on the rim. So this is a good option, particularly for beginners. Make sure you choose thin CA glue and don't use so much that it pools on the side of the tyre.

If you use too much, quickly wipe away any excess with a rag, taking care that the excess doesn't run over the surface of the tyre.

Setup Diary

Take a notebook with you to the track and write down:

- Your starting setup (most manufacturers provide a blank setup sheet for you to note this information. Fill it out and tape it into your notebook).
- Each change made. Make one change at a time.
- Any affect the change had. If you can't tell any difference, then undo the change before you try something else.
- The track conditions at the time you made the change (dusty/damp, hot/cold).

This will help you understand what each adjustment does to your car's handling and will become a good reference tool for you.

I still have my setup diary for every car I've ever run.

Tools

You can save yourself a great deal of frustration trying to remove stripped screws by preventing them from stripping in the first place. This is achieved using a set of quality drivers where the tip is machined to fit the screw head precisely and is made of a hard metal which will not wear out quickly.

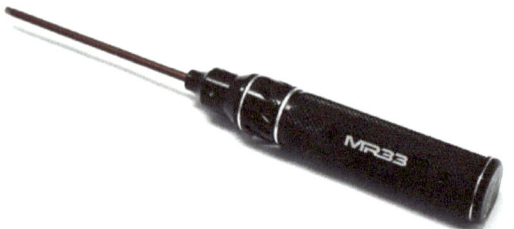

There are typically three types of screw heads used across the various manufacturers:

1. The most popular are hex heads using metric measurements, typically 1.5mm, 2mm, 2.5mm and 3mm.
2. Hex heads using imperial measurements, typically .050 inch, 1/16 inch, 5/64 inch and 3/32 inch.
3. Phillips or cross-head screws. These are predominantly used by Tamiya, a Japanese company, and Tamiya screws use the Japanese Industry Standard (JIS) screw head. Using a non-JIS screwdriver such as a Phillips screwdriver will often result in stripped screws.

Assuming your car uses metric drivers, then you will use the 2mm most frequently, followed closely by the 1.5mm. If you have a limited budget, you won't be sorry you spent the money on these drivers. The heads of the tools are usually replaceable and should be replaced whenever wear becomes noticeable.

Pinion gears are attached to the motor using a 1.5mm grub screw and tightening these sufficiently to not come off, while not stripping, can be a challenge with a cheap driver. If you do strip a pinion grub screw, take it to someone in the pits with a good quality hex driver, they may be able to get it out for you.

Lipo Battery Safety

Make sure you charge your lipo battery using a lipo charger, place the battery in a lipo safety bag during charging, and follow the manufacturer's advice on charge settings. Failure to follow basic safety guidelines can cause the battery to catch fire.

MR33 Lipo Safety Bag

Appendix D – Checklists

Quick Reference

Maintenance _____ 311
After Run Checks _____ 311
Maintenance Checklist _____ 312
Rebuilding a Car _____ 313
Correcting Key Balance Issues _____ 314
Traction – How to Increase _____ 314
Steering _____ 315
   Too Much Steering (Oversteer) _____ 315
   Not Enough Steering (Understeer) _____ 317
Easier to Drive – How-to _____ 319
Troubleshooting _____ 320
Acceleration/Forward Traction _____ 320
Bump Handling _____ 320
Change of Direction (Chicane) _____ 321
Changing Tracks – Low-Grip to High-Grip (or vice versa) _____ 321
Fast Sweeper Cornering _____ 322
Flipping _____ 323
"Hops" or "Chatters" Across the Track _____ 323
Inconsistent Handling _____ 323
Jumping Issues _____ 324
   More Distance _____ 324
   Hard Landings _____ 324
   Jumps Nose Up _____ 324
Traction Rolling _____ 325
Unexplained – Handling Changes for No Apparent Reason ____ 326
   Lacking Acceleration or Started Oversteering _____ 326
   Steering Response Changes for No Apparent Reason _____ 326
   Traction – Unexplained Loss of Traction _____ 327
Wanders on the Straight _____ 327

Maintenance

After Run Checks

After a race or practice run, check your car over. The car should have a battery installed.

1. Check tyres:

    a. Are they still glued to their rims? Try and peel the tyre edge gently back with your thumb and if it comes away from the rim, add some CA glue to fix it in place.

    b. Look for cracks on the rim. If cracked, then replace, or CA glue may help for a short period.

2. Check the wheel nuts are tight.

3. Check the drive train is free and gear mesh remains correct. Note: with high torque motors (stiff to turn), remove the pinion gear to check the drive train is free.

4. Check that each wheel rotates as you'd expect – looking for drive wheels freewheeling or not turning freely.

5. Check each of the shocks pumps up and down as you'd expect – looking for leaks, ball joints popped off, springs not sitting correctly.

6. Check that all the electronic components are still secure (ESC, receiver, transponder, servo) and haven't moved after a crash.

7. Push the front wheels to full lock in both directions and check for binding when the wheels turn.

8. Check the gear diff(s) are not leaking/tightness of the ball diff (refer to page 141).

9. If you had to change the steering trim during/after the race then the servo may have moved.

Some racers put their car on a setup station after each run and partially disassemble the car to ensure it is operating correctly. This may identify issues and, while not necessary after every run, can be a good idea prior to a critical race.

Maintenance Checklist

By Ray Munday

	Start of Race Day	Before each Race	After each club day	Before Each Big Race	Comment
Clean	(should be clean)	Compressed air / rag with sample green. If muddy, baby wipes and sample green	Remove wheels / shocks / wing. Compressed air and sample green. If arms binding, polish hinge pins and pipe cleaner in arms	Take apart and clean CVA (brake clean), CVA rebuild kit, replace driveshaft if parts badly worn	A clean car looks good, but more importantly cleaning the car helps you see damaged parts more easily
Driveshafts	(should be clean)	Clean excess dirt / dust (toothbrush)	Take off, clean with brake clean, and re-grease		Clean CVA gives more traction. Regular maintenance increases life.
Shocks	Bleed (always) bleed after the car has been sitting on a car stand for a few minutes to allow air to settle)	Bleed if temperature has changed (if often check mid morning / mid afternoon) Brush off dirt from weld area		New Shock Seals, bushings, oils. New shock bushes (if very worn). Check shock length with vernier, set to within 0.1mm around seal area. ★	Shock bleeding is important for outdoor racing as temps vary widely from morning to afternoon. Keep dirt from building up around seal area. ★
Differential	(should be set)	Gear diffs: warm up imperceivably before race (hold 1 wheel, use ~20% power for ~5 sec)	Check tightness, inspect outdrives for wear. Rebuild if gritty (Flip thrust race and diff rings or use rebuild kit).	Diff rebuild. New balls every few rebuilds. New outdrives if badly worn. Gear Diff: Replace oil	After building ball diff, MUST run in correctly and set tight for first runs. Diff will last a long time if this is done correctly
Pinion / Spur	(mesh should be set)	Check motor screws, arc pinion between quals and finals. If mossy, check for dirt in mesh (clean with pick).	Check mesh, look for damage	Replace if badly worn	A worn pinion will destroy spurs. Always loctite your pinion
Slipper Clutch	Set at start of day (2wd usual setting front tyres just lift off ground)	Re-adjust if track conditions or temp major change	Loosen clutch (if car will sit for a while. Re-set at track.	Inspect slipper pads. Flip pads if badly scored	Slipper clutch setting is critical in 2wd. Clutches can become sticky, so loosen off in advance before raceday
Ride Height	Check (always) setup change (always shock bleed before ride height / after changing tyres).	Check if spring / setup change (always shock bleed before ride height / after changing tyres).	Set after shock bleed	Check before rebuild (always bleed shocks before ride height check). Start with shock collars equal left and right	Always bleed shocks before ride height check. Shouldn't need adjustment unless you change setup (springs / weight / tyres)
Camber / Toe	(should be set)	Check camber if change links / ride height / after big crash.	Check camber and toe (always after shock bleed and ride height are set).	Re-check after rebuild (after ride height check). Use setup station	Set before start of meeting. With BRP64 1/4 turnbuckle rotation adjustment = 0.5 deg camber
Screw Check	Wheel nuts	Wheel nuts and shock screws.	Check all screws (especially metal to metal screws).	Check all screws. Re-loctite any metal-metal screws. Replace screws with damaged heads (otherwise will strip at worst time)	Preventative maintenance helps reduce frustrating failures
Broken Arm / Part Check	(should be checked)	Visual check of arms / covers each race.	Visual check of car for any cracks or breakages (especially arms / towers)	Visual check of all parts after cleaning (cleaner car is much easier to check for damage). Check for bent chassis, driveshaft, shock shafts. Wipe dirt off all bearings and check for smooth rotation. If nylock nuts are free, replace	Preventative maintenance helps reduce frustrating failures. Prioritise fixing breakages over setup.
Tyres	Choose tyres after doing track walk	Take wheels off. Clean if muddy (sample green and brush). Check bead is not coming unglued	Wipe off dust / mud (Pledge or rag with sample green). Check for wing cracks (major crack in rear wing reduces downforce a lot)	Make sure tyres are bagged in groups and arranged so easy to find. All tyres should be marked with a sharpie (date, compound, left/right)	Tyre maintenance improves lap time. Bulk buy large zip lock bags and store off vehicle
Body / Wing	(should be clean)			Fresh wings (cut out several to save time / space)	
Batteries	(should be charged)	Balance Charge in LiPo sack after battery cools. Record mAh used.	Check with Pledge (furniture polish). Check for crack / velcro OK.	Clean battery terminals with cotton buds and brake clean.	Always look after your batteries safely. Change in a Lipo sack, balance charge, don't store in high temperature, don't serve in low voltage.
Motor	(should be maintained)		Check voltage (if don't leave batteries less than ~7.6V). Store in cool area (if leave in my shed fridge). Charge night before race. Charge transmitter batteries if needed.	Re-oil motor bearing. Check sensor wire in ESC and motor	Brushless motors last a long time - most common problem is bearing seizing if no maintenance
Notes	Note down starting setup	Note change made each run	Compressed air to blow dust out. Brush dust off bearing. Check sensor wire	Create starting setup	Keeping notes is important to analysing what worked / what didn't last race. Create setup sheet in advance, then make notes each run

* Shock Bleeding - When changing tyres due to a change in temperature, that's a good time to bleed the shocks. There is no need to take them off the car.

312

Rebuilding a Car

If you buy a car second-hand, then we recommend checking it as follows and rebuilding if necessary:

1. Check the shocks and rebuild if necessary.
2. Check that the front shock springs are both the same length and of the same type. Repeat for the rear springs.
3. Check the various shims which control the setup and ensure the same number and thickness of shims are used on both sides of the car (left = right).
4. Check the bearings spin freely.
5. Check the diff action (page *141*) and rebuild if necessary.
6. Check the gearing (refer to page *160*).
7. Place the electronics but don't fix in place yet. Balance the car side-to-side and fix the electronics in place (refer to page *192*).
8. Check that the motor wires don't bind on the chassis or the body.
9. Program the ESC (refer to page *158*).
10. Program the radio (refer to page *166*).
11. Set the ride height (refer to page *168*).
12. Check the car is not tweaked. Follow the instructions on page *201*.
13. Set the toe (refer to page *185*).
14. Set the camber (refer to page *118*).
15. Recheck the ride height as changing the camber will change the ride height. If you change the ride height, recheck the camber.
16. Set the steering throw (refer to page *183*).
17. When you first test the car, keep an eye on motor temperature (refer to page *164*).

Note that the above does not list every single setting that can be checked, but it is the minimum that we recommend.

Checklists – Appendix D

Correcting Key Balance Issues

Sometimes our cars have an inherent balance problem due to the style of the track or the amount of traction. Tracks can be so different that we need to make changes in order to make the car more gripped up, or in some cases take grip away, to make the car driveable. Here are the extreme situations where you may have a balance issue, and what to look for in order to get your car dialled.

If you make a change and it does not improve the car's handling, then undo it before making the next change.

Traction – How to Increase

Having no traction on low-grip tracks isn't much fun. There are ways of making the car work harder to generate traction from the tyres. Here are things you can do in order to make the car more aggressive and increase overall traction in low-grip.

Front and Rear Traction

Listed in the recommended order. Make one change at a time and check the result:

1. **Additive (if used)** – let it soak into tyres for longer and/or consider a second application. Page 82.
2. **Ride height** – higher (within reason). Page 168.
3. **Shock position** – stand shocks up on shock tower (especially at rear). Page 128.
4. **Shock springs** – softer (rear first, then front if needed). Page 132.
5. **Shock oil** – softer. Page 126.
6. **Roll bar** – thinner or remove. Page 177.
7. **Roll centre** – lower front and rear. Page 178.
8. **Camber** – increase. Page 118.
9. **Flex** – increase (remove manufacturer recommended flex option screws). Page 160.
10. **Diff height** – lower front and rear. Page 146.
11. **Camber gain** – increase front and rear. Page 121.

Rear Traction Only

1. **Diff (rear)** – gear diff thinner oil. Page *141*.
2. **Toe-in (rear)** – increase. Page *187*.
3. **Ride height split** – make the front ride height the same, or higher, than the rear ride height. Page *170*.
4. **Wing** – to assist with higher speed corners, move the wing rearwards or use a high downforce wing (if local rules allow it). Page *197*.
5. For more rear traction ideas refer to *Oversteer* below.

Steering

Too Much Steering (Oversteer)

If the car has too much steering, it can be difficult to drive and may oversteer.

Oversteer is an imbalance in the car with weight transfer biased towards the front. This means that the front is generating more traction than the rear. The aim when trying to achieve more rear traction is to add grip to the rear, not take too much traction away from the front. Rear traction is really important for forward drive, predictability and consistency. Not enough rear traction will cause you to be fighting your car throughout your runs. Here are some things you can do in order to achieve more rear traction in all grip levels.

Listed in the recommended order. Make one change at a time and check the result:

1. **Additive (if used)** – reduce on front tyres. Page *82*.
2. **Roll bar** – thicker front roll bar and/or thinner rear roll bar. Page *177*.
3. **Shock springs** – softer on rear first, then harder on front if needed. Page *132*.
4. **Shock oil** – thinner at rear first, then thicker at front if needed. Page *126*.
5. **Weight** (particularly in 2WD) – if practical, move weight from the rear to the front. Page *192*.
6. **Diff (front)** – thicker gear diff oil. Page *142*.
7. **Diff (rear)** – thinner gear diff oil. Page *142*.
8. **Ride height split** – make the front ride height the same, or higher, than the rear ride height. Page *168*.
9. **Roll centre** – lower the rear first, then raise the front. Page *177*.
10. **Droop** – more front droop and/or less rear droop. Page *152*.

11. **Camber** – decrease front first, then if needed increase rear. Page *118*.
12. **Toe-out (front)** – increase. Page *186*.
13. **Toe-in (rear)** – increase. Page *187*.
14. **Shock position** – stand rear shocks up on tower. Page *128*.
15. **Track width (front)** – wider. Page *188*.
16. **Radio** – reduce steering lock (dual rate). However, if the amount of steering is correct, but you'd like to reduce how quickly the car turns into the corner, then reduce the Steering Curve (Expo). Page *166*.
17. **Bump steer** – less shims. Page *117*.
18. **Camber gain** – decrease. Page *121*.
19. **Wheelbase** – longer front and/or rear wheelbase. Page *196*.

If the above does not resolve the oversteer, then undo the changes, identify when the oversteer occurs, and address as follows:

Oversteer at Corner Entry

1. **Weight (particularly in 2WD)** – if practical, move weight from the rear to the front. Page *192*.
2. **Caster** – increase. Page *124*.
3. **Track width (rear)** – wider. Page *188*.
4. **Ackermann** – decrease. Page *105*.

Oversteer at Mid-corner

1. **Track width (rear)** – wider. Page *188*.
2. **Wheelbase (front)** – longer. Page *196*.

Oversteer at Corner Exit

Track width (rear) – narrower. Narrower rear track width increases rear grip at corner exit. Page *188*.

Oversteer On-power

1. **Weight (particularly in 2WD)** – if practical, move weight from the front to the rear. Page *192*.
2. **Caster** – reduce. Page *124*.
3. **Spring (front)** – softer spring to reduce on-power steering. Page *132*.

Not Enough Steering (Understeer)

Understeer is an imbalance in the car with weight transfer biased towards the rear. This means that the rear is generating more traction than the front. The aim when trying to achieve more steering is to add steering to the front, not take away traction from the rear. Rear traction is really important for forward drive, predictability and consistency. However, a loose car (oversteering) is often a fast car, and having too much rear stability can slow you down and cause the car to bind up in the corners. Here are some things you can do in order to achieve more steering in all grip levels.

Listed in the recommended order. Make one change at a time and check the result. If the car has insufficient steering:

1. **Ride height** – set the front ride height lower than the rear ride height. Page *168*.
2. **Additive (if used)** – increase on front tyres. Page *82*.
3. **Roll bar (front)** – thinner. Page *180*.
4. **Weight (particularly in 2WD)** – shift weight from the front to the rear if practical. Page *192*.
5. **Shock springs** – softer on front first, then harder on rear if needed. Page *132*.
6. **Shock oil** – thinner at front first, then thicker on rear if needed. Page *126*.
7. **Shock position (rear)** – move bottom of shock towards the chassis on the suspension arm. Works better on smaller tracks. Page *128*.
8. **Droop** – increase rear droop. Page *152*.
9. **Camber** – increase. Page *118*.
10. **Diff (rear)** – gear diff thicker oil. Page *142*.
11. **Toe-out (front)** – reduce. Page *186*.
12. **Toe-in (rear)** – reduce. Page *187*.
13. **Steering throw** – if not already against the stops then increase. Page *182*.
14. **Roll centre** – first raise the rear roll centre then lower the front roll centre. Page *178*.
15. **Track width (front)** – narrower. Page *188*.
16. **Bump steer** – more shims. Page *117*.
17. **Flex** – increase (track dependant). Page *160*.

18. **Camber gain (front)** – increase. Page *121*.

19. **Wheelbase** – shorter. Page *196*.

If the above does not resolve the understeer, then undo the changes, identify when the understeer occurs, and address as follows:

Understeer at High-speed

If the car has insufficient steering:

1. **Wing (front)** – install.

2. **Wing position (rear)** – move wing further forward or reduce size of gurney. Page *197*.

Understeer at Corner Entry

If the car has insufficient steering:

1. **Weight (particularly in 2WD)** – shift weight from the front to the rear if practical. Moving weight to the rear gives more steering overall but reduces exit steering. Page *192*.

2. **Diff (front)** – gear diff thinner oil. Page *143*.

3. **Caster** – reduce. Page *124*.

4. **Shock position (front)** – stand up shocks by moving top of shock towards the outside of the shock tower. Page *128*.

5. **Shock position (rear)** – lay down shocks by moving top of shock towards the chassis on the shock tower. Page *128*.

6. **Roll bar (rear)** – thinner. Page *180*.

7. **Ackermann** – increase. Page *107*.

8. **Roll centre (front)** – higher. Page *178*.

Understeer at Mid to Exit of the Corner or On-power

If the car has insufficient steering:

1. **Weight (particularly in 2WD)** – shift weight from the rear to the front if practical. Moving weight to the front gives less steering overall but increases exit steering. Page *192*.

2. **Diff (front)** – gear diff thicker oil. Page *143*.

3. **Caster** – increase. Page *124*.

4. **Shock position (front)** – lay down shocks by moving top of shock towards the chassis on the shock tower. Page *128*.

5. **Shock position (rear)** – stand up shocks by moving top of shock towards the outside of the shock tower. Page *128*.

6. **Roll bar (rear)** – thicker. Page *180*.

Easier to Drive – How-to

Listed in the recommended order. Make one change at a time and check the result:

1. **Toe-out (front)** – increase. Page *186*.
2. **Diff height** – high. Page *146*.
3. **Droop (rear)** – decrease. Page *156*.
4. **Roll bar (front)** – thinner. Page *174*.
5. **Camber** – decrease. Page *118*.
6. **Camber gain** – decrease. Page *121*.
7. **Ackermann** – reduce. Page *105*.
8. **Bump steer** – more shims. Page *182*.
9. **Caster** – increase. Page *124*.
10. **Weight balance (front-to-rear)** – move weight forwards if practical. Page *194*.
11. **Track width (rear)** – wider. Page *188*.
12. **Track width (front)** – wider. Page *188*.
13. **Wheelbase** – longer. Page *196*.
14. **Roll centre (rear)** – higher. Page *178*.
15. **Shock oil** – thicker. Page *126*.
16. **Shock rebound** – less rebound will make the car easier to drive on a bumpy track. Page *130*.
17. **Shock position on arm (rear)** – outside. Page *129*.

Troubleshooting

In alphabetical order.

Acceleration/Forward Traction

With a 4WD the rear may provide slightly more drive than the front but both ends of the car are important. In a 2WD, focus on the rear of the car. For greater acceleration/forward traction:

1. **Weight balance (front-to-rear)** – move weight rearwards if practical. Page *194*.
2. **Anti-squat** – increase. Page *111*.
3. **Gearing** – smaller pinion. Page *160*.
4. **Slipper clutch** – tighten. Page *180*.
5. **Ball diff** – tighter. Page *145*.
6. **Gear diffs** – thicker oil in all diffs (front, centre and rear) for greater acceleration. Page *144*.
7. **Roll centre** – lower. Page *178*.
8. **Wings** – larger wings will provide greater forward traction but reduce top speed. Page *197*.
9. **Tyres** – square profile. Page *92*.
10. **Shock position** – running the rear shock position higher on the shock tower than the front generates more forward traction. Page *128*.
11. **Track width** – widen the rear. Page *188*.

Bump Handling

If the track has many bumps around the whole track, consider:

1. **Tyres** – make sure your wheels have ventilation holes. Page *77*.
2. **Inserts** – softer and/or use Open Cell inserts. If using Close Cell inserts consider cutting a V into them. Page *81*.
3. **Camber** – increase (rear first, then front). Page *118*.
4. **Droop** – increase. Page *152*.

5. **Ride height** – higher, if practical. In very bumpy conditions set the front higher than the rear. Page *168*.
6. **Shock pistons** – bigger holes. Page *127*.
7. **Shock oil** – thinner. Page *126*.
8. **Shock rebound** – less or zero rebound. Page *130*.
9. **Anti-squat** – reduce. Page *111*.
10. **Arm sweep** – less. Page *112*.
11. **Bump steer** – more shims. Page *117*.
12. **Camber gain** – increase. Page *121*.
13. **Caster** – increase. Page *124*.
14. **Kick-up** – increase. Page *165*.
15. **Roll bars** – thinner. Page *173*.
16. **Track width (front)** – narrower, front and rear. Page *188*.
17. **Wheelbase** – longer. Page *196*.
18. **4WD – Centre Diff** – thinner oil. Page *144*.

Change of Direction (Chicane)

If the car does not change directions quickly:

1. **Ride height** – lower, if practical. Page *168*.
2. **Ackermann** – reduce. Page *107*.
3. **Shock oil** – thicker. Page *126*.
4. **Diff height (rear)** – lower. Page *146*.
5. **Roll bar (rear)** – thicker. Page *174*.

Changing Tracks – Low-Grip to High-Grip (or vice versa)

What to do first on a high-traction track

To prevent traction rolling we are aiming to slow down responsiveness and reduce mechanical grip.

1. **Weight (particularly in 2WD)** – shift weight from the rear to the front if practical. Page *192*.

2. **Tyres** – on carpet or astroturf use tyres with larger, harder pins which are more spaced out. On high-grip dirt or clay consider slicks or tyres with a minimal pattern. Page *86*.

3. **Ride height** – lower. Page *169*.

4. **Axle height** – raise. Page *113*.

5. **Toe-in (rear)** – reduce. Page *187*.

6. **Shocks** – thicker oil and stiffer springs. Page *126*.

7. **Roll bars** – stiffer. Page *173*.

8. **2WD** – use a lay down transmission (page *188*) and a gear diff with 7K oil (page *142*).

9. **4WD** – 1/10 use front diff oil 15K, centre 500K and rear 10K. 1/8 use 15K–10K–8K. Page *142*.

10. **Motor Temp** – keep an eye on motor temperature as the gearing may need to be changed. Page *164*.

What to do first on a low-traction track

If you've been running on a high-traction track, then refer to the checklist for high-traction above and do the inverse. For example, point 3 above says lower the ride height; the inverse is to raise the ride height so that's what you'd do when moving from high-traction to low-traction.

If you still need more traction after following the above, then refer to the *Traction – How to Increase* checklist on page *314*.

From Low-Grip Dirt to High-Grip Carpet (or Astroturf)

This is discussed in detail under *Carpet Setup* on page *257*. The Case Studies chapter includes further advice for carpet and astroturf surfaces.

Fast Sweeper Cornering

To increase steering through fast sweepers:

1. **Caster** – increase. Page *124*.

2. **Toe-out (front)** – reduce. Page *186*.

3. **Wheelbase** – increase. Page *196*.

To increase stability through fast sweepers:

1. **Shock springs (front)** – harder. Page 132.
2. **Roll bars** – thicker. Page 174.
3. **Gear diffs** – thicker oil in all diffs (front, centre and rear). Page 144.

Flipping

When a tyre catches the edge of a rut in the track the car can flip over. This is a different situation to traction rolling (separate checklist below).

1. **Camber** – increase. Page 119.
2. **Tyre profile** – use a tyre with a rounded profile. Page 92.
3. **Tyre insert** – if using a square profile tyre, cutting the edge off a square insert can make the tyre less likely to grab. Page 81.

"Hops" or "Chatters" Across the Track

If the car "hops" (also called "chatter" or "judder") when cornering, then the springs are too stiff (refer to Springs on page 132).

Inconsistent Handling

The following issues can also cause inconsistent handling:

1. If the roll bars are not set correctly (refer to page 175).
2. Suspension arms should move up and down smoothly when the suspension is compressed.
3. Track width shims are not the same on the left as on the right (refer to page 188).
4. Remove the front springs and place them next to each other on a flat surface. They should be the same length. Replace if needed. Repeat this test for the rear springs.

Jumping Issues

More Distance

Assuming you are maximising your jump approach (page *69*) and are nailing your run-up and take-off (page *56*), but still need more distance, then:

1. **Shock springs** – harder, front and rear, to achieve a little more jump height. Page *132*.
2. **Anti-squat** – increase for greater forward traction. Page *111*.
3. **Gearing** – if there is little run-up to the jump then a smaller pinion will provide better acceleration. If there is a long straight before the jump then a larger pinion will provide a higher top speed. Page *160*.
4. **2WD only** – tighten the slipper clutch for greater acceleration. Page *180*.

Hard Landings

If the chassis slaps the ground on landing then:

1. **Shock oil** – increase oil thickness front and rear. It is recommended to increase both front and rear the same amount (try 5 WT or 50 cSt). Page *126*.
2. **Shock pistons** – fewer holes. Page *127*.
3. **Droop** – increase. Page *152*.
4. **Ride height** – increase. Try making the front higher than the rear. Page *169*.

Jumps Nose Up

If the car jumps nose up then the front-to-back weight distribution may be biased to the rear (page *194*). Or, the rear wing may be too large or mounted too far back (page *200*).

Traction Rolling

Traction rolling is when the car is cornering, and it rolls over. It often occurs because the chassis has reached the limit of the amount it can roll, but needs to roll more. Because the chassis cannot roll any further, the car rolls over. This is different to flipping because the tyre has caught the edge of a rut in the track (refer to the Flipping checklist above).

> Traction rolling can be just as annoying as having no traction. You do nothing wrong, but your car ends up on its lid ... great! It can be frustrating, but if you work through ways to decrease the risk of this, you can make your car less edgy, more enjoyable to drive and more consistent. Most traction rolling comes from the rear of the car.

Listed in the recommended order. Make one change at a time and check the result. To reduce or eliminate traction rolling:

1. **Ride height** – reduce. Page *168*.
2. **Additive (if used)** – reduce traction additive on front tyres. Page *82*.
3. **Additive (if used)** – shorten traction additive time to five minutes or less. Page *82*.
4. **Roll centre** – lower. Page *177*.
5. **Roll bar (front)** – thinner. Page *174*.
6. **Shock springs** – softer. Page *132*.
7. **Shock oil** – thicker (as slows down weight transfer). Start at rear. Page *126*.
8. **Shock position** – lay the shocks over more on the shock tower. Page *128*.
9. **Shock rebound** – reduce if high-traction. Page *130*.
10. **Toe-out (front)** – increase. Page *186*.
11. **Diff height** – raise front and rear. Page *146*.
12. **Ride height split** – reduce. Page *170*.
13. **Droop** – decrease rear droop and/or increase front droop. Page *152*.
14. **Camber (front)** – reduce. Page *118*.
15. **Camber gain** – decrease front and rear. Page *121*.
16. **Weight** – in high-grip move weight to the front of the car. Page *194*.
17. **Bump steer** – reduce shims. Page *117*.
18. **Arm sweep** – add. Page *112*.

19. **Glue front tyre sidewalls** – a thin layer of glue on the tyre sidewall helps stop the traction roll. This stiffens the sidewall and in some cases allows the tyre to slide on the glue rather than fold under the car. Gluing the front sidewalls will reduce steering and may be best used on high-grip carpet.
20. **Radio** – increase radio exponential and/or decrease steering lock (dual rate). Page 166.
21. **Flex** – reduce, especially the front of the car. Page 160.
22. **Track width (front)** – wider. Page 188.
23. **Ackermann** – reduce. Page 107.

Unexplained – Handling Changes for No Apparent Reason

Lacking Acceleration or Started Oversteering

If the car was working well but is now lacking acceleration or has started oversteering, then:

1. Check CVAs/CVDs are working properly (not binding), set screws haven't come loose and pins haven't worn a groove in the diff outdrives.
2. Check motor temperature (refer to page 164).
3. Diffs – Gear diff leaking or ball diff may be slipping too much (tighten using the recommendations on page 141).
4. If the car has belts then check they are not worn or slipping.

Steering Response Changes for No Apparent Reason

If the car was steering correctly and no longer is, then:

1. Are the front linkages bent?
2. Are there any cracks, or loose screws, on any of the steering arms or parts?
3. Do the front arms move up and down on the springs and return to rest correctly?
4. If you disconnect the shocks are the suspension arms moving completely freely?
5. Has the servo horn stripped?
6. Is the servo working correctly?
7. Is the car tweaked? (Refer to page 201).

Traction – Unexplained Loss of Traction

If your car has been handling well and then suddenly loses grip, here is a checklist of potential causes:

1. **Tyre temperature** – are the tyres cold? (Mostly an issue when the air temperature is cold). If so, make sure to do a couple of warm-up laps or use tyre warmers if necessary (page *84*).

2. **Track temperature** – has the track temperature changed? Are the tyres you are using the correct ones for the new temperature?

3. **All tyres** – tyre gluing – check your tyres to see if any of them have come unglued.

4. **Differential** – is the gear diff leaking/ball diff still set correctly? Page *141*.

5. **Rear wing** – has the rear wing been damaged?

6. **Screws** – are all the chassis screws done up properly? Losing screws can cause unpredictable handling.

7. **Shocks** – are any of the shocks leaking?

8. **Tweak** – has your car become tweaked? Page *201*.

Wanders on the Straight

1. **Toe-out (front)** – increase. Page *186*.
2. **Caster** – increase. Page *124*.

Check out my other RC books and eBooks at www.DaveBStevens.com

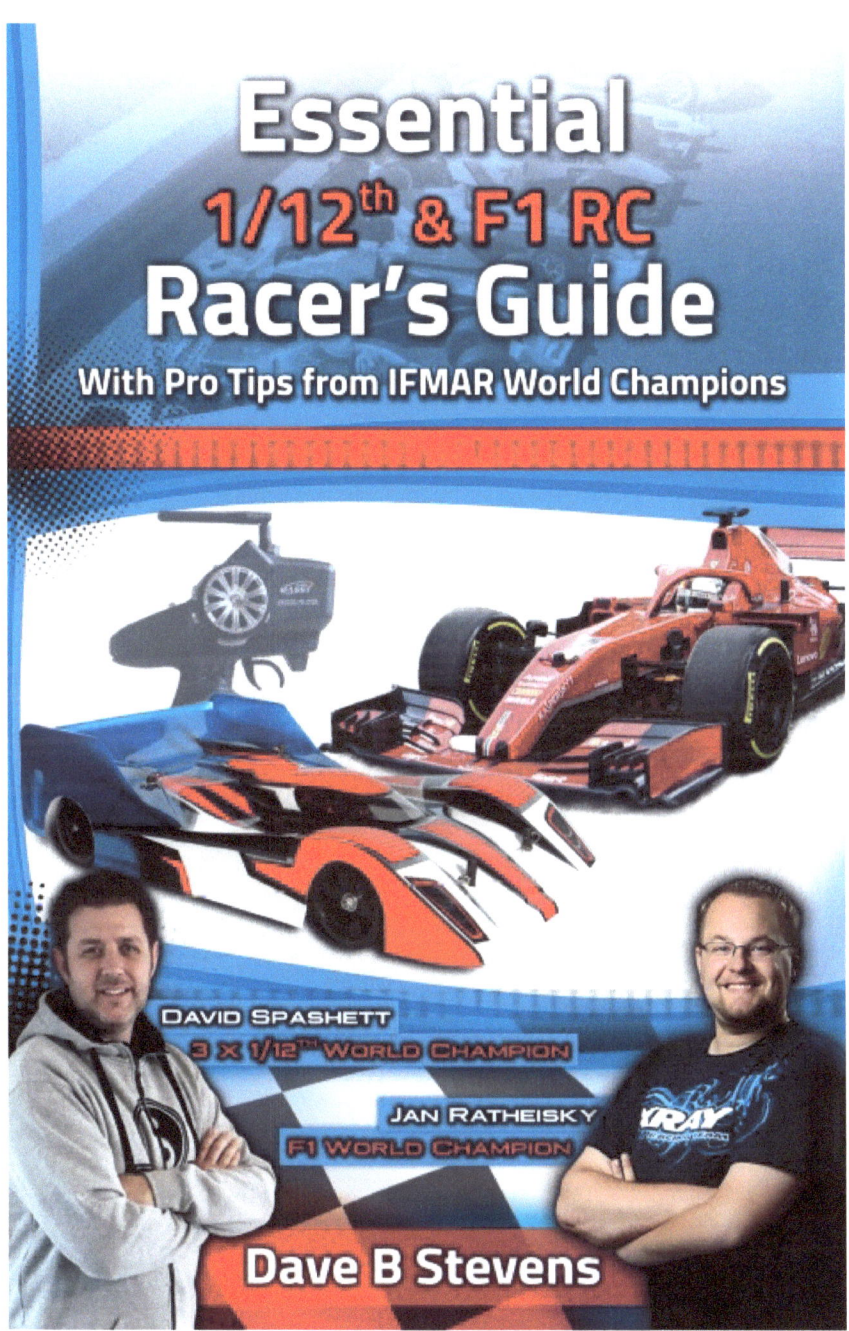

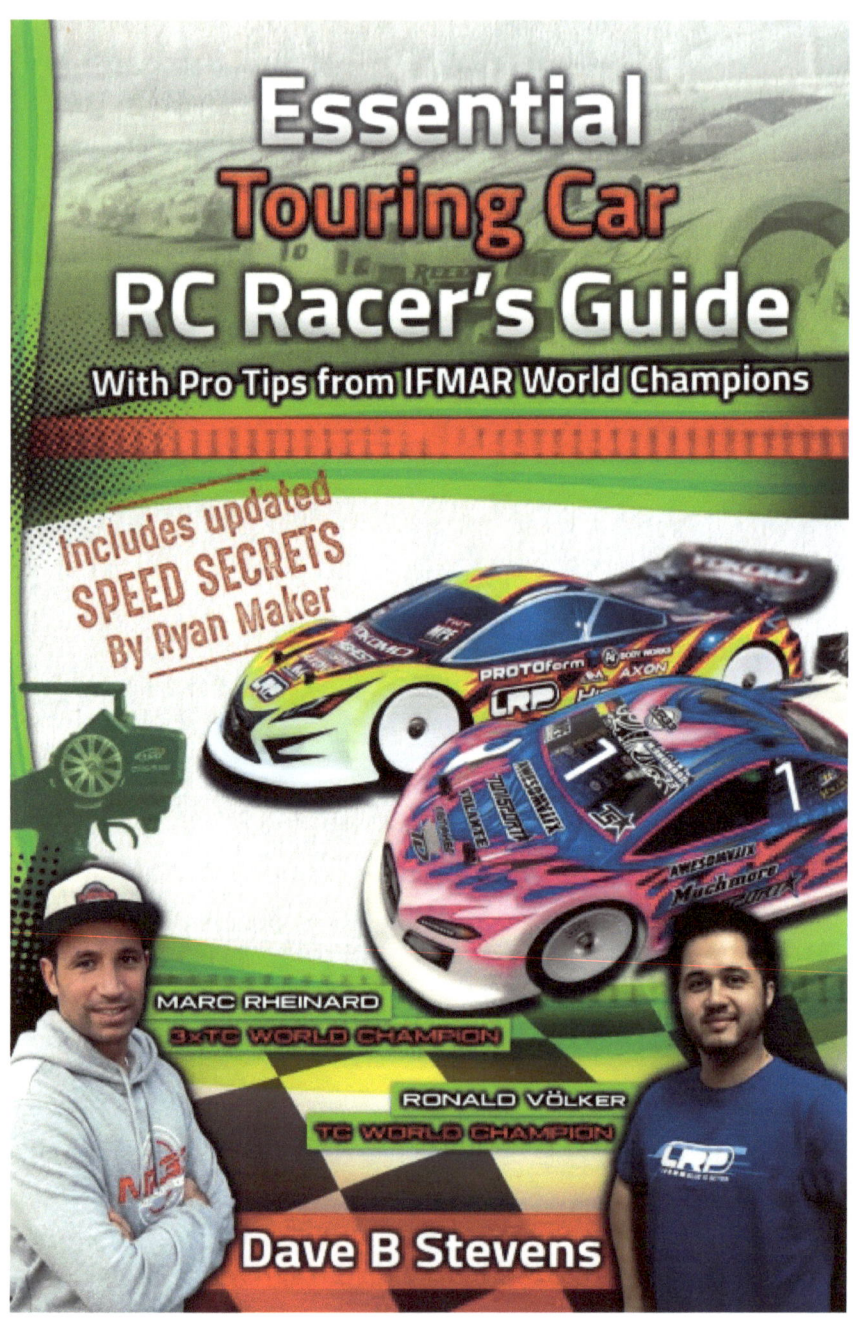

Quick Reference

Maintenance	311
After Run Checks	*311*
Maintenance Checklist	*312*
Rebuilding a Car	*313*
Correcting Key Balance Issues	314
Traction – How to Increase	*314*
Steering	*315*
Too Much Steering (Oversteer)	315
Not Enough Steering (Understeer)	317
Easier to Drive – How-to	*319*
Troubleshooting	320
Acceleration/Forward Traction	*320*
Bump Handling	*320*
Change of Direction (Chicane)	*321*
Changing Tracks – Low-Grip to High-Grip (or vice versa)	*321*
Fast Sweeper Cornering	*322*
Flipping	*323*
"Hops" or "Chatters" Across the Track	*323*
Inconsistent Handling	*323*
Jumping Issues	*324*
More Distance	324
Hard Landings	324
Jumps Nose Up	324
Traction Rolling	*325*
Unexplained – Handling Changes for No Apparent Reason	*326*
Lacking Acceleration or Started Oversteering	326
Steering Response Changes for No Apparent Reason	326
Traction – Unexplained Loss of Traction	327
Wanders on the Straight	*327*

www.ingramcontent.com/pod-product-compliance
Lightning Source LLC
Chambersburg PA
CBHW041459010526
44107CB00044B/1501